BUILDING A NEW
LEGAL ORDER
FOR THE OCEANS

BUILDING A NEW LEGAL ORDER FOR THE OCEANS

by

Tommy Koh

NUS PRESS
SINGAPORE

© 2020 Tommy Koh

Published by:

NUS Press
National University of Singapore
AS3-01-02, 3 Arts Link
Singapore 117569

Fax: (65) 6774-0652
E-mail: nusbooks@nus.edu.sg
Website: http://nuspress.nus.edu.sg

ISBN: 978-981-3250-89-5

National Library Board, Singapore Cataloguing in Publication Data

Name(s): Koh, Tommy T.B. (Tommy Thong Bee), 1937– |Seah, Sharon, editor.
Title: Building a new legal order for the oceans/by Tommy Koh; editor, Sharon Seah Li-Lian.
Description: Singapore: NUS Press, 2020.|Includes index.
Identifier(s): OCN 1112867109 |I SBN 978-981-32-5089-5 (paperback)
Subject(s): LCSH: Law of the sea.|United Nations Conference on the Law of the Sea.
Classification: DDC 341.45--dc23

Front cover image: Tommy Koh introducing the draft resolution (document A/38/L.18/Rev.1) before the vote (14 December 1983).
Back cover image: Tommy Koh addresses the General Assembly at the 30th Anniversary of the launch of UNCLOS (10 December 2012).

Printed by: Ho Printing Singapore Pte Ltd

Contents

CONTENTS

Essays and Lectures

Academic Essays

List of Images

(Between pages 141 and 142)

Ambassador Tommy Koh with Ambassador Jens Evensen just prior to the beginning of the signing session of the Conference of the Law of the Sea in Montego Bay on 6 December 1982. Ambassador Evensen was later appointed as Judge of the International Court. Credit: UN Photo 266302 by UN Photo.

Press Briefing by Tommy Koh, President of Law of Sea Conference (24 March 1981). Credit: UN Photo by Yutaka Nagata.

At the United Nations on the day Tommy Koh was elected President of UNCLOS III (13 March 1981). Credit: UN Photo 145796 by Saw Lwin.

Professor Tommy Koh with judges outside ITLOS at Hamburg during Singapore's Land Reclamation Case (2003). Credit: Author's own.

The 20th anniversary of the establishment of the International Seabed Authority (ISA). Credit: Author's own.

Tommy Koh introducing the draft resolution (document A/38/L.18/Rev.1) before the vote (14 December 1983). Credit: UN Photo by Saw Lwin.

Tommy Koh addresses the General Assembly at the 30th Anniversary of the launch of UNCLOS (10 December 2012). Credit: UN Photo 537401 by Devra Berkowitz.

Foreword

The Third United Nations Conference on the Law of the Sea, which spanned many years, ended with the adoption of the United Nations Convention on the Law of the Sea (UNCLOS). The negotiation process in the Conference was most unusual—with informal processes alongside the formal processes, with secret negotiating groups and, above all, an unprecedented influential role of a few individuals.

It was Singapore's good fortune that one of the leading lights at the Conference was Professor Tommy Koh. He was the leader of Singapore delegation, but his impact was beyond that. He was admired for his legal acumen, and his negotiation and mediation skills. The delegates turned to him whenever there was an impasse. Unsurprisingly, he was elected President of the Third United Nations Conference on the Law of the Sea.

No one can speak as authoritatively about the UNCLOS as Professor Tommy Koh can. I am therefore very glad that his various speeches and writings about the Convention have been put together in this volume.

Professor S Jayakumar

Introduction

I want to begin my introduction with several expressions of gratitude. First, I want to thank Professor Lucy Reed, the Director of the Centre for International Law, at the National University of Singapore, for showing my Stimson Lectures to Mr Peter Schoppert, the Director of the National University of Singapore Press. Second, I want to thank Mr Schoppert for his interest in publishing the Stimson Lectures. I persuaded him to include some of my other writings on the law of the sea. Third, I wish to thank my friend and colleague, Sharon Seah, for accepting my request to edit the book. Sharon went through a massive amount of my writings on the law of the sea and picked what she considered the best and the most relevant. Fourth, I thank my old comrade, Professor S Jayakumar, for accepting my request to write the foreword of the book.

I spent more than ten years of my life in the Third United Nations Conference on the Law of the Sea (1973–1982) and in the preparatory committee, called the United Nations Seabed Committee.

In my work, I was guided by a vision and a mission. The vision was to help build a new legal order for the oceans. The mission was to treat the oceans as an ecological unity and to protect the health and conserve the resources of this unity. The mission was to help negotiate a new treaty on the law of the sea which would be fair and just and which would be universally accepted. The mission was to end the state of legal chaos and conflict then prevailing with order and peace.

The United Nations Convention on the Law of the Sea was adopted thirty-seven years ago. It came into force twenty-five years ago. I am grateful that the Convention has been a great success. I am humbled by the fact that, in the final year of the Conference, I was chosen to be the second President of the Conference and to bring the Conference to a successful conclusion.

Professor Tommy Koh

Editor's Preface

This volume started as a project to publish four lectures that Professor Tommy Koh had delivered at Yale University in 1982. The Stimson Lectures are historical gems to the international law of the sea community and deserve to be read and appreciated by those interested in the United Nations Convention on the Law of the Sea (UNCLOS).

The Henry L Stimson Lectures

Professor Koh was invited by Yale University to deliver a series of four lectures in 1982 as President of the Third United Nations Conference on the Law of the Sea. The lectures are reproduced in the first section to give readers an insight into the genesis of the UNCLOS, the thinking behind the 320 Articles and 9 Annexes of the Convention and the negotiating techniques used in order for 160 countries to reach agreement on the Convention.

The Henry L Stimson Lecture series is a Yale University project started in honour of Henry L Stimson (1867–1950), a Yale alumnus, distinguished American lawyer and statesman who had served his country with distinction. Best known for the 1932 Stimson Doctrine, Stimson, who was the United States Secretary of State at the time of Japanese occupation of Manchuria, advocated the non-recognition of territories acquired by force. The Stimson Lecture series has featured many distinguished speakers including Samuel P Huntington, Susan Dunn and William R Polk, to name a few.

The first section of this book contains four lectures centred on the building of a new legal order of the sea. Each lecture covers specific topics relating to the negotiations of the UNCLOS. The first lecture talks about the collapse of the old order; the second lecture addresses the competing claims to the resources and uses of the sea; the third lecture focuses on the concept of the common heritage of mankind and, finally, the last lecture focuses on the unique negotiating process of the Third United Nations Conference on the Law of the Sea.

Selected Essays and Lectures

The second section comprises nine of the best essays and lectures written, published and delivered by Professor Tommy Koh from the late 1980s to 2017 either in his capacity as Ambassador-at-Large at the Ministry of Foreign Affairs of Singapore, or as the Chairman of the Governing Board of the Centre for International Law (CIL) at the National University of Singapore. These essays and lectures capture his views on the latest developments involving the interpretation and application of the UNCLOS, including the South China Sea dispute and the Australia-Timor Leste maritime boundary conciliation case.

Academic Essays

The last section comprises three academic essays written by Professor Tommy Koh that were published by the *Malaya Law Review* (the predecessor of the *Singapore Journal of Legal Studies*) between 1987 to 1988. The essays were written six years after the successful conclusion of the Third United Nations Conference on the Law of the Sea. These essays reveal the academic thinking and discussions at the time surrounding the many new legal concepts contained in the Convention.

The first in the series, entitled "The Origins of the 1982 Convention on the Law of the Sea", traces the evolution of the law of the sea. An international legal order, based upon a three-mile territorial sea, was increasingly challenged by the unilateral claims of coastal States. Faced with the threat of a legal chaos, the international community decided to convene the Third United Nations Conference on the Law of the Sea in an attempt to build a new international legal order for the sea in 1970. The first essay was published in July 1987.

The second essay, entitled "The Territorial Sea, Contiguous Zone, Straits and Archipelagoes under the 1982 Convention on the Law of the Sea", was published in December 1987. The article discusses the provisions of the Convention relating to the territorial sea, contiguous zone, straits and archipelagos and the special regimes of passage for ships and aircraft through, over and under straits used for international navigation and archipelagic sea lanes. Professor Koh also discusses the negotiating process leading to the adoption of these provisions.

The final essay, "The Exclusive Economic Zone", discusses the evolution of the concept of the exclusive economic zone (EEZ), its basic principles and legal status. Professor Koh discusses the conservation, management and exploitation of the fishing resources in the EEZ and the negotiating process leading to the adoption of the provisions in the Convention relating to the EEZ. This last academic essay was published in 1988.

The book concludes with a letter penned by Professor Koh to his colleagues reflecting on the UNCLOS and what it has achieved.

Conclusion

Before I conclude, I wish to thank our publisher's editor Lindsay Davis for her time and effort, friendship and camaraderie. I also wish to thank my intern Keila Garcia for her assistance.

Last but not least, I wish to thank Professor Koh for entrusting me with the project. It has been a great honour and privilege.

Sharon Seah

BUILDING A NEW LEGAL ORDER FOR THE OCEANS

LECTURE 1

---⚬⚬⚬---

The Collapse
of the Old Order

In 1609, Hugo Grotius propounded the thesis that the freedom of the seas was part of international law. According to Grotius, coastal States could assert their sovereignty only over a narrow belt of territorial sea. As a result of State practice, it was generally recognised that the maximum permissible breadth of the territorial sea was three miles. Beyond the territorial seas was the high seas which could not be divided or appropriated for exclusive use by any nation. The only limitations on the principle of freedom of the seas were those which recognised the right of coastal States to deal with customs, fiscal, immigration and health matters and the right of all States to act against slavery and piracy.

The international law of the sea, as propounded by Grotius, survived for more than 300 years. It survived for such an impressive length of time because it served the needs of the world community, as it was constituted in the past. It served the needs of the maritime powers for navigation, the interest in commerce and the interests of the colonial empires.

Since 1945, the old legal order of the seas came increasingly under challenge. By the 1960s, it could fairly be said that the old legal order had collapsed and the world was faced with a plethora of conflicting claims for jurisdiction and resources by coastal States. Instead of order, we had chaos.

It is ironical that the rush by coastal States to grab the resources of the seas was started, wittingly or unwittingly, by the United States. On 28 September 1945, President Truman issued a proclamation in which the US asserted its jurisdiction and control of the natural resources of the subsoil and seabed of the continental shelf contiguous to the US coast. The term "continental shelf" was described in an accompanying press release as generally extending to the point where the waters reached a depth of 600 feet or 200 metres isobath.

The example of the US was soon emulated by other coastal States. Three years later, Chile and Peru, followed by Ecuador, claimed maritime zones extending 200 miles from their coast and embracing the water column as well as the seabed. Argentina, Brazil, El Salvador, Nicaragua, Panama and Uruguay also claimed some form of jurisdiction out to 200 miles. Canada claimed jurisdiction over shipping which could cause pollution in a zone up to 100 miles from its Arctic coast. Norway successfully broadened its fishing jurisdiction by the use of straight baselines. Iceland claimed a fishery zone of 50 miles and engaged briefly in a cod war with the United Kingdom. In 1960, Indonesia enacted a law proclaiming that the waters enclosed by baselines connecting the outermost points of the outermost islands forming the Indonesian archipelago were internal waters. The Philippines followed suit in 1961. By 1974, 76 countries had claimed territorial seas ranging from 12 to 200 miles. Since then, the number has increased to over 100. Of the world's 137 independent coastal States, only 24 States still adhere to the traditional territorial sea limit of three nautical miles. Over 70 States have claimed some form of resource jurisdiction of 200 miles.

What led to the breakdown of the old legal order? What were the underlying reasons for the unilateral claims by the coastal States?

There were three essential reasons or pressures behind the coastal States' expansion. The first is resources, the second is security and the third is concern for the marine environment.

The old legal order collapsed under the weight of:

1. progress in technology;
2. new uses of the ocean;
3. the failure of the traditional law to deal adequately with the concerns of coastal States regarding the utilisation of oceanic resources; and
4. the emergence of the developing countries.

The combination of a narrow territorial sea and the freedom to fish in the high seas served the interests of the world community as long as there was plenty of fish for all. The advent of factory fishing vessels equipped with electronic tracking gear led to overfishing and to the depletion of fish stocks. The possession of such advanced technology by a few distant-water fishing States naturally led to the perception by developing coastal States, dependent on coastal fisheries, of the situation as being inequitable. Developing coastal States, which are dependent upon coastal fisheries for their economic survival and welfare, claim that they have a better equity to such resources than the developed distant-water fishing States.

The statistics showing the impact of technology on the harvest of fish are revealing. In 1950, the world harvested 16 million tonnes of fish. In 1974, the global harvest of fish had increased to 69 million tonnes. Progress in the field of ship-building technology has also had an impact on navigation and on the marine environment. The emergence of very large crude carriers, such as the 500,000 tonne supertankers, nuclear-powered and nuclear-armed submarines, are some examples. There has been a vast increase in both the number and tonnage of vessels. In 1950, the world merchant tonnage was 76 million tonnes. In 1973, it had increased to 306 million tonnes. This vast increase posed serious problems of congestion and navigational safety in important shipping lanes.

The progress of technology has also led to new uses of the ocean. The exploitation of oil and gas in the continental shelf is one such example. Another example is the development of technology to mine the polymetallic nodules which lie on the deep seabed and ocean floor.

Confronted with the problems of overfishing and the depletion of fish stocks, some coastal States have attacked the traditional law as being inadequate to meet their concerns and interests. They have extended their jurisdiction over the fish stocks in the waters off their coasts, in the interest of conservation, and on the grounds that they had a better equity to harvest such fish stocks than other States.

In the period since 1945, especially in the decades of the 1950s and 1960s, most of the colonial empires were liquidated and a great number of the former colonies acceded to independence. The developing countries generally felt that they had no part in the moulding of the traditional law and that it did not serve their interests. They, therefore, demanded that the traditional law of the sea be re-moulded in order to take their interests into account. The fusion of the interests of developed and developing coastal States brought about a historic movement for the expansion of the jurisdiction and resource rights of coastal States. One American expert on the law of the sea, Leigh Ratiner, has described it as a coastal State/developing country revolution.

Why didn't the major maritime powers oppose the expansionism of the coastal States? Why were the great powers, especially the two superpowers (US and USSR), reluctant to use force in order to check the unilateral claims of the coastal States?

Initially, the great maritime powers protested, by diplomatic means, all unilateral claims by coastal States. When these diplomatic protests failed to stem the tide of coastal States expansion, the great powers did not resort to force to check the tide. For example, the UK did not use its superior firepower against Iceland during the cod war. The US did not send its navy to protect its tuna boats against seizure by Chile, Ecuador and Peru. Why did they not do so? I believe that they did not do so for four reasons. First, the US had itself been the first to make a unilateral claim to the resources of the continental shelf. Its moral authority was therefore not impeccable. Second, most of the coastal States that had made unilateral claims were friends and allies of the great powers. It is easier to use military force against an adversary than against a country which is an ally or friend. The use of force by a great power against an ally or friend would have serious repercussions on its alliance interest and on its foreign policy. Third, the use of force is arguably unlawful under the United Nations Charter and is, in any case, impolitic. Great powers would be condemned by world public opinion for bullying small or militarily weak coastal States, irrespective of the merit or demerit of the unilateral claims of the coastal States. Fourth, the coastal States were perceived to be claiming the resources of the sea in order to feed their hungry peoples and to augment their developing economies.

By the late 1960s, the great powers and the coastal States felt a need for a new legal order for the oceans. The four Geneva Conventions of 1958 had been ratified by very few States and were being rapidly overtaken by State practice. They had been adopted at a time when most of the countries of the Third World had not yet attained their independence. The great powers needed "a new consensus regarding the rules of ocean law that is compatible with the mobility, flexibility and credibility of a routine global deployment of forces." The coastal States wanted a new legal order to ratify the unilateral claims which they have made for oceanic jurisdiction, oceanic resources, for the protection of the marine environment, and for their greater security. The opportunity to build a new consensus on oceanic law was first presented in 1967 when the then Ambassador of Malta to the United Nations, Dr Arvid Pardo, drew the attention of the world to the immense resources of the seabed and ocean floor beyond the limits of the then prevailing national jurisdiction and proposed that such resources be considered the common heritage of mankind.

The coastal States immediately saw the advantage of broadening Pardo's proposal to include all aspects of the uses and resources of the sea. Their basic thought was that trade-offs could be made between the demand of the great powers for navigational and overflight rights and the demand of the coastal States for expanded resource rights. In 1967, the USSR approached the US and other countries on the idea of recognising a 12-mile territorial sea provided that a high seas corridor is preserved in international straits. In 1968 and 1969, the US started sounding out the views of some NATO countries, the USSR and others, on the idea of conceding 12 miles as the maximum permissible breadth of the territorial sea in return for free navigation of warships and overflight of military aircraft. The confluence of these three streams of thought led in 1970 to the decision to convene the Third United Nations Conference on the Law of the Sea in 1973.

In the summer of 1974, the Third United Nations Conference on the Law of the Sea held its first substantive session in Caracas, Venezuela. Eight years later, on 30 April 1982, the Conference, meeting in New York, adopted the United Nations Convention on the Law of the Sea and four related resolutions by a recorded vote of 130 States in favour, 4 States (Israel, Turkey, US and Venezuela) against, with 17 States abstaining. The Convention has been hailed by some and denounced by others. The former Foreign Minister of Canada, Dr Mark McGuigan, has described the new Convention as the most important legal instrument adopted since the adoption of the United Nations Charter.

I shall proceed to discuss some of the salient features of the Convention and of the unique process by which it has evolved. In my discussion of the Convention, I shall pay particular attention to the accommodation of competing interests, for example, between coastal fishermen and distant-water fishermen; between coastal States and landlocked and geographically disadvantaged States; between those with broad continental shelves and those with narrow continental shelves; between developed and developing countries; between the major maritime powers and the coastal States, etc. I shall also attempt to answer the question whether the Convention has adequately promoted the interests of the world community, such as:

1. the maintenance of peace and security;
2. the conservation and optimum utilisation of the living resources of the sea;
3. the preservation of the marine environment;

4. the freedom of navigation;
5. the promotion of world economic stability;
6. the narrowing of the gap between developed and developing countries;
7. the promotion of marine scientific research; and
8. the promotion of the peaceful settlement of disputes.

The Territorial Sea

The territorial sea is the belt of sea adjacent to the coast over which a coastal State may claim sovereignty. Under the traditional law, the territorial sea was supposed to have a maximum breadth of three miles. The First United Nations Conference on the Law of the Sea, held in 1958 in Geneva, failed to reach an agreement on the maximum permissible breadth of the territorial sea. Two years later, another attempt was made at the Second United Nations Conference on the Law of the Sea also held in Geneva. The second attempt also failed.

In 1981, of the 137 independent coastal States, only 24 claim a territorial sea of three miles. Seventy-nine States, by far the majority, claim a territorial sea of 12 miles. Twenty-six States claim a territorial sea of more than 12 miles.

Under international law, the coastal State has sovereignty in the territorial sea. The sovereignty of the coastal State is subject only to a right of "innocent passage" for foreign ships, including warships, but not for aircraft or submerged submarines.

What is innocent passage? What is the extent of the regulatory power of the coastal State over ships in the territorial sea?

The new Convention repeats the provisions of the 1958 Convention on innocent passage. The term is defined as that which is "not prejudicial to the peace, good order or security of the coastal state". In addition, it adds a list of activities which are not innocent passage. It prohibits discrimination by the coastal States based on the flag or destination of a ship. It also clarifies the right of the coastal State to establish sea lanes and traffic separation schemes and to control pollution. The provisions of the new Convention on innocent passage are a major improvement on the 1958 Convention.

A question that has often been asked is whether warships have a right to enjoy the regime of innocent passage through the territorial sea or must they seek the prior authorisation of the coastal States or give prior notification to the coastal States? This issue was heatedly debated in the Conference and was not resolved until its final day.

Article 17 of the Convention states that, "ships of all States whether coastal or landlocked, enjoy the right of innocent passage through the territorial sea." Since the Convention makes no distinction between merchant ships and warships, it follows logically that the right of innocent passage is applicable to all ships including warships. This interpretation of the text is also consistent with the legislative history of the question.

The delegation of Gabon submitted an amendment to Article 21 to require prior authorisation or notification for the passage of warships through the territorial sea. This amendment was strongly opposed by the major maritime powers, especially by the US and the USSR. In order to preserve consensus on the provisions relating to the territorial sea and on the Convention as a whole, the President of the Conference, aided by his colleagues in the Collegium persuaded Gabon not to insist on its amendment. After much persuasion, the delegation of Gabon agreed.

There was, however, another amendment, co-sponsored by 29 delegations to Article 21(1). This article gives the coastal States the power to make laws and regulations relating to innocent passage through the territorial sea, in respect of a list of eight matters. The amendment would add "security" as an additional matter on which such laws and regulations may be made. The two superpowers opposed the amendment because they feared that its adoption would confer on the coastal States extremely broad powers over navigation in the territorial sea, not restricted necessarily to warships. The US and the USSR threatened that if the amendment were adopted, their attitude towards the Convention, as a whole, would be affected. In view of the stand taken by the two superpowers, the Conference could not afford to take the risk of putting the amendment to vote. The burden of persuading the co-sponsors of the amendment not to insist on putting it to the vote fell on the Conference President.

In the frantic hours of the last day of the Conference, the President, with the help of his colleagues in the Collegium, had to undertake shuttle diplomacy between the group of co-sponsors of the amendment, locked in one room, and the delegations of the US and USSR in another room. Various texts were tried but none of them satisfied the two opposing sides. At one point, the Conference President asked the Secretary-General of the United Nations to help by speaking to the representative of Romania, the most insistent of all the co-sponsors. At the last minute, the President succeeded in persuading the co-sponsors not to insist on putting their amendment to the vote in return for a statement which the President would read into the record. The statement stated that the co-sponsors of the amendment agreed to respond to the appeal of the Conference President not to insist on putting their amendment to the vote and that their decision was "without prejudice to the rights of coastal States to adopt measures to safeguard their security interests, in accordance with Articles 19 and 25 of this Convention." It was agreed that no delegation would attempt to interpret the President's statement at the meeting. However, it is likely that the maritime powers and the co-sponsors of the draft amendment would give differing interpretations to the outcome. The co-sponsors would probably claim that there is sufficient latitude under Articles 19 and 25 to enable them to enact laws restricting the passage of warships through their territorial seas. The maritime powers, on the other hand, would argue the contrary and would seek support from the fact that there would have been no sense in submitting the two amendments if Articles 19 and 25 do confer such powers on coastal States.

Straits Used for International Navigation

The expansion of the maximum permissible breadth of the territorial sea from three to twelve miles has a very important impact on the freedom of navigation through straits. This is because there are 116 straits which have been recognised as international waterways and whose breadths are between six and twenty-four miles. With the extension of the territorial sea from three miles to twelve miles, the high seas corridor in these straits is lost. From the outset of the Conference, the US conditioned its willingness to agree to a 12-mile territorial sea upon obtaining recognition of a treaty right to unimpeded transit through, under and over straits used for international navigation. At the very first substantive session of the Conference in 1974, the US delegation stated:

> Unlike the territorial sea in general, international straits serve as access and connecting points for large areas of the oceans. As such, transit through straits is essential to the meaningful exercise of the high seas and rights of all States in these vast areas. Functionally, then, straits are quite distinct from other territorial sea areas.

The new Convention provides a special regime of passage through, under and over straits used for international navigation. Such straits are defined as straits connecting one part of the high seas or an exclusive economic zone and another part of the high seas or an exclusive economic zone. The special regime of passage is called transit passage. Unlike the regime of innocent passage, the regime of transit passage permits both overflight by aircraft and submerged transit by submarines.

Do the provisions of the new Convention on the regime of transit passage through straits used for international navigation offer better protection of navigational and overflight rights than the pre-existing law? Writing in the same issue of the *American Journal of International Law*, John Norton Moore said yes and Michael Riesman said no. Which of the two learned scholars is right?

Before answering this question it is well to remember that the pre-existing rule, under the 1958 Convention, was non-suspendable innocent passage. We should also remember that with the extension of the breadth of the territorial sea from three to twelve miles, the high seas corridor in the 116 straits whose breadths are between 6 and 24 miles has disappeared. In the absence of the Convention, the strait States will argue, as they did during the early part of the Conference, that since the waters in the straits were territorial seas, therefore the applicable regime is innocent passage.

The new Convention offers better protection than the pre-existing law in several ways. First, unlike the 1958 Convention, the new Convention clearly includes aircraft in the concept of transit passage. Article 38, paragraph 1, states that "all ships and aircraft enjoy the right of transit passage". Article 38, paragraph 2, refers to the "freedom of navigation and overflight solely for the purpose of continuous and expeditious transit of the strait". Article 39, paragraph 3, lays down the duties of aircraft in transit passage.

Second, unlike the pre-existing law, the new Convention allows submarines to transit the straits in submerged passage. This conclusion is not explicitly stated in the text but has to be derived from the text by way of interpretation. The conclusion was, however, agreed by the negotiators and the text was intended to convey that meaning. Article 38, paragraph 2, uses the term "freedom of navigation" when referring to transit passage. That expression is a term of art. It is used in Article 87 of the Convention dealing with the freedom of the high seas. The term was taken from Article 2 of the Geneva Convention on the High Seas. The term was deliberately chosen for use in the straits articles and none of the negotiators ever seriously argued that it was meant to exclude submerged transit. The phrase, "their normal modes of continuous and expeditious transit" in Article 3, paragraph 1(c) was also understood by the negotiators to be a term of art and to cover submerged passage by submarines.

It may be helpful to summarise the main provisions of the Convention relating to the regime of transit passage. Article 38 specifies the right of transit passage. Article 39 sets out the duties of vessels and aircraft in transit passage. It is important to note that these duties are not set out in the same manner as the activities specified in Article 19 which would remove the offending vessels from the regime of innocent passage. In the provisions of Article 39, these are duties which, if violated, entail international responsibility and liability under the Convention but do not give rise to a right of action by a coastal State. The laws and regulations that a strait State may adopt relating to transit passage, under Article 42, are limited to four categories. The first two, dealing with safety of navigation and the prevention of pollution, restricts the acts of coastal States to those consistent with internationally approved standards. The second and third categories, relating to fishing and the violations of customs, fiscal and immigration laws are subject to the general requirement that laws enacted with respect thereto, must not hamper transit passage, nor must they discriminate among foreign ships. Warships and State aircraft are immune from the enforcement of such regulations and are not subject to pollution regulations.

Why is the regime of transit passage through straits used for international navigation so important to the strategic and military interest of great powers?

Writing in *Foreign Affairs*, Elliot Richardson reasoned that "our fleet missile submarines ... depend on complete mobility in the oceans and unimpeded passage through international straits. Only such freedom makes possible the secrecy on which their survival is based." Writing in another journal, Richardson concluded that: "in sum, the transit passage regime will satisfactorily protect and enhance the legal regime in straits that is essential for the continued mobility and flexibility of air and naval forces."

Archipelagic States

In recent decades, a number of States, whose territories are composed of groups of islands lying in close proximity to one another, have claimed a special status under international law. They want to be recognised as archipelagic States. They have enacted domestic laws authorising the drawing of baselines connecting the outermost points of the outermost islands and claiming the waters within such baselines as internal waters. Indonesia did so in 1960. The Philippines followed in 1961.

The rationale put forward by the archipelagic States is that their special geographical characteristics pose a serious challenge to their national security, unity and integrity. They claim that it is necessary for the waters between the islands to be recognised as internal waters in order to assure their security, unity and integrity. Archipelagic States, such as Indonesia, which have experienced rebellions and attempts at secession by some of the islands comprising the archipelago, are particularly sensitive and insistent on this point. The archipelagic States tried to obtain recognition of their status at the First United Nations Conference on the Law of the Sea in 1958. They failed so they resorted to unilateral national legislation to accomplish the same end. Resistance to the concept, especially by the great powers, sprang from the fact that in some cases, the waters for which archipelagic status was claimed were not only vast in area, such as the Java Sea, but covered important straits and navigation and over-flight routes critical to the movement of their military forces.

The Convention has tried to respond to the needs of the archipelagic States and the interests of the international community. Under the Convention, the concept of archipelagic States is applicable only to island States, such as Indonesia, the Philippines and Fiji. The concept does not apply to archipelagos belonging to a continental State, for example, Hawaii and the Greek islands. While an archipelagic State may draw baselines joining the outermost points of the outer islands, they are subject to certain specific geographical limitations. The waters landward of the baselines are archipelagic waters under the sovereignty of the archipelagic States. The sovereignty of the archipelagic State is, however, subject to a number of limitations. The most important limitation is the preservation of the right of ships and aircraft of foreign States to enjoy continuous, expeditious and unobstructed transit in, over and under sea lanes and air routes which traverse the archipelagic waters and innocent passage in the adjacent territorial sea. Archipelagic sea lanes are defined by courses and distances from a point of entry into and a point of exit from the archipelagic waters, and which extend 25 miles on each side of its axis. The archipelagic sea lanes must be approved by the International Maritime Organization before they are applied by the archipelagic State. The right of archipelagic sea lanes passage must be at least as broad with respect to navigation and overflight as is transit passage through straits used for international navigation.

It will be recalled that in the late 1960s the primary interest of the US in convening a new conference on the law of the sea was to secure international recognition of its navigational and overflight rights. In the face of unilateral claims by coastal States to extend their territorial sea from three to twelve miles, thereby abolishing the high seas corridor in 116 straits used for international navigation, and in the face of claims by archipelagic States such as Indonesia and the Philippines, the US felt the need for a new international consensus concerning the maximum permissible breadth of the territorial sea, concerning a special regime of passage for ships and aircraft through, under and over straits used for international navigation and through the archipelagos. The provisions of the Convention have first, strengthened the regime of innocent passage through the territorial sea and second, prescribed a new regime called transit passage for ships and aircraft through, under and over straits and a new regime called archipelagic sea lanes passage through archipelagos.

The US government has decided not to become a party to the new Convention. The question therefore arises whether the US can, on the one hand, stay outside the Convention and, on the other hand, claim to enjoy the navigational and overflight rights contained in the Convention. Let us examine the regimes of innocent passage of territorial sea, the regime of transit passage through straits and the regime of archipelagic sea lanes passage *seriatim*.

Representatives of the US government have argued that it may remain outside the Convention and yet enjoy the navigational and overflight rights of the new Convention. They based their argument on the ground that these provisions of the Convention do not create new law but merely codify the existing international law. At the final plenary meeting of the Conference, on 30 April 1982, the Chairman of the Group of 77 stated that no rights could accrue to States which are not parties to the Convention. He argued that the rights in the Convention are contractual in nature, that they are not customary international law and that States have no right to pick and choose among the provisions of the Convention taking those they like and rejecting the rest.

The *North Sea Continental Shelf Case* dealt, *inter alia*, with the question when a rule in a convention becomes part of the general international law. The court answered that it could do so in three instances. First, when the rule in the convention merely codifies the pre-existing law. Second, when the rule in the convention reflects the emerging customary law. Third, when the subsequent practice of States subsumes a rule of law in the convention into the body of general international law. Using this analytical tool let us look at the provisions of the Convention. In the case of the regime of innocent passage through territorial sea, although the Convention makes some improvements to the pre-existing law, it is probably right to argue that this aspect of the Convention satisfies the first and second criteria in the *North Sea Continental Shelf Case*. Therefore, a State which stays outside the Convention may enjoy the rights conferred by the Convention on innocent passage through the territorial sea.

In the case of the regime of transit passage through straits used for international navigation, the position is more doubtful. Under the pre-existing law, the applicable rule for passage of ships through straits formed by territorial sea is non-suspendable innocent passage. The provisions of the Convention on transit passage through straits was the result of intensive negotiations between the parties and reflect a *quid pro quo*. In view of this, it may be difficult to argue convincingly that the regime of transit passage through straits used for international navigation is "either customary international law, the best evidence of international law or, at the very least, a pattern of understanding reflecting the foundation upon which customary law will undoubtedly develop."

What is true of the regime of transit passage through straits is equally true of the regime of archipelagic sea lanes passage through archipelagos. Representatives of archipelagic States have claimed that since their failure to win acceptance of the concept at the 1958 Conference, the status of archipelagic States has become part of general international law by virtue of State practice. The question is whether the regime of archipelagic sea lanes passage is also part of customary international law. One representative of an archipelagic State has said recently that his government does not regard it to be part of customary international law and if a State, which is not a party to the Convention, claims to exercise such a right, it will have to enter into a bilateral agreement with the archipelagic State.

The law is, to put it mildly, unclear. In practice, strait States and archipelagic States may apply the rules of the Convention uniformly, not differentiating between States which are parties to the Convention and those which are not. If this were to happen, then the US would have succeeded in its policy of pick and choose. However, one cannot exclude the possibility of a dispute arising between the US and a strait State or an archipelagic State, parties to the Convention, over the assertion by the US of the right of transit passage or archipelagic sea lanes passage.

In that event, the US could find itself in an awkward position. Some authors of this country have written to the effect that if any strait State or archipelagic State were to impose restrictions on the passage of US ships or aircraft through their straits or archipelagos, the US, the mightiest military power in the world, would simply blast its way through the straits and archipelagos. I have already said there are limits to the efficacy of the use of force. When force is to be used, it is surely better to use it with the law on your side than to do so with the law on the side of your adversary or in the context of legal uncertainty.

The Protection and Preservation of the Marine Environment

The protection and preservation of the marine environment is clearly one of the interests of the world community. The oceans constitute one of our global commons. It is a source of food, of recreation, of energy and a frontier to be explored in the advancement of our knowledge. As a result of the dumping of wastes, pollution from ships, and offshore exploitation for oil, the ecology of the oceans has been seriously threatened. Accidents involving oil tankers such as the *Showa Maru*, in the Straits of Malacca and Singapore, and the *Amoco Cadiz*, off the shore of France, have helped to raise the consciousness of the world concerning this important problem.

Part XII of the Convention has strengthened the international legal system in protecting and preserving the marine environment. The Convention deals with the problem by examining each of the sources of pollution. These are: land-based sources, pollution resulting from seabed exploitation within the national jurisdiction of a coastal State, pollution resulting from seabed activities in the international area of the seabed and ocean floor, pollution by dumping, pollution from ships and pollution from and through the atmosphere.

The Convention codifies the existing law under which each State has the right to legislate and to implement its laws to protect the sea from pollution emanating from the land territory of such State. In the case of pollution resulting from seabed activities within the jurisdiction of a coastal State, the coastal State has the power to legislate as well as to enforce its laws against such pollution. However, the Conference feels that there was a need to ensure the implementation by the coastal States of minimum international standards. As a result, the Convention requires coastal States to make and implement laws at least as effective as the international rules and standards for pollution prevention when engaging in the exploration and exploitation of the seabed within national jurisdiction. The International Seabed Authority is required by Article 145 to adopt rules and regulations for the protection of the marine environment in the international area of the seabed and ocean floor.

Pollution by Dumping

As for the problem of pollution by dumping, the Conference took note of the existence of the London Convention to prevent pollution of the sea by dumping of harmful substances and other matters. The Convention recognises the right of coastal States to control dumping within their territorial seas, their exclusive economic zones and their continental shelves.

Pollution from Ships

The problem of pollution from ships was, by far, the most difficult. The debate in the Conference centred on the need to strike a proper balance between navigational rights and environmental concerns. The debate on this issue did not polarise along north-south lines. Instead, coalitions were formed representing the interests of flag States, port States and the environmentalists.

At first, many coastal States argued that they should have the power to legislate and to implement national laws and regulations to protect their marine environment from pollution by vessels. They rest their argument on the grounds that pollution by ships could adversely affect the living resources in the exclusive economic zone. The maritime powers were concerned that coastal States may abuse such power to interfere with the freedom of navigation in the exclusive economic zone. In the final compromise, the Convention tilts towards navigation by placing principal reliance on the port States and giving very limited competence to the coastal States.

The salient features of this part of the Convention can be summarised as follows. First, the port State has plenary power to set and to enforce pollution standards. The port States would have the jurisdiction to take action against ships for pollution wherever it might have taken place. Second, in the territorial sea, the right of the coastal State to set standards is circumscribed but its power of enforcement is generally unlimited. The coastal State can set standards for discharges but not for the construction, design, equipment and manning, unless they are giving effect to generally accepted international rules and standards. Third, in the exclusive economic zone, the coastal State has no real latitude in the setting of standards because they must conform to international rules and standards, meaning those adopted by the International Maritime Organization. The power of enforcement by the coastal State in the exclusive economic zone is limited to discharges of pollutants causing or threatening major damage to the environment.

The provisions of the Convention have succeeded in accommodating the concern for the protection of the marine environment and concern for the freedom of navigation. The Convention recognises certain rights of coastal States to protect the maritime zones under their jurisdiction and, at the same time, ensures the universal and uniform character of the environmental rules and standards applicable to all ships, thereby preventing unilateral actions by coastal States.

LECTURE 2

―⸺∞⸺―

Reconciling Competing Claims to the Resources and the Uses of the Sea

The two most important resources of the sea are oil and fish. I will begin this lecture by discussing the question of fish and the innovation by the Conference of the concept of the exclusive economic zone to deal with the problem.

Fish is the world's most important source of animal protein. For some countries, it is also the cheapest and the most common form of animal protein. In many countries, fishing provides an important source of occupation and income for its coastal populations. In 1974, Dr S Holt of the Woods Hole Oceanographic Research Institute estimated the value of the world marine catch, excluding whales, at US$15 billion. In dealing with the problem of fish, it is well to remember that it falls under several important classifications which have an impact on the legal regime.

There is, first of all, the sedentary species such as lobsters, which live on the sea bottom. Second, there are some species of fish which are highly migratory. They travel great distances from one part of the ocean to another. The most important example of a species which falls within this category is tuna. The third category consists of the anadromous species. The salmon is a classic example of an anadromous fish which lives most of its life in the sea but ascends rivers to spawn. The fourth category of fish, by far the largest, embraces all the species which are not sedentary, not highly migratory and not anadromous. It includes the catadromous species, that is fish which descend to the lower river or to the sea to spawn.

In my first lecture, I have already discussed the impact of advanced fishing technology on the world's fish resources. As a result of overfishing, some species of fish have become or are in danger of being depleted. If this tendency were not checked, it would pose a serious threat to an important interest of the world community. The response of the coastal States has been that the problem could not be adequately dealt with under the traditional law. Their argument was that if most of the world's fish stocks were in the high seas and, therefore, governed by the high seas freedom, the fishing problem becomes what has been called a common pool problem. Under the common pool problem, the participants have a built-in disincentive to conserve, thus making it a classic example of a zero-sum game. Spokesmen for the coastal States have argued that the various international and regional fisheries commissions have been ineffective in adopting and enforcing adequate conservation measures.

If the traditional law governing fishing was inadequate, what were the alternatives available to deal with the problem? There were two schools of thought. There were those who, like Dr Arvid Pardo, advocated the establishment of an international oceans authority with extensive powers to regulate the resources and uses of the sea, including the problem of fish. This approach was, however, rejected by the coastal States. Why did the coastal States reject such an approach? They rejected it because, as one spokesman for a coastal State said, "Whether we like it or not, international relations are based still on the principle of State sovereignty." The point he was making was that we still live in an era of nation States, and the political will to cooperate at the international level and to establish international institutions to solve global problems is still a very weak impulse. Some have, however, objected to this approach on the ground that it is impractical.

The second approach, which was ultimately accepted by the Conference and embodied in the Convention, was to accept the view of the coastal States that they are the best means to manage the fish resources of the world. The Convention allows every coastal State to establish an exclusive economic zone seaward of its territorial sea and extending up to 200 miles from its coast. Why 200 miles? Why not 25 miles or 50 miles? Is there any rationale for choosing 200 miles? The figure of 200 miles has no particular rational basis other than the fact that the Latin American coastal States had unilaterally claimed various forms of maritime zones extending to that limit. Initially, the Asian and African coastal States regarded the Latin American claim as being rather extreme and were prepared to settle for a narrower limit. The insistence of the Latin Americans and the growing mood by the coastal States to claim as much of the resources of the sea as possible, eventually led the other coastal States to embrace the 200-mile limit.

Where did the term "exclusive economic zone" come from? Why not call it the fisheries conservation zone as it is known in United States domestic law? Some Latin American coastal

States had claimed a territorial sea of 200 miles. Other Latin American coastal States refer to the 200-mile maritime zone as their "patrimonial sea". It was the delegation of Kenya which first used the term exclusive economic zone at a meeting of the Asian African Legal Consultative Committee at Lagos, Nigeria, in January 1972. In June 1972, the Kenyan proposal was accepted by an African seminar on the Law of the Sea held in Yaounde, Cameroon. Finally, Kenya submitted draft articles on the exclusive economic zone on 7 August 1972 to the United Nations Seabed Committee. A strenuous effort was made by a group of countries at the Conference called landlocked and geographically disadvantaged States to knock off the word "exclusive" but this effort failed. The coastal States insisted on the retention of the word in order to symbolise their exclusive rights to the resources of the zone.

What are the rights of a coastal State in its exclusive economic zone? First, the coastal State has exclusive sovereign rights to control the exploration, exploitation, conservation and management of all living and non-living natural resources in the waters and on the seabed. Second, the coastal State has exclusive sovereign rights to control other activities for the economic exploration and exploitation of the zone, such as the production of energy from the water, currents and wind. Third, the coastal State has the exclusive right to control the construction and use of all artificial islands and most installations and structures, especially those used for resources and other economic purposes. Fourth, the coastal State has the right to be informed of and participate in proposed marine scientific research projects of other States in its exclusive economic zone and to withhold consent for a project in a timely manner and under certain specified circumstances. Fifth, the coastal State has the right to control the dumping of wastes. Sixth, the coastal State has the right to board, to inspect and, where there is a threat of major damage, to arrest a merchant ship for discharging pollution in the zone in violation of internationally approved standards. This right is, however, subject to substantial safeguards to protect shippers and consumers. The safeguards are similar to those which apply to straits used for international navigation.

What are the rights of the international community in the exclusive economic zone? The rights of the international community can be classified under two categories: first, the high seas freedoms of navigation, overflight, the laying of submarine cables and pipelines; and second, other internationally lawful uses of the sea related to these freedoms. The second category may cover a variety of uses, such as recreational swimming, weather monitoring and certain naval operations. What about activities that are covered neither by the rights of the coastal States, on the one hand, or the rights of the international community, on the other? The Convention provides that the matter shall be resolved on the basis of equity and in the light of all the relevant circumstances.

How will the establishment of the exclusive economic zone enhance the world community's interest in the conservation of the living resources of the sea? Under the Convention, the coastal State is required to ensure the conservation of the living resources in the exclusive economic zone. Except in respect of marine mammals, the coastal State is also required to ensure their optimum utilisation. This duty was imposed on coastal States in view of the world's demand for animal protein. Therefore, the coastal State must, within conservation limits, grant access under reasonable conditions to foreign vessels to fish for stocks in excess of what the coastal State can harvest for the time being. The Convention also prescribes regional regulation of the highly migratory species, such as tuna, outside the exclusive economic zone. As for anadromous stocks, the Convention states that the

States in whose rivers anadromous stocks originate shall have the primary interest in and responsibility for such stocks. The State of origin shall ensure the conservation of the anadromous stocks by the establishment of appropriate regulatory measures for the fishing of such stocks in its exclusive economic zone. In the case where anadromous stocks migrate from the State of origin into the exclusive economic zone of another State, such State shall cooperate with the State of origin with regard to the conservation and management of such stocks. Where the anadromous stocks pass beyond the exclusive economic zone of the State of origin into the high seas, the States which have been fishing such stocks shall maintain consultations with a view to achieving agreement on terms and conditions of such fishing, giving due regard to the conservation requirements and the needs of the State of origin in respect of such stocks. The enforcement of regulations regarding anadromous stocks beyond the exclusive economic zone shall be by agreement between the State of origin and the other States concerned.

According to one expert, 99 per cent of the total world catch of marine fish is caught within 200 miles of shore. Only 1 per cent is caught outside the exclusive economic zone and consists mainly of tuna. If the coastal States pursue an enlightened policy towards the conservation and management of the living resources of their exclusive economic zones, then it can be argued that the problems of overfishing and of the depletion of certain species will be overcome. If, on the other hand, some coastal States ignore their long-term interests in favour of their short-term benefits and indulge in overfishing of certain species, then the problems would remain unsolved. There is, however, provision for dispute settlement procedure to challenge inadequate conservation by coastal States. Therefore, whether the world community's interests in the conservation of the living resources of the seas will be enhanced by the establishment of the exclusive economic zone, will depend upon the present and future performances of the coastal States. It is fair, however, to say that the new law will probably work better than the pre-existing law.

What about the question of international equity? What is the effect of the exclusive economic zone on the redistribution of world income from fish? The result of the exclusive economic zone is to redistribute income from fish from nations with long-distance fishing fleets to States with long coasts bordering on rich fishing grounds. It can be argued that the new law is more equitable than the old because it recognises that the coastal States, especially developing ones, have a greater equity to the fish off their coasts than the distant-water fishing fleets. However, since the richest fishing grounds, like the richest countries, are located in the temperate zones, the benefits go mainly to developed coastal States. It is somewhat ironical that the size of the combined exclusive economic zones of the 50 African States is less than the size of the exclusive economic zone of the US alone. Twenty-five countries will gain control of 76 per cent of the world's economic zones. Out of these 25, 13 are developed countries. Some of the biggest winners of the Conference are the US, Canada, Australia, New Zealand and Norway. It is also a lamentable fact that none of the income from fish will be re-distributed to the developing landlocked countries, most of which belong to the group of Least Developed Countries. Until 1976, the group of landlocked and geographically disadvantaged States resisted the concept of the exclusive economic zone. The resistance would have lasted longer if not for the fact that in 1976, in the expediency of an election year, the US took one of its U-turns and enacted its own 200-mile Fisheries Conservation Zone. With the US joining the unilateralists, the group of landlocked and geographically disadvantaged States realised that further resistance was futile and settled for the best it could extract from the coastal States. Only the delegation of Zambia resisted the idea to the end, insisting on the superior merit of regional economic zones. The Convention does contain some provisions giving to landlocked States and geographically disadvantaged States some preferential rights to the surplus of the allowable catch of their neighbouring States.

There is one other aspect of the exclusive economic zone that I would like to touch upon. What is the status of the exclusive economic zone? Is it a zone of national jurisdiction? Is it part of the high seas? Is it a *sui generis* zone? The struggle over this question occupied the Conference for several years until it was finally resolved in an informal negotiating group convened by Foreign Minister Castañeda of Mexico in 1977. Article 56 of the Convention summarises the rights of coastal States. Paragraph 1(a) confers sovereign rights on coastal States for various economic purposes. Paragraphs 1(b) and 1(c) refer to jurisdiction and other rights and duties specifically provided for elsewhere in the Convention. Taken together, Article 56 and the articles to which it refers, incorporate State practice regarding fisheries and make detailed provisions for additional coastal State rights.

But a coastal State, in exercising its rights and performing its duties in the exclusive economic zone, is required to have due regard to the rights and duties of other States and to act in a manner compatible with the Convention. By placing the exclusive economic zone in the context of the Convention as a whole, Article 56 draws attention to the two sources of limitation on coastal States' rights in the zone: first, the specificity of their enumeration; and second, their subjection to the due regard and compatibility provision. These limiting provisions, which have no counterpart in any pre-existing Convention, are reinforced by the cross reference in Article 58, paragraph 2, to Article 89, the effect of which is that no State may validly purport to subject any part of the exclusive economic zone to its sovereignty. Paragraph 1 of Article 58 identifies the safeguarded freedoms as those referred to in Article 87, which is captioned "Freedom of the high seas". Article 87 defines "freedom of the high seas" by setting forth a list of freedoms whose non-exhaustive character is made clear by the prefatory phrase *"inter alia"*. The non-inclusiveness of Article 58 with respect to both the quality and quantity of the freedoms thereby safeguarded, is further reinforced by the phrase "other internationally lawful uses of the sea related to these freedoms". In sum, although the exclusive economic zone is not explicitly characterised as part of the high seas, the net result of the provisions is that the high seas freedoms exercisable in the zone are qualitatively and quantitatively the same as the traditional high seas freedoms recognised by international law.

The Continental Shelf

Oil and gas are the most important economic resources beneath the sea. In 1974, of the approximately 20 billion barrels of oil produced worldwide, 20 per cent came from offshore production. Of the more than 2.5 trillion barrels worth of oil estimated to lie beneath the sea, the United States National Petroleum Council has estimated that 30 to 45 per cent lies in those portions of the continental margin beyond the depth of 200 metres.

Geomorphologically, the continental shelf is that area of the underwater continental land mass lying immediately adjacent to the shoreline and generally extending out for a distance that can be as little as 2 miles or as much as 600 miles, with an average gradient of less than one-tenth of a degree and the outer edge of which is usually found at a depth of between 130 and

200 metres. The continental shelf, together with a steeper area lying adjacent to it, known as the continental slope, and the continental rise make up the continental margin. The continental slope has a steeper gradient than the continental shelf, is often narrower in width and can drop at its outer edge to a depth between 2,000 and 2,500 metres. The continental rise is an area largely composed of continental sediments that have been transported down the slope through the ages and that merge gradually with the deep seabed, which is called the abyssal plain. It is within the continental margin, consisting of the continental shelf, the continental slope and the continental rise, that virtually all of the oceans' non-living organic resources, including oil and gas, are to be found.

I have already referred to the fact that US was the first country to claim exclusive rights over the resources of the continental shelf through the Truman Proclamation of 1945. The rights claimed by the US extended to the point where the waters reached a depth of 200 metres isobath. The 1958 Convention on the Continental Shelf recognised the sovereign rights of coastal States to the resources of the continental shelf "to a depth of 200 metres or, beyond that limit, to where the depth of the superjacent waters admits of the exploitation of the natural resources of the said areas." The problem with this definition is that it prescribes an indeterminate boundary since the progress of offshore drilling technology makes it possible to exploit the continental shelf at greater and greater depths. One of the objectives of the Third United Nations Conference on the Law of the Sea was to replace the definition in the 1958 Convention with a more precise definition.

Has the new Convention succeeded in prescribing a more precise definition than that of the 1958 Convention? The answer is probably yes, although the term "continental shelf" has now acquired a legal meaning quite distinct from its geomorphological meaning. Geomorphologically, the continental shelf does not include the continental slope and the continental rise. Indeed, these three components form the continental margin. Under the new Convention, the concept of the continental shelf has been expanded to include both the continental slope and the continental margin.

The boundary of the continental margin falling within the jurisdiction and rights of coastal States is determined in the following manner. First, if the outer edge of the continental margin does not extend beyond 200 miles, the rights of coastal States end either at the outer edge of the continental margin or at 200 miles from the baselines. Second, if the continental margin extends beyond 200 miles, the boundary will be drawn in accordance with one of the following two criteria. The first criterion is a line not more than 60 miles from the foot of the continental slope. The second criterion is a line drawn at a point where the thickness of the sedimentary rock is at least 1 per cent of the shortest distance from such point to the foot of the continental slope. These two criteria are, however, governed by two provisos. The line drawn in accordance with the two criteria must not exceed 350 miles from the baselines or 100 miles from the point at which the water is 2,500 metres isobath in depth.

If a coastal State claims a continental shelf beyond 200 miles, it is required by Article 76, paragraph 8 of the Convention, to submit information on the limits of its continental shelf to the Commission on the Limits of the Continental Shelf, established by Annex II of the Convention. The Commission shall make recommendations to coastal States and the coastal States shall establish the limits of the shelf on the basis of such recommendations. The coastal State shall deposit with the Secretary-General of the United Nations charts and relevant information, including geodetic data, permanently describing the outer limits of its continental shelf. The Secretary-General shall give publicity to such information.

One effect of the provisions of the new Convention on the continental shelf is that all the areas of the seabed which contain commercially exploitable deposits of oil and gas have been taken out of the common heritage of mankind and given to coastal States.

How did the Conference come to accept this result? Did the representatives of States consider other proposals which would result in a more equitable redistribution of this form of oceanic wealth?

In 1970, the US put forward a proposal to the United Nations Seabed Committee that in the area beyond the depth of 200 metres to the outer edge of the continental margin, to be known as the "trusteeship zone", the coastal State would have to contribute part of the revenues derived from the exploitation of oil and gas into an international fund. At one point, the delegation of Canada also put forward a similar proposal for revenue sharing which would extend not from 200 metres isobath, but from the coastal States' internal waters. These proposals were strongly opposed by the coastal States with broad continental margins. The proposal by the US, which would have benefited most of the developing countries, whether coastal or landlocked, was rejected by the Group of 77. It was rejected for four reasons. First, the proposal by the US was part of a large and comprehensive proposal which was not fully understood. Second, the fact that the proposal was made by the US made it suspect in the eyes of some of the developing countries. Third, the internationalist sentiment underlining the concept of revenue sharing ran counter to the strong tide of nationalism. Fourth, the choice of the word "trusteeship" to describe the zone was unfortunate because of its colonial connotations. This was a classic example of a good concept that was rendered suspicious because of the infelicitous choice of its name. It is a paradigm case of what linguistic philosophers would call "word magic".

In the negotiations on the continental shelf, two groups of States strongly opposed the demands of the broad margin States. They were the group of landlocked and geographically disadvantaged States and the Arab group. The group of landlocked and geographically disadvantaged States argued strongly in favour of applying the same limit to the exclusive economic zone and to the continental shelf. It put forward numerous proposals of revenue sharing, starting from a point to be fixed by depth or distance from the baselines. To make its proposals attractive, the group suggested that both the formula for contributions to the international fund and the formula for payments to States should favour the developing countries. An attempt was made to ensure that no developing coastal State would be a net contributor to the international fund. The Arab group insisted that the limit of the continental shelf must, under no circumstances, extend beyond 200 miles. In the later stages of the Conference, another attempt was made by a number of the landlocked and geographically disadvantaged States to gather support for the idea of a common heritage fund which would be based essentially on revenue sharing. All such proposals failed to obtain the support of the coastal States, especially the broad margin States.

In the end, a compromise proposal was agreed upon whereby revenue sharing would be applicable only to the area of the continental shelf beyond 200 miles. This is contained in Article 82 of the Convention. The first five years of production shall be exempted. During the sixth year, the rate of payment shall be 1 per cent of the value or volume of production at the site. The rate shall increase by 1 per cent for each subsequent year until the 12th year and the rate shall remain at 7 per cent thereafter. A developing country which is a net importer of oil or gas, is exempt from making such payments. This aspect of the Convention is clearly new law. Although it is very inadequate compared to the proposal made by the US in 1970 and the various proposals of the group of landlocked and geographically disadvantaged States, it is, nevertheless, an attempt to redistribute the income derived from offshore deposits of oil and gas in a more equitable way than simply to let the coastal States have it all.

Marine Scientific Research

I have earlier described the promotion of marine scientific research as one of the interests of the world community. This is because mankind has an interest in expanding its knowledge about the oceans which cover two-thirds of the earth's surface. Knowledge about the living resources of the seas is essential for the proper management and conservation of such resources. Knowledge about non-living resources in the continental shelf and in the deep seabed will enable us to explore and exploit such resources. Knowledge about the currents and the differential temperatures of waters have led to new uses of the sea.

If the promotion of marine scientific research is so clearly in the interest of the world community, why was it such a divisive issue in the Conference? Why was the cause of freedom of scientific research advocated by only five or six States and opposed by most of the coastal States? There are many reasons to explain this. First, marine scientific research is an expensive business and there are only six countries—US, USSR, United Kingdom, France, Federal Republic of Germany (FRG) and Japan—which have major programmes in marine scientific research. This means that the rest of the world, especially the developing countries, does not feel that they have a stake in the promotion of marine scientific research. Second, some developing countries fear that marine scientific research may disguise other less wholesome activities conducted off their coasts or on their continental shelves. Third, the research States had, in the past, made the mistake of not inviting the personnel from the developing coastal States to participate in the research. Fourth, some research States had failed to share the results derived from the research with the coastal States concerned. Fifth, some coastal States fear that the research States will acquire valuable economic information which would then give them an advantage in their bilateral negotiations.

What is the pre-existing law governing marine scientific research? Has the Convention improved the position of marine scientists or has it made it worse? Under the pre-existing law, no research can be carried out in the territorial sea of a coastal State without its consent. This rule is reproduced in the new Convention. Under the 1958 Convention on the Continental Shelf, the consent of the coastal State is required. The exclusive economic zone is a new concept and there is, therefore, no pre-existing rule applicable to research in such zones. The representatives of coastal States, however, argued that the regime applicable under the 1958 Convention on the Continental Shelf should, by analogy, apply to research in the exclusive economic zone. This view was strongly opposed by the research States, especially by the US, which advocated freedom of research in both the exclusive economic zone and on the continental shelf. In this, as in all the other areas, compromises were arrived at which reconciled the competing concerns of the research States and of the coastal States.

The main provisions of Part XIII, which is new law, can be summarised as follows. Article 246, paragraph 2, states that marine scientific research in the exclusive economic zone and on the continental shelf, shall be conducted with the consent of the coastal State. Paragraph 3, however, states the proposition that coastal States must, in normal circumstances, grant their consent. Paragraph 4 states that "normal circumstances" may exist in spite of the absence of diplomatic relations between the coastal State and the research State.

Under paragraph 5, the coastal State may withhold its consent only under four circumstances: one, if the research project is of direct significance for the exploration and exploitation of natural resources; two, if it involves drilling into the continental shelf, the use of explosives or the introduction of harmful substances in the marine environment; three, if it involves the construction, operation or use of artificial islands, installations and structures; or four, if the information provided regarding the nature and objectives of the project is inaccurate or if the researcher has an outstanding obligation to the coastal State from a prior research project. The discretion of the coastal State to withhold consent is, therefore, limited. Also, under Article 296, paragraph 2, disputes between the research State and the coastal State shall be referred to conciliation.

In the case of research on the continental shelf, outside 200 nautical miles, the coastal State may withhold its consent only if the research project is to be conducted in the specific areas of the shelf that the coastal State has publicly designated as areas in which exploitation or detailed exploratory operations are occurring or will occur within a reasonable period.

The provisions of the Convention on marine scientific research have wisely sought to achieve the objective of mutual benefits. The coastal State will be fully informed of the nature and objectives of the research project. The coastal State will be given an opportunity to participate in the research project. The coastal State will have access to the results of the research project. In these ways, the coastal State will have an interest to cooperate with the research State.

What have been the reactions of the marine scientific community to the provisions of Part XIII of the Convention? Donald Walsh, the Director of Marine and Coastal Studies of the University of Southern California, has said that the provisions of the new Convention are a definite improvement to the pre-existing situation. He has said that although Part XIII is not optimal, it is the best that we can get. He has described this part of the new Convention as a blessing to marine scientific research.

Before leaving the subject of marine scientific research, I want to draw your attention to a strange curiosity. Congressman John Breaux of Louisiana has submitted a bill to the House of Representatives entitled, "Exclusive Economic Zone Establishment Act". H.R. 7225, Section 104 of the bill deals with marine scientific research in the exclusive economic zone. The proposal is that a US citizen who wishes to undertake marine scientific research in the zone must seek the consent of the Secretary of State. A foreign citizen must not only seek the consent of the US Secretary of State but he must be from a reciprocating State. It is difficult to reconcile this proposal with the stand taken by the US at the Conference.

The Settlement of Disputes

Almost all international treaties do not contain mandatory provisions on the settlement of disputes. In the 1958 Conventions, for example, the effort to include such provisions failed. The Optional Protocol containing provisions for the settlement of disputes has been ratified by very few States. There are several reasons for the reluctance of States to include in treaties mandatory provisions for the settlement of disputes. First, most States, whether big or small, have a reluctance to tie their hands in advance. Second, the more powerful States are reluctant to commit themselves to binding third-party procedures and prefer negotiations because they hope to be able to use their weight and influence to extract better terms in such negotiations. Third, States can seldom agree on the fora to which their disputes should be referred. Some States prefer the International Court of Justice. Other States are opposed to the Court. Some prefer arbitration. Still others, as a matter of ideology and principle, refuse to commit themselves to any form of binding third-party procedures. Viewed in this light, the success of the Conference in including in the Convention a system for the settlement of disputes is a landmark achievement in international law. It is the first time that the USSR has subscribed to such a system in a treaty.

Why have States been willing to accept a system for the settlement of disputes in this Convention? They have done so because they have very important interests at stake. These interests have been reflected by a series of delicately balanced compromises. It is in everybody's interests to protect these compromises from being unravelled through varied interpretations. It was for this reason that the USSR and the African States were prepared, for the first time, to put aside their objections and to embrace a binding system of dispute settlement.

The broad outline of the system of dispute settlement in the Convention can be described as follows. First, the parties to the Convention can agree between themselves and select any dispute settlement method they wish. The choice of the parties prevails over all the other provisions of the Convention. Similarly, if the two parties to a dispute have previously agreed, in a bilateral, regional or general agreement to settle their disputes in reference to any particular procedure entailing a binding decision, this procedure supersedes those provided for in the Convention. To give an example, if the two parties to a dispute have accepted unconditionally the jurisdiction of the International Court of Justice, then either of them can refer the dispute to the Court.

However, if the procedure chosen by the parties does not lead to a binding decision, the jurisdiction of the institutions established by the Convention is revived and a party to the dispute can resort to them. Similarly, the provisions of the Convention come into play whenever the parties have not been able to settle the dispute by negotiation or conciliation and have not succeeded in agreeing on another method of settlement.

The Convention provides four methods for the settlement of dispute. These are:

1. the International Tribunal for the Law of the Sea, to be established in accordance with Annex VI of the Convention;
2. the International Court of Justice;
3. an arbitral tribunal constituted in accordance with Annex VII of the Convention; and
4. a special arbitral tribunal for one or more of the categories of disputes specified in Annex VIII.

If the two parties to a dispute have chosen different methods for settling their dispute, Article 287 of the Convention provides that the dispute shall be submitted to arbitration. The logic for this rule is that whilst arbitration was not everyone's first choice, it was a method acceptable to all States because it is the parties to the dispute that choose the arbiters.

There are three important exceptions to the system I have described. The first exception concerns disputes relating to the exclusive economic zone. The second covers disputes relating to sea-boundary delimitations, to military or law enforcement activities or to disputes submitted to the United Nations Security Council. The third exception concerns disputes relating to sea-bed mining.

I will deal first with the third exception. As a general rule, disputes relating to the provisions of Part XI and its related Annexes concerning the international area of the seabed and ocean floor, will be referred to the Seabed Disputes Chamber of the International Tribunal for the Law of the Sea. The Tribunal will have 21 members. The Seabed Disputes Chamber will consist of 11 members chosen by the Tribunal from among its members. The jurisdiction of the Seabed Disputes Chamber covers disputes between States, concerning interpretation or application of the relevant part of the Convention; disputes between States and the International Seabed Authority (ISA) for alleged violations of that part of the Convention or abuses or misuse of power by the ISA; disputes between States and the Enterprise, as well as disputes between entities other than States, such as State enterprises, consortia, corporations and either the ISA or the Enterprise concerning mining contracts. Article 188, paragraph 1, enables States which have disputes concerning the interpretation or the application of Part XV of the Convention and its related Annexes to refer such disputes to a smaller chamber, chosen either from the Tribunal as a whole or from the Seabed Disputes Chamber.

In the case of disputes over the interpretation or application of mining contracts, the transfer of technology to the Enterprise and the financial terms of mining contracts, such disputes can be submitted to binding commercial arbitration in accordance with the United Nations Commission on International Trade Law arbitration rules. In the case of a dispute which involves both the interpretation of the Convention and of a mining contract, the question concerning the interpretation of the Convention will be referred by the Arbitral Tribunal to the Seabed Disputes Chamber for a ruling. The Arbitral Tribunal's award should be in accordance with such ruling. The Seabed Disputes Chamber has the power to redress any party for any act of the ISA that is outside its competence or is based upon an abuse of its powers. The Chamber does not, however, have jurisdiction in respect of the exercise by the ISA of its discretionary powers.

The second exception permits States by declaration to exclude from binding settlement disputes relating to sea-boundary delimitations, to military or law enforcement activities or to disputes submitted to the United Nations Security Council. Disputes which are being dealt with by the Security Council are totally exempt from the disputes settlement system under the Convention. Disputes concerning military activities and law enforcement activities in regard to the exercise of sovereign rights or jurisdiction by a coastal State, may also be taken out of the binding disputes settlement system by a State when it signs, ratifies or accedes to the Convention or at any time thereafter.

Where States have so elected by a declaration, disputes concerning sea-boundary delimitations or involving historic bays or titles are dealt with in the following ways. First, those which arose before the entry into force of the Convention are totally exempt from the dispute settlement procedures of the Convention. Second, those which arise after the entry into force of the Convention will be subject to compulsory conciliation. Third, mixed disputes which involve the concurrent consideration of sea boundaries or of any unsettled dispute concerning sovereignty or other rights over continental or insular land territory are totally excluded from disputes settlement under the Convention. Fourth, sea-boundary disputes which have been finally settled by an arrangement between the parties or which are to be settled in accordance with an agreement between them are also excluded from the dispute settlement procedures of the Convention.

Disputes relating to violations by either a coastal State or by any other State of the provisions of the Convention with respect to freedoms and rights of navigation, overflight, the laying of submarine cables and pipelines, or other internationally lawful uses of the sea, as well as those relating to violations by the coastal State of international rules and standards for the protection and preservation of the marine environment, are subject to the general system for compulsory and binding dispute settlement.

Disputes relating to marine scientific research are divided into three categories: some are subject to the general system of binding dispute settlement, some are completely excluded from that system due to their discretionary character and some are subject to compulsory conciliation. Disputes relating to fisheries, like those relating to marine scientific research, are also divided into three categories.

It is generally agreed that the inclusion in the Convention of a mandatory and binding system for the settlement of disputes is one of the most important accomplishments of the Conference. The system offers to State parties a choice of four methods for the settlement of disputes. While the general system is simple and straightforward, the many exceptions to the system are complex and difficult to understand. Despite the complexity of the exceptions, however, Part XV of the Convention constitutes an important contribution to the peaceful settlement of disputes between States and to the rule of law. The disputes settlement provisions of the Convention are available only to States which are parties to the Convention. If a dispute were to arise between a State which is a party to the Convention and a State, such as the US, which is not a party thereto, such disputes would have to be solved in accordance with procedures available to the parties outside the Convention. At present, such procedures are not often available. In the last few decades, the US has been involved in a number of disputes with Canada and with a number of Latin American countries. As a result of these disputes, the US has found that, in the absence of a satisfactory system for the settlement of disputes, even a powerful country cannot adequately protect its citizens and ships against the acts of foreign governments that are not willing to submit their actions to impartial adjudication. The decision of the US not to become a party to the Convention means that it will not be able to enjoy the benefits of the system of disputes settlement under the Convention.

A Common Heritage
of Mankind

In 1967, the Maltese Ambassador to the United Nations, Dr Arvid Pardo, proposed that the seabed and the ocean floor outside the then prevailing limits of national jurisdiction, and the resources therein, should be declared a common heritage of mankind. In Pardo's view, the concept meant that any member of the international community is entitled to exploit the resources, but no one could take the resources without the consent of all. He also intended the concept to mean that the resources could not be subject to the appropriation or exclusive occupation by any State.

"The sea is a common heritage of mankind," Prince Wan Waithayakon of Thailand, the President of the First and the Second United Nations Conferences on the Law of the Sea is reported to have said in the first Plenary Meeting of the Conference in 1958. Apparently, he was the first person to use the phrase "a common heritage of mankind" in relation to the sea.

In the light of recent developments, it may be ironic that the next person who contributed to the evolution of the concept of the sea and its resources as a common heritage of mankind was an American. Speaking at the dedication of a United States research ship, *Oceanographer*, on 18 July 1966, President Johnson said:

> Under no circumstances, we believe, must we ever allow the prospects of rich harvest and mineral wealth to create a new form of colonial competition among the maritime nations. We must be careful to avoid a race to grab and to hold the lands under the high seas. We must ensure that the deep seabed and the ocean bottoms are, and remain, the legacy of all human beings.

The Declaration of Principles

On 17 December 1970, the United Nations General Assembly adopted the declaration of principles governing the seabed and ocean floor, and the subsoil thereof, beyond the limits of national jurisdiction. The declaration was adopted by 108 votes in favour (including the US), none against, with 14 abstentions. The Soviet bloc countries abstained in the vote but subsequently declared their support for the declaration. The declaration states that the seabed and ocean floor, and the subsoil thereof, beyond the limits of national jurisdiction as well as the resources of the Area are a common heritage of mankind. The declaration also states that the Area shall not be subject to appropriation by States or by other entities and no State shall claim or exercise sovereignty or sovereign rights over any part thereof. The declaration also adds that no State or other entity shall claim, exercise or acquire rights with respect to the Area or its resources incompatible with the international regime to be established, and with the principles of the declaration. All activities regarding the exploration and exploitation of the resources of the Area shall be governed by the international regime to be established.

The Common Heritage Reduced

In the short space of time between 1967 and the commencement of the Conference in 1973, an American expert on the law of the sea, John Temple Swing, estimated that 35 per cent of the common heritage of mankind, including the continental margins in which oil and gas resources are likely to be found, have been claimed by coastal States. The most significant mineral resource found in the international area of the seabed and ocean floor is manganese nodules. More recently, scientists have also discovered deposits of polymetallic sulphides.

Manganese Nodules

Polymetallic nodules, more commonly referred to as manganese nodules, come in various shapes and forms. They are often described in the literature as looking like potatoes. The formation processes of nodules are not yet fully understood. The world's interest in manganese nodules is due to the fact that they contain, among other metals, manganese, copper, nickel and cobalt, four important metals. Manganese is essential for the making of steel. Nickel is required for the making of stainless steel. Cobalt is needed for high-technology alloys and magnets. Because of their importance, they have sometimes been described as strategic metals.

Most of the known deposits of manganese nodules lie outside the jurisdiction of coastal States. Although our knowledge of the distribution of manganese nodules is incomplete, the most promising deposits are thought to lie within the so-called Clarion-Clipperton Fracture Zone. The nodules within this zone are said to contain on the average, 25 per cent manganese, 1.4 per cent nickel, 1.1 per cent copper and 0.25 per cent cobalt. The zone extends westward from Clarion Island and Clipperton Island in the eastern Pacific to a point approximately 1,600 kilometres directly south of Hawaii in the west. The area, irregular in shape, is approximately 4,500 kilometres from east to west and 1,000 kilometres from north to south totalling approximately 2.5 million square kilometres. It is the largest known single deposit of nodules that are presently of commercial grade.

Commercial grade manganese nodules are found only in very deep water, between 3,000 to 5,000 metres. Because of the technical difficulties of mining the nodules, and because of the enormous financial resources and sophisticated skills required, only a few countries now possess and are likely to develop a capacity to mine this resource. At present, there are four multinational consortia which have carried out extensive research and development. Of these, two of the consortia have succeeded in intermittent tests of prototype mining systems. The other two have tested individual components but not entire systems. The governments of France, Japan, the USSR and India have also carried out research and development in this field.

The Parallel System

From 1968 until 1976, the developed and the developing countries were unable to agree on the nature of the international regime and related institutions for the exploration and exploitation of the manganese nodules. The highly industrialised countries held the view that the proposed International Seabed Authority (ISA) should simply grant licences to mining consortia and State enterprises to mine the nodules. The developing countries, on the other hand, felt that since these resources constitute a common heritage of mankind, they should therefore be exploited by an international public enterprise belonging to the whole of mankind. The socialist countries did not favour either approach. They argued in favour of the division of the international area of the seabed and ocean floor into lots which could then be allocated to States. This deadlock was broken in 1976 as a result of an ingenuous proposal by the then US Secretary of State Dr Henry Kissinger. Kissinger proposed a compromise which has come to be known as a parallel system. Under this compromise proposal, the resources of the area will be exploited, on the one hand, by an international public enterprise called "the Enterprise" and, on the other hand, by States, State enterprises, private enterprises or any grouping of them. In response to fears expressed by representatives of developing countries that the Enterprise might be stillborn because of the lack of capital and technology, Secretary Kissinger said that the industrialised countries will help to provide the Enterprise with the capital necessary to undertake its first mining project and will ensure that the Enterprise will be able to obtain seabed mining technology. To make the compromise proposal even more attractive to the developing countries, Kissinger agreed that the parallel system would be reviewed after 20 years in order to determine whether it had worked well and in order to enable modifications to be made to the system, if necessary. After much agonising and a bitter internal debate, the developing countries, commonly known as the Group of 77 (although the group now includes about 120 countries) accepted the parallel system.

Elliot Richardson

After the breakthrough on the parallel system in 1976 and the appointment of Elliot Richardson as the new leader of the US delegation, rapid progress was made in the negotiations on Part XI of the Convention and its related Annexes dealing with the international area of the seabed and ocean floor. By the end of the session in the Summer of 1980, the Conference thought that general consensus had been achieved on the international regime as well as on the institutions for the exploration and the exploitation of the resources of the international area of the seabed and ocean floor. The Conference thought that it had only three remaining issues to negotiate, which were the resolution establishing the Preparatory Commission for the ISA, the protection of the preparatory investments of pioneer investors who have already expended considerable sums, and the question of what entities, in addition to States, may become parties to the Convention. The election of a new administration in the US in November 1980 brought about a radical shift in the oceans policy of the US which had remained constant through the Nixon, Ford and Carter administrations.

President Reagan

When the Conference reconvened in New York in March 1981, it was shocked to learn from the US delegation that its government was undertaking a fundamental review of the draft Convention and that until the review was completed, it would not be in a position to participate in the negotiations of the Conference. The US delegation further demanded that, pending the completion of its review, the negotiating process must be kept open so as to give the US the opportunity to ask for changes in the provisions of the Convention. Although the Conference was close to the termination of its work, and although changes of governments in other countries had not led to similar demands, the Conference waited a whole year for the US to complete its review. In March 1982, President Reagan announced that the US would return to the Conference. He further declared that although most of the provisions of the Convention were acceptable to his administration, there were important defects in Part XI of the Convention which must be cured if the Convention was to be acceptable to the US. He set out six objectives that would guide his delegation in seeking changes to Part XI.

The Group of 12

At the March/April 1982 session of the Conference, the US delegation presented a paper setting out the various options by which the six objectives of President Reagan could be achieved. The Group of 77 responded to the options paper by requesting the US to translate its demands into the form of draft amendments to Part XI. In compliance with this request, the US compiled a book of amendments which, because of its green cover, came to be known as the Green Book. The amendments were so numerous and so extensive in character that it became clear to the President of the Conference that the Green Book would not be acceptable to the Group of 77 as a basis for negotiations. The President turned to a group of medium-sized industrialised countries for help. This group, comprising Australia, Austria, Canada, Denmark, Finland, Iceland, Ireland, New Zealand, Norway, Sweden, Switzerland and the Netherlands, which came to be known as the Group of 12, proceeded to prepare a series of compromise proposals in order to bridge the gap between the US and the Group of 77. In preparing these amendments, the Group of 12 kept in mind the six objectives contained in President Reagan's statement.

The President of the Conference appealed to the US to accept the compromise proposals of the Group of 12. He was confident that if the US had been willing to accept those compromises, he would have succeeded in persuading the Group of 77 and the Socialist countries of Eastern Europe to accept them. The US, however, rejected the compromise proposals of the Group of 12 and insisted on its own amendments. After the US had demanded a vote on the Convention package and had voted against it, it explained its vote by stating that if the compromise proposals of the Group of 12 had been incorporated in the Convention, it would have made a difference to the position of the US. One cannot help thinking that, if this explanation was not merely an excuse for its negative vote, why didn't the US accept the compromise proposals of the Group of 12 during the negotiations?

The US has explained its decision not to sign the Convention on the ground that Part XI of the Convention will deter and not attract investment in seabed mining. It reached this conclusion on the grounds that the Convention does not provide the industrialised countries with reasonable access to the resources of the Area, that the provisions on the mandatory transfer of technology are unacceptable, that the provisions of the Convention on production limitation are objectionable in practice and in principle, that the Enterprise is given a competitive edge, and that the structure of governance does not adequately reflect the interests of the large industrialised countries.

Access to the Resources

Because of the strategic value of the metals contained in the manganese nodules, because of the scarcity of some of these minerals in the territories of the major western industrialised countries and because they perceive the supply of these metals from the developing countries as insecure, the industrialised countries attach the highest importance to access to the mineral resources of the deep seabed. The question is therefore whether the Convention gives reasonable assurance that all qualified applicants will be granted contracts for exploration and exploitation. Under the Convention, a determination has to be made on the qualification of the applicant by the Legal and Technical Commission. This determination must be made in accordance with the rules, regulations and procedures of the ISA. There are two uncertainties in this procedure. First, we do not yet have the rules, regulations and procedures. These will be drafted by the Preparatory Commission which will be established once the Convention has been signed by 50 States. The second uncertainty is over the manner in which the Legal and Technical Commission will make its decisions. The Commission is to consist of experts in various fields related to ocean mining and they are supposed to base their decisions on objective criteria. The Commission does, however, possess some discretion and one cannot therefore guarantee that no qualified applicant will ever be turned down by the Legal and Technical Commission.

The uncertainties of the procedure for the approval of contracts have, however, been made irrelevant by virtue of Resolution II adopted by the Conference. This resolution governs the preparatory investment of pioneer investors. Under this resolution, the four western consortia, along with France, Japan, India and the USSR, have been recognised as pioneer investors. A pioneer investor may apply to the Preparatory Commission to become a registered pioneer investor. If the pioneer investor is a State or State enterprise, the State in question must have signed the Convention. If the pioneer investor is an incorporated consortium or corporation, the sponsoring State must have signed the Convention. If the pioneer investor is an unincorporated consortium, only one of the States whose corporation is a partner of the consortium needs to sign the Convention. The Commission must accept the application of every pioneer investor. Upon registration, the pioneer investor is granted the exclusive right to conduct exploration activities on its mine site. Once the Convention comes into force, the pioneer investor has the right to ask the ISA for a mining contract so long as its application is filed in accordance with the Convention and with its rules and regulations. The only requirement is that the sponsoring State must be a party to the Convention. In the case of an unincorporated consortium, all the States whose corporations make up the consortium, must be parties to the Convention. In view of this resolution, we can conclude that the pioneer investors have a guaranteed right to a mining contract. This should, therefore, satisfy the demand of the industrialised countries for access to the strategic minerals.

Financial Payments to the Authority

Under the Convention, a miner must make financial payments to the ISA. The Convention provides two systems for determining the payments. The first is a simple royalty payment, based on the gross revenue from the sale of metals from the nodules. This system was included primarily for the sake of the socialist countries which have problems in accepting the concept of profit. The second system, which is favoured by the market economy countries, combines a considerably reduced royalty payment with a system of profit sharing.

The second system of financial payment has been designed to take into account explicitly the risks involved in ocean mining ventures. Both the royalty payment and the share of the profits taken by the ISA vary depending upon the profitability of the mining project. The profit-sharing provisions are responsive to both project-long and annual profitability variations. Thus, the investor is protected when the overall outcome of the project is unfavourable, as well as when the financial picture in a particular year is unfavourable. In other words, the tax system in the Convention is a progressive one, both in terms of overall project profitability and of year-to-year profitability. The tax system would be even more favourable if governments of the developed countries were to treat the financial payments to the ISA as akin to the payment of taxes to foreign governments and were to refrain from double taxation. The tax system in the Convention is more advanced than the tax systems governing land-based projects. According to the analysis of Ronald Katz, the magnitude of financial payments under the Convention also compare favourably with those made by land-based mining operations in developing countries.

Production Limitation

In order that the supply of minerals from the seabed can ease into the existing world markets, the Convention establishes a limit on the amount of nickel which can be produced from the seabed during the initial years of the seabed mining industry. The effective period during which the production limitation applies is 15 years. The limit is calculated as the sum of the growth of world nickel consumption over the five years prior to the first commercial mining operation, plus 60 per cent of the growth of world nickel consumption thereafter. The Convention also imposes a 3 per cent growth rate for world nickel consumption as the floor for the purpose of the calculation. Projections made by two American experts, Lance Antrim and James Sebenius, of the number of mine sites which will be available under the production limitation, based upon 2.4 per cent, 3 per cent and 4 per cent growth rates, show that the production limitation is unlikely to have any practical effect in view of the small number of prospective entrants to the seabed mining industry. The conclusion is, therefore, that while the production limitation in the Convention is offensive ideologically to those who believe in free market principles, it is unlikely to have any "bite" in practice.

Transfer of Technology

The Convention contains provisions requiring a miner to sell his technology, on fair and reasonable commercial terms, to the Enterprise only when technology is not available on the open market. These provisions have aroused the opposition of both the US government and of the industry. The provisions are ideologically offensive to those who believe that no owner of technology should be compelled to sell his technology against his wishes. It is not clear, however, that these provisions are ever likely to be implemented in practice.

The Convention forbids the Enterprise from invoking the mandatory transfer of technology unless it has failed to obtain the technology by other means, including tenders for bids. A recent study by the Interior Department of the US government indicates that there are at least four suppliers for every component of an ocean mining system, as well as for the design and construction of the system itself. If this study is correct, and if the technology is available on the open market, the provisions of the Convention on the mandatory transfer of technology will never be invoked. The Reagan administration's objection to mandatory transfer of technology and to production limitation may be based more on their "precedential value" than on their practical effect on seabed mining.

Fears of the Enterprise

Under the parallel system, the international community will establish a public Enterprise to explore and exploit the mineral resources of the Area. The Convention guarantees that the Enterprise will be provided with the capital necessary to undertake a fully integrated, four-metal mining project.

Why did the developing countries insist on the establishment of the Enterprise? The developing countries were not satisfied to share the common heritage by way of financial means alone. Developing countries feel a psychological need to participate directly in seabed mining. They do not want to be bystanders and to receive financial payments. It would leave them with a feeling of inadequacy. They want to be part of the action. The Enterprise therefore became a proxy for the developing countries. It enables States that would otherwise have no chance of participating in seabed mining to have a vehicle through which they can feel that they are participating directly in the exploitation of the common heritage. To quote William C Brewer Jr: "the Enterprise, therefore, fills a deep-rooted psychological need."

Some developed countries have expressed a fear of the Enterprise. They fear that the ISA would favour the Enterprise over the private entities. They fear the tax holiday which the Enterprise will enjoy during the first ten years of its operation will give it an undue advantage in comparison with the private entities. They fear that, in the long term, the Enterprise may become so powerful as to dominate seabed mining. They fear that the mining consortia will be unable to compete with the Enterprise. These fears of the developed countries concerning the Enterprise are not well-founded. The Enterprise will have to be created from scratch. It has no personnel, no technology, no management, no know-how and no track record. It will be a long time before the Enterprise will pose a serious challenge to the private entities. Indeed, in the early years, it would be extremely difficult for the Enterprise to go it alone. The most likely scenario is for the Enterprise to enter into joint ventures with the private entities. This would be in the mutual interests of both the Enterprise and such entities. Therefore, rather than competition, I foresee cooperation between the two arms of the parallel system.

The System of Governance

Another area in the Convention which has drawn the criticism of the US is the system of governance. The ISA consists of an Assembly and a Council. The Assembly is the plenary body in which all State parties are represented. Decisions are made on the basis of one State, one vote. The Council is the principal executive body of the ISA. Its composition and its decision-making procedures were the result of extremely difficult negotiations. These are issues which are being raised in the Bretton Woods institutions and are relevant to all future international organisations.

Concerning the composition of the Council, an accommodation has been reached between those who want the Council to be composed in accordance with the principle of geographical representation and those who argue that the members of the Council should represent countries which have an economic stake in seabed mining. In the final compromise, half of the 36 members of the Council will be elected to represent special interests such as the biggest consumers of the metals retrieved from the seabed, the countries having the largest investments in seabed mining and land-based producers. The remaining 18 members of the Council will be elected so that the overall composition of the Council satisfies equitable geographical representation. In order to satisfy the US, a permanent seat on the Council has been created for the largest consumer. The US is not satisfied with this compromise. It wants permanent seats on the Council not only for itself but for the seven largest contributors to the regular budget of the United Nations.

Decision-Making in the Council

On the decision-making procedures of the Council, the developed and the developing countries had very conflicting views. The developing countries invoked the sovereign equality of States and the majoritarian principle. They argued that decisions in a Council should be made on the basis of one State one vote and by a simple majority or by two-thirds majority. The developing countries were opposed to any system of weighted voting and of vetoes. In contrast, the developed countries urged realism. They argue that the decision-making process should take into account the fact that countries have different interests and that some countries have more at stake in seabed mining than others. The French advocated a system of chambered voting. The US insisted on a system of weighted voting.

In the final compromise, a three-tiered voting system was arrived at. Substantive questions before the Council are divided into three lists. The items on the least important list would be decided by a two-thirds majority. The developing countries on the Council, voting together, would have a two-thirds majority. It should not, however, be assumed that they will necessarily vote together since their interests are not identical. The items in the intermediate list would be decided by a three-quarters majority. This would make it impossible for the developing countries, voting as a bloc, to impose their views on the other members of the Council. The third list, containing the most sensitive questions, can only be decided by consensus. The procedure of consensus would compel members of the Council to seek to accommodate one another. However, any one member of the Council can block a consensus. The net effect of the three-tiered voting procedure in the Council is that it affords reasonable protection of the minority. This did not, however, satisfy the US because it wanted a system under which it would be possible for six western members of the Council to impose their view on the majority. This was unacceptable.

The Lawfulness of Seabed Mining Outside the Convention

The US has decided not to sign the Convention. In 1980, the US enacted the Deep Seabed Hard Minerals Resources Act. The US has announced its intention to authorise seabed mining under this Act and under a reciprocating States regime which it hopes to establish with some of its allies. A reciprocating States regime or "mini treaty" means an arrangement under which several countries that have enacted unilateral national legislation, recognise each other's laws as well as the licences and contracts granted under their respective laws. In this way, an alternative legal regime is sought to be established to the regime in the Convention.

Will the US succeed in creating a mini treaty? A mini treaty can be successful only if it has the participation of all or nearly all the seabed mining countries. If it does not have the participation of all or nearly all the seabed mining countries, then it cannot avoid the possibility of conflicts between contracts granted under national legislation and contracts granted under the Convention. My guess is that the US is unlikely to succeed in establishing an effective mini treaty because it will not be able to get all or even most of the seabed mining countries to join in such an arrangement. The governments of France and the USSR have already announced their intentions to sign the Convention. The prospects are that the government of Japan is also likely to sign the Convention. The position of the United Kingdom and the Federal Republic of Germany (FRG) is uncertain. Let us assume that the British and the FRG governments decide to join the US in staying outside the Convention. Can these three countries succeed in establishing a workable reciprocating States regime? The answer is probably no because the mine sites granted to France, Japan and the USSR by the ISA may conflict with the mine sites granted under the mini treaty. In that event, and if a request were made to the International Court of Justice for its advisory opinion, the Court will very likely rule in favour of the claims of those who were granted their mine sites under the Convention rather than under a mini treaty.

Since the US has decided to proceed to mine the deep seabed outside the Convention, the question of the lawfulness of such action has naturally been discussed. Representatives of the US hold the view that it is lawful to mine the seabed outside the Convention. They rest their conclusion on the argument that the nodules in the deep seabed are like fish in the high seas. Under the freedom of the high seas, a State has the right to catch the fish in the high seas. By analogy, it is argued that any State has the right to mine manganese nodules. According to this view, the 1970 declaration of principles is not international law and is not even evidence of emerging international law. The most thoughtful exposition of this point of view is by Theodore Kronmiller in his book *The Lawfulness of Deep Seabed Mining*.

It is correct to say that there was no body of customary international law dealing specifically with the exploitation of deep seabed resources. It is true that the novelty of deep seabed mining does not, in and of itself, affect its lawfulness. The analogy between high seas fisheries and the manganese nodules is not, however, a very appropriate one. Manganese nodules, unlike fish, are not mobile but are resource *in situ*. The nature of a mining operation requires the assertion of one's exclusive right to the manganese nodules in a large area of the seabed. It is true that resolutions of the United Nations General Assembly are not normally regarded as a source of international law. However, a resolution containing a declaration of normative principles adopted without objection, could be cited as evidence of customary law or as reflecting an emerging rule of international law. In addition, if the Convention is widely ratified, that, too, is a factor which would be taken into account. If the US were to proceed to mine the seabed outside the Convention, it is more than likely that the United Nations General Assembly will ask the International Court of Justice for an advisory opinion on the lawfulness of such action.

Conclusion

From the above analysis, it is difficult to accept the conclusion of the US that Part XI of the Convention is fundamentally flawed and unworkable. It is true that some of the provisions of the Convention such as production limitation and transfer of technology are ideologically offensive to the Reagan administration. According to the analysis of two American experts, Antrim and

Sebenius, these and other provisions of the Convention to which the US takes objection, are unlikely to pose a "significant deterrence to ocean investment" under the Convention. Given the legal uncertainty surrounding the mining of the seabed outside the Convention, one cannot help wondering whether the financial community will be prepared to back such ventures. Perhaps the US government would be prepared to abandon its free market principles and support seabed mining outside the Convention by a programme of government-backed political risk insurance. Reviewing the whole situation, one is compelled to come to the conclusion that the opposition of the US to the provisions of the Convention on deep seabed mining is based not on functional or pragmatic interests but on philosophical and ideological grounds. One can't help suspecting that the real reason for the opposition of the US is based upon its rejection of the concept of the common heritage of mankind as applied to seabed resources and the fear that the concept may be extended to apply to other global commons.

LECTURE 4

❦

Reflections on the
Negotiating Process

The Third United Nations Conference on the Law of the Sea is said to be the biggest international conference ever held. At its first substantive session held in Caracas in the summer of 1974, there were 143 participating delegations with over 2,000 delegates. In the subsequent eight years, the number of participating delegations rose to almost 160. The Conference had a long and complex agenda. The subjects and issues on the agenda involved important economic, strategic, environmental, scientific and other interests of States as well as of the international community as a whole. In the years ahead, the international community will, no doubt, hold other global conferences, dealing with other important questions on the planetary agenda.

It may, therefore, be useful to look back on the negotiating process of the Conference and to ask whether we could learn any valuable lessons from it. Does the experience of the Law of the Sea Conference teach us anything on how to manage a large multilateral conference? Does it tell us anything about how to structure negotiations, what rules of procedure to follow, what methods of work are likely to be the most productive and what pitfalls to avoid?

Rules of Procedure

One of the most important innovations of the Conference is its rules of procedure. The rules of procedure contain an appendix which, *inter alia*, states: "The Conference should make every effort to reach agreement on substantive matters by way of consensus and there should be no voting on such matters until all efforts at consensus have been exhausted."

Consensus

The letter and spirit of this "gentleman's agreement" was scrupulously observed by the Conference. Not a single article in the Convention was adopted by vote. All the provisions of the Convention were negotiated until satisfactory accommodation was reached between the competing interests and there was general agreement on the provisions.

Cooling Off

Another interesting feature of the rules of procedure is the provision in Rule 37 for a cooling-off period before a vote is taken. Under Rule 37, paragraph 2, when a matter of substance comes up for voting for the first time, either the President or 15 delegations may request a deferment of a vote for a period not exceeding ten days. During the period of deferment, the President shall make every effort to facilitate the achievement of general agreement. At the end of the period, the President shall inform the Conference of the results of his efforts. A vote on the proposal may be taken only after the Conference has determined that all efforts at reaching agreement have been exhausted.

Required Majority

The majority required for the adoption of a proposal by vote is also of interest. On all matters of substance, the decisions of the Conference shall be taken by a two-thirds majority of the representatives present and voting provided that such majority shall include at least a majority of the States participating in that session of the Conference. What this means is that even though there may be a two-thirds majority in favour of a proposal, it will not be adopted unless the number of positive votes is greater than half the number of delegations attending that session of the Conference.

How did the rules of procedure work in practice? In practice, the rules of procedure worked very well. When the gate was opened for the submission of amendments to the draft Convention, altogether 33 amendments were submitted. The President invoked Rule 37 and declared a cooling-off period of ten days. During this period, he and his colleagues in the Collegium, contacted the co-sponsors of all the amendments in order to do two things. First, they tried to see whether any of the amendments enjoyed widespread and substantial support and which, if accepted, would enhance the prospects of achieving general agreement. Of the 33 amendments, only one fell into this category. This was an amendment submitted by the Council of Namibia concerning its right to become a party to the Convention. Following consultations conducted by one of the vice presidents from Ireland, a compromise proposal was accepted by the Conference. Second, after the President had ascertained that the other amendments did not satisfy the two criteria stated above, he tried to persuade their co-sponsors to withdraw or, at least, not to insist on putting them to the vote. After much persuasion, he succeeded in respect of all the amendments except three. Spain insisted on putting its amendments to Articles 39 and 32 to the vote. Neither amendment was adopted. The second Spanish amendment obtained the required two-thirds majority but not the second requirement of a majority of the delegations attending that session of the Conference. Turkey also insisted on putting its amendment to Article 309 to the vote. Turkey's amendment was also rejected. The rejections of these amendments, especially of Spain's amendment to Article 42, which had considerable merit, confirmed the Conference's commitment to the consensus procedure.

Reconciling the Package Deal with a Broad Agenda

The Conference had an extremely long agenda. It contained no less than 25 subjects and issues. At the same time, delegations insisted that both because the different aspects of ocean space are inter-related, as well as for tactical reasons, all the subjects and issues on the agenda must be dealt with together in a package and a single Convention must be adopted. A problem similar to this will arise when the global economic negotiations are launched. How did the Conference on the Law of the Sea deal with this problem? The Conference decided that it was simply impossible to deal with all these subjects and issues in one negotiating forum. The Conference decided that the package deal approach did not preclude the allocation of the different subjects and issues to different negotiating bodies, so long as their inter-relatedness was always borne in mind and so long as it was understood that the solutions to the different subjects and issues must be brought together into a single convention. Therefore, the Conference established four principal fora to deal with the subjects and issues: the Plenary, which dealt with the preamble, the final clauses and disputes settlement; the First Committee which dealt with Part XI of the Convention and related Annexes; the Second Committee which dealt with Parts I to X of the Convention and related Annexes; and the Third Committee which dealt with the preservation and protection of marine environment, marine scientific research and marine technology. The point to be made here is that the package deal approach does not preclude the allocation of different subjects and issues on an agenda to different negotiating fora so long as the negotiators in the different fora bear in mind their inter-relatedness, and so long as the different components will be welded together at a later point.

Miniaturising the Negotiating Groups

A conference with 160 participants is obviously a large and un-wieldy body. It is impossible to conduct meaningful negotiations in such a large body. The problem is how to transform such a large conference into small, efficient and representative negotiating groups. This is by no means an easy task. In the Law of the Sea Conference, all delegations felt that they had important national interests at stake. They therefore wanted to participate directly in the negotiations so as to promote or to protect their national interests. They resisted the idea that they should allow others to represent their interests. The Conference eventually solved this problem in the following way. Let us take, as an example, the negotiations on the financial terms of mining contracts. The Chairman of the Negotiating Group first held meetings at the level of the Plenary so that all delegations could participate in them. The second step he took was to establish an open-ended group of financial experts. Although the meetings were open to all, the very name of the group intimidated many from coming and the group of financial experts had a regular attendance of approximately 30 delegations, or one-fifth of the membership of the Conference. To miniaturise this further, when the Chairman considered that the time was ripe for negotiating an agreement, he invited the representative of the United States to represent all the market-economy countries, and three representatives of the Group of 77, one each from Africa, Asia and Latin America to represent the developing countries. Simultaneously, the Chairman conducted negotiations with the USSR, representing the centrally planned economies. The results of these negotiations were subsequently ratified by the Conference. The technique of miniaturising the negotiating groups requires political finesse, obtaining the trust of the interest groups, good feedback from the negotiators to their interest groups and good judgement on timing.

Negotiating Groups

Reference has already been made to the fact that the Conference had four principal negotiating fora: the Plenary, the First, Second and Third Committees. At various times, informal negotiating groups were established within each of these fora. Within the Third Committee, for example, two working groups were established, one dealing with the protection and preservation of the marine environment and the other dealing with marine scientific research.

In addition to the above, the Conference also established seven negotiating groups to deal with seven hardcore problems. Negotiating Group 1 dealt with the international regime for the exploration and exploitation of the international area of the sea-bed and ocean floor and was chaired by Francis Njenga of Kenya. Negotiating Group 2 dealt with financial arrangements and was chaired by Tommy Koh of Singapore. Negotiating Group 3 dealt with the organs of the International Seabed Authority and was chaired by Paul Bamela Engo of the Cameroon. Negotiating Group 4 dealt with the relationship between coastal States and landlocked and geographically disadvantaged States with respect to the living resources of the exclusive economic zone and was chaired by Satya Nandan of Fiji. Negotiating Group 5 dealt with the dispute settlement aspect of the subject of Negotiating Group 4 and was chaired by Constantin Stavropoulos of Greece. Negotiating Group 6 dealt with the continental shelf and was chaired by Andrés Aguilar of Venezuela. Negotiating Group 7 dealt with the question of sea-boundary delimitation and was chaired by Judge Eero Manner of Finland.

A remarkable feature of the Conference was that some of the most important and intractable problems were negotiated and resolved, not in any of the principal fora or negotiating groups established by the Conference, but in informal negotiating groups that were privately convened. Jens Evensen of Norway convened a group which dealt with the exclusive economic zone and with marine pollution. Jorge Castañeda of Mexico, convened a group which resolved the difficult question concerning the status of the exclusive economic zone. A group was convened, under the joint initiative of Fiji and the United Kingdom, to negotiate the question of passage through straits used for inter-national navigation. At the initiative of Professor Louis Sohn of the US, a group was convened under the co-chairmanship of Australia, El Salvador and Kenya, on the question of disputes settlement.

The experience of the Conference has been that both the formal and the informal negotiating groups were extremely useful. Sometimes, when a problem eludes a solution in a formal negotiating group, it is necessary to take it into a smaller and more informal negotiating group. If the private negotiating group is to succeed in getting its result ratified by the Conference, it must comprise all those who have a real interest at stake as well as those who are regarded as the leaders of the Conference. The fact that such an effort is being made should not be kept secret from the Conference because secrecy tends to breed suspicion.

Interest Groups

Some commentators have characterised the Third United Nations Conference on the Law of the Sea as primarily a north-south negotiation. This characterisation is incorrect. On most issues before the Conference, the interests and positions of a country were determined not by its development status or its ideological orientation, but by geography. Hence, most negotiating groups were not composed along north-south lines. Part XI of the Convention, dealing with deep seabed mining, was the only area in which the delegations were polarised between north and south.

Delegations at the Conference belong to a whole variety of groups. With a few exceptions, they belong to regional groups. Of the five regional groups, only the Eastern European Group was able to work with a high degree of coherence on all issues. The African group was usually able to take a unified position on First Committee matters. Members of the other regional groups were split on most of the issues. The Group of 77, consisting of nearly 120 developing countries, was effective only in the area of the mining of the deep seabed. Some of the most important interest groups established at the Conference were the following:

1. the coastal States Group;
2. the group of landlocked and geographically disadvantaged States;
3. the territorialist group consisting of coastal States which have claimed a 200-mile territorial sea;
4. the group of strait States;
5. the group of archipelagic States;
6. the group of coastal States with broad continental margins, sometimes referred to as the "margineers";
7. the group of island States;
8. the European Economic Community;
9. the group favouring the medium-line or equidistance principle in sea-boundary delimitation;
10. the group favouring equitable principles in sea-boundary delimitation;
11. the group of land-based producers;
12. the western Gang of Five consisting of the US, UK, France, the Federal Republic of Germany and Japan also called the "Coordinating Group of Five";
13. The East-West Gang of Five consisting of the US, USSR, UK, France and Japan called the "Group of Five"; and
14. the two superpowers.

What purpose did these interest groups serve? The establishment of the interest groups was an important prelude to serious negotiations. It took some time for countries to identify their own interests and for those with kindred interests to form coalitions or groups. It was only after the interest groups had been established, that negotiations could be held between the representatives of the competing interest groups.

Were there any disadvantages to the group system? There were two disadvantages to the group system. First, it was often difficult for the groups to come to an agreed position. Negotiations were often held up for days in order to allow the Group of 77 to come to a common position. Once they had done so, the groups tended to get locked into that position and it was often difficult for them to reconsider their positions and to modify them in the course of negotiations. The second disadvantage was that the groups often gave a very narrow mandate to their negotiators. This often meant that the negotiators had little or no flexibility and were not able to give and take in the course of the negotiations. The conclusion is that, although the group system serves a useful function and will probably be a feature of any major multilateral conference, it should be used with flexibility. When an impasse occurs, the group system should not prevent the emergence of sub-groups of delegations in the competing groups which could seek to build bridges between the groups.

Role of Conference Leaders

The principal officers of the Conference were the President, the Chairmen of the First, Second and Third Committees, the Chairman of the Drafting Committee and the Rapporteur General. These six officers comprise the Collegium. The Special Representative of the Secretary-General attended all meetings of the Collegium as an observer. The Collegium worked extremely well during the Conference and provided it with the administrative, managerial, political and negotiating leadership. The Conference would have floundered if the Collegium was not united and if it had failed to provide the Conference with leadership. The Conference conferred extensive powers on the principal officers of the Conference. This came about by accident and not by design. The Conference had commenced without a basic text. At the second substantive session of the Conference held in Geneva in 1975, the Conference requested the chairmen of the three main committees to produce a negotiating text which came to be known as the Informal Single Negotiating Text. The President of the Conference contributed a text on dispute settlement. The Informal Single Negotiating Text underwent many revisions culminating in the Convention. These revisions were undertaken by the Collegium in accordance with certain criteria established by the Conference. The criteria were that the modifications must be based upon compromise proposals emerging from negotiations and consultations which, when presented to the Plenary, were found to enjoy widespread and substantial support and which would substantially improve the prospects of achieving consensus.

The leaders of the Conference did not, however, consist only of the members of the Collegium and of the chairmen of the seven negotiating groups. A handful of other individuals, by virtue of their knowledge, ability, negotiating skill and initiative, were recognised by their peers as leaders of the Conference. These include Jens Evensen of Norway, Jorge Castañeda of Mexico, Keith Brennan of Australia, Elliot Richardson of the US, Joseph Warioba of Tanzania, Alfonso Arias-Schreiber of Peru, SP Jagota of India, Alvaro de Soto of Peru, Christopher Pinto of Sri Lanka, Inam Ul-Haq of Pakistan, Fernando Zegers of Chile, Karl Wolf of Austria and Semyon Kozyrev of the USSR.

The Role of Personality in Multilateral Negotiations

In a multilateral conference, the importance and effectiveness of a delegate depends on both the weight and influence of his country and on his own qualities. In the case of the five major powers, the US, USSR, UK, France and the Federal Republic of Germany, the power of the country is probably more important than the personal attributes of its representative. This is not the case with the other countries. In a multilateral conference, apart from the Big Five, the personal qualities of a delegate determine his influence and effectiveness. Let me give the following example. Fiji is a relatively small developing country, and yet its chief representative to the Conference, Satya Nandan, played one of the most important roles in the Conference. He co-chaired the negotiating group on passage through straits. He was instrumental in negotiating the compromise text between the archipelagic States and the major maritime powers. He chaired the difficult negotiations between coastal States and landlocked and geographically disadvantaged States with respect to the living resources of the exclusive economic zone. He chaired the negotiations on the provisions of the Convention dealing with production limitation. Finally, he assisted the President in resolving the problem of sea-boundary delimitation.

Making Negotiations Succeed

The first pre-condition for successful negotiations is to establish mutual trust and confidence. If the two sides are separated by mutual mistrust and suspicion, it is very difficult to make the negotiations work. This was the situation prevailing in the First Committee between 1974 and 1976. The developed countries suspected that the developing countries were out to prevent them from having access, under reasonable terms and conditions, to the resources of the deep seabed. The developing countries suspected that the developed countries were determined to exploit the common heritage of mankind without their participation and without the equitable sharing of the benefits. The fog of suspicion and mistrust lifted when Elliot Richardson was appointed as the leader of the US delegation in 1974. He was able to win the trust and confidence of his negotiating adversaries. He was able to convince them that solutions could be found which could accommodate the interests of both sides.

Qualities of Negotiators and Chairmen

The second precondition for a successful negotiation is the quality of the negotiators and of the chairmen of negotiating conferences. A good negotiator should be a person possessing technical competence, negotiating skills, personal integrity, a calm temperament and a likeable personality. A good chairman should possess, in addition to those qualities, objectivity, a judicial temperament, a capacity to reconcile differences, the ability to think of creative solutions to seemingly intractable problems and the courage to put forward compromise proposals.

Third, it is helpful if the two or more sides to a negotiation could agree on what the facts were. In the difficult negotiations on the financial terms of mining contracts, for example, the chairman was able to convince the negotiators to accept a computer model developed by a team of scholars at the Massachusetts Institute of Technology, as a means of comparing the economic performance of a hypothetical seabed mining system under different conditions. The acceptance of the model contributed greatly to the success of the negotiations. In establishing the facts on which the negotiations are to be conducted, the use of experts is sometimes helpful. In the Law of the Sea Conference, the non-governmental organisations contributed a great deal to the education of the delegates on many technical issues, such as the financial terms of mining contracts, transfer of technology, the continental shelf, and by bringing experts to talk to the delegates.

Techniques of Chairmanship

There are many different techniques of chairing a negotiation. Some chairmen are good at shuttle diplomacy. Others prefer to have the negotiating adversaries meet face-to-face. Some chairmen listen to the negotiators without putting a single question to them. Others prefer to play a more active role by analysing the issues and putting questions to the negotiators. The different techniques of chairmanship all seem to work. The choice of the technique and style must depend upon each chairman's cultural and intellectual preferences and on his personality. Whatever the technique of the chairman, he must understand that each party to a negotiation has certain irreducible minimum interests. He must try to meet those interests and to think of a solution which accommodates the interests of both parties. He should try to create a good negotiating atmosphere and control the tempers of the negotiators. He should try to win the trust and confidence of the negotiators. He should have a creative mind and not be afraid to think of novel solutions to seemingly intractable problems. He could prevent delay and prevarication by setting strict time limits. Finally, when an important breakthrough occurs, he should maintain the momentum and persuade the negotiators to continue, if necessary, skipping meals, working late into the night and over the weekend. Very often, one breakthrough will lead to another and it is important for the chairman to understand this and to practise the doctrine of "hot pursuit" in negotiations.

Conclusion

I have tried to describe the complex process by which the new Convention on the Law of the Sea was negotiated and adopted. What were the unique features of that process? What were the procedural rules, arrangements and innovations that made the process succeed? What generalisations can be drawn from that experience about the art and science of negotiations? The negotiating process succeeded for a whole variety of reasons. First, I would point to the rules of procedure and the "gentleman's agreement" which laid primary emphasis on the objective of achieving consensus. The cooling-off period before voting and the double majority requirement for substantive decisions served to reinforce the commitment of the Conference to the goal of achieving consensus. Second, we have learnt that it is possible to reconcile the package deal approach with the allocation of different subjects and issues to different negotiating bodies. Third, we have seen the importance for the leadership of the Conference, the Collegium, to work as a cohesive team and to provide the Conference with its managerial, diplomatic and negotiating leadership. Fourth, it is absolutely essential to transform a large, unwieldy conference of 160 players into small, representative and efficient negotiating groups. Although efforts to miniaturise the negotiating fora will encounter resistance, they are essential and can be done. Fifth, a conference needs formal, informal and even privately convened negotiating groups. As a general rule, the more informal the nature of the group the easier it is to resolve a problem. However, secrecy must be avoided and if the results of a negotiating group are to have any chance of winning the support of the conference, then the group must include all those who have a real interest at stake and the conference leaders. Sixth, interest groups play a useful function and are probably a permanent feature of any global negotiation. The group system should, however, be operated with flexibility. We must avoid the twin dangers of groups adopting rigid positions which cannot be modified and giving their negotiators a mandate with no room for give and take. Seventh, negotiation is both an art and a science. There are probably some qualities of a negotiator which are inborn and cannot be taught. There are other attributes, skills and techniques which can probably be identified, analysed and taught. A good negotiator should possess technical competence, negotiating skills, personal integrity, a calm and likeable personality. A good chairman should possess, in addition to those qualities, objectivity, a judicial temperament, a capacity to reconcile differences, the ability to think of creative solutions to seemingly intractable problems and courage. In the final analysis, the Third United Nations Conference on the Law of the Sea succeeded because it brought together a group of negotiators and chairmen who possess many of these qualities. They did not regard one another as an enemy who had to be conquered. They regarded the issue or question under negotiation as the enemy that had to be conquered. While pursuing the interests of their respective countries, they also felt inspired by the fact that what they were doing was no less than writing a constitution for the oceans.

SECTION TWO

ESSAYS AND LECTURES

"A Constitution
for the Oceans"

On 10 December 1982, we created a new record in legal history. Never in the annals of international law had a Convention been signed by 119 countries on the very first day on which it was open for signature. Not only was the number of signatories a remarkable fact but just as important was the fact that the Convention had been signed by States from every region of the world, from the north and from the south, from the east and from the west, by coastal States as well as landlocked and geographically disadvantaged States.

When we set out on the long and arduous journey to secure a new Convention on the Law of the Sea, covering 25 subjects and issues, there were many who told us that our goal was too ambitious and not attainable. We proved the sceptics wrong and we succeeded in adopting a Convention covering every aspect of the uses and resources of the sea.

The question is whether we achieved our fundamental objective of producing a comprehensive constitution for the oceans which will stand the test of time. My answer is in the affirmative for the following reasons:

- The Convention will promote the maintenance of international peace and security because it will replace a plethora of conflicting claims by coastal States with universally agreed limits on the territorial sea, on the contiguous zone, on the exclusive economic zone and on the continental shelf.
- The world community's interest in the freedom of navigation will be facilitated by the important compromises on the status of the exclusive economic zone, by the regime of innocent passage through the territorial sea, by the regime of transit passage through straits used for international navigation and by the regime of archipelagic sea lanes passage.
- The world community's interest in the conservation and optimum utilisation of the living resources of the sea will be enhanced by the conscientious implementation of the provisions in the Convention relating to the exclusive economic zone.
- The Convention contains important new rules for the protection and preservation of the marine environment from pollution.
- The Convention contains new rules on marine scientific research which strike an equitable balance between the interests of the research States and the interests of the coastal States in whose economic zones or continental shelves the research is to be carried out.
- The world community's interest in the peaceful settlement of disputes and the prevention of use of force in the settlement of disputes between States have been advanced

by the mandatory system of dispute settlement in the Convention.

- The Convention has succeeded in translating the principle that the resources of the deep seabed constitute the common heritage of mankind into fair and workable institutions and arrangements.

- Though far from ideal, we can nevertheless find elements of international equity in the Convention, such as revenue sharing on the continental shelf beyond 200 miles, giving landlocked and geographically disadvantaged States access to the living resources of the exclusive economic zones of their neighbouring States, the relationship between coastal fishermen and distant-water fishermen, and the sharing of the benefits derived from the exploitation of the resources of the deep seabed.

I would like to highlight the major themes which I found in the statements made by delegations at Montego Bay.

First, delegations said that the Convention does not fully satisfy the interests and objectives of any State. Nevertheless, they were of the view that it represents a monumental achievement of the international community, second only to the Charter of the United Nations. The Convention is the first comprehensive treaty dealing with practically every aspect of the uses and resources of the seas and the oceans. It has successfully accommodated the competing interests of all nations.

The second theme that emerged from the statements is that the provisions of the Convention are closely inter-related and form an integral package. Thus, it is not possible for a State to pick what it likes and to disregard what it does not like. It was also said that rights and obligations go hand-in-hand, and it is not permissible to claim rights under the Convention without being willing to shoulder the corresponding obligations.

The third theme I heard was that this Convention is not a codification Convention. The argument that, except for Part XI, the Convention codifies customary law or reflects existing international practice is factually incorrect and legally insupportable. The regime of transit passage through straits used for international navigation and the regime of archipelagic sea lanes passage are two examples of the many new concepts in the Convention. Even in the case of Article 76 on the continental shelf, the article contains new law in that it has expanded the concept of the continental shelf to include the continental slope and the continental rise. This concession to the broad margin States was in return for their agreement for revenue sharing on the continental shelf beyond 200 miles. It is therefore my view that a State which is not a party to this Convention cannot invoke the benefits of Article 76.

The fourth theme relates to the lawfulness of any attempt to mine the resources of the international area of the seabed and ocean floor. Speakers from every regional and interest group expressed the view that the doctrine of the freedom of the high seas can provide no legal basis for the grant by any State of exclusive title to a specific mine site in the international area. Many are of the view that Article 137 of the Convention has become as much a part of customary international law as the freedom of navigation. An attempt by any State to mine the resources of the deep seabed outside the Convention will earn the universal condemnation of the international community and will incur grave political and legal consequences. All speakers have addressed an earnest appeal to the United States to reconsider its position. The US is a country that has, throughout its history, supported the progressive development of international law and has fought for the rule of law in the relations between States. The present position of the US government towards this Convention is, therefore, inexplicable in the light of its history, in the light of its specific law of the sea interests and in the light of the leading role which it has played in negotiating the many compromises which have made this treaty possible.

A final theme that emerged from the statements concerns the Preparatory Commission. Now that the required number of States have signed the Convention, the Preparatory Commission for the establishment of the International Seabed Authority and the International Tribunal for the Law of the Sea will begin its work. The Commission will have to adopt the rules and procedures for the implementation of Resolution ll, relating to pioneer investors. It will, *inter alia*, draft the detailed rules, regulations and procedures for the mining of the seabed. If it carries out its work in an efficient, objective and business-like manner, we will have a viable system for the mining of the deep seabed. This will induce those who are standing on the sidelines to come in and support the Convention. If, on the other hand, the Preparatory Commission does not carry out its tasks in an efficient, objective and practical manner, then all our efforts in the last 14 years will have been in vain.

In the report of the Secretary-General on the work of the United Nations (A/37/1) dated 7 September 1982, he wrote: "We have seen, in the case of the law of the sea ..., what remarkable results can be achieved in well-organised negotiations within the United Nations framework, even on the most complex of issues...."

It may be helpful to identify those features of the negotiating process of this Conference which were productive, and to distil some wisdom from our experience.

I would point, first of all, to the importance of reaching agreements on substantive matters on which States have important interests by consensus. The Conference was wise to resist the temptation of putting substantive proposals to the vote, because those who vote against a proposal would naturally not feel bound by it. The consensus procedure, however, requires all delegations, those in the majority as well as those in the minority, to make efforts, in good faith, to accommodate the interests of others.

Second, the Conference took the wise decision that the package deal approach did not preclude it from allocating the 25 different subjects and issues to different negotiating forums, so long as the results were brought together to form an integral whole.

Third, the group system in the Conference contributed to its work by helping delegations to identify their positions and by enabling negotiations to take place between competing interest groups. The group system should, however, be used with flexibility and not be allowed to paralyse the negotiating process with rigidity.

Fourth, the negotiations in this Conference could not have been brought to a successful conclusion if we had failed to progressively miniaturise them. It is obvious that no meaningful negotiations can take place in a forum consisting of 160 delegations.

Fifth, there is a role for the main committees, for formal negotiating groups, for informal negotiating groups and even for privately convened negotiating groups. In general, the more informal a negotiating group, the more likely it is to make progress. Some of the most intractable problems of the Conference were resolved in privately convened negotiating groups, such as the Evensen Group and the Castañeda Group.

Sixth, the Drafting Committee and its language groups played a very important role in the negotiating process. It was due to their hard work that we have one treaty in six languages and not six treaties in six languages.

Seventh, the leaders of a conference can play a significant role in determining the success or failure of a conference. In our case, we were extremely fortunate that the Collegium worked well together. The Conference could well have floundered during its many crises if the Collegium had not been united and if it had failed to provide the Conference with leadership.

Eighth, the Secretariat played an important role in the work of this Conference. The members of the Secretariat, under the able leadership of the Special Representative of the Secretary-General, not only provided the Conference with excellent services but also ably assisted the President and the Chairmen of the various committees and groups in the negotiations. I should like to take this opportunity to thank Mr Bernardo Zuleta and his loyal deputy, Mr David Hall.

Ninth, I should also acknowledge the role played by the non-governmental organisations. such as the Neptune Group. They provided the Conference with three valuable services. They brought independent experts to meet with delegations, thus enabling us to have an independent source of information on technical issues. They assisted representatives from developing countries to narrow the technical gap between them and their counterparts from developed countries They also provided us with opportunities to meet, away from the Conference, in a more relaxed atmosphere, to discuss some of the most difficult issues confronted by the Conference.

Although the Convention consists of a series of compromises, it forms an integral whole. This is why the Convention does not provide for reservations. It is therefore not possible for States to pick what they like and disregard what they do not like. In international law, as in domestic law, rights and duties go hand-in-hand. It is therefore legally impermissible to claim rights under the Convention without being willing to assume the correlative duties.

Let no nation put asunder this landmark achievement of the international community.

I cannot conclude without recalling, once more, our collective debt to two men, Hamilton Shirley Amerasinghe (former President of the Conference) and Dr Arvid Pardo (former Permanent Representative of Malta to the United Nations). Pardo contributed two seminal ideas to our work: first, that the resources at the deep seabed constitute the common heritage of mankind, and second, that all aspects of ocean space are inter-related and should be treated as an integral whole. Amerasinghe led our efforts from 1968 until his untimely death in 1980.

In the final analysis, I believe that this Conference succeeded because it brought together a "critical mass" of colleagues who were outstanding lawyers and negotiators. We succeeded because we did not regard our counterparts in the negotiations as the enemies to be conquered. We considered the issues under dispute as the common obstacles to be overcome. We worked not only to promote our individual national interests but also in pursuit of our common dream of writing a constitution for the oceans.

We have strengthened the United Nations by proving that with political will, nations can use the organisation as a centre to harmonise their actions. We have shown that with good leadership and management, the United Nations can be an efficient forum for the negotiation of complex issues. We celebrate the victory of the rule of law and of the principle of the peaceful settlement of disputes. Finally, we celebrate human solidarity and the reality of interdependence which is symbolised by the United Nations Convention on the Law of the Sea.

"A Constitution for the Oceans" was adapted from statements made by Ambassador Tommy Koh, President of the Third United Nations Conference on the Law of the Sea on 6 and 11 December 1982 at the final session of the Conference at Montego Bay, Jamaica and subsequently published in the official United Nations volume containing the official text of the Convention and the Final Act in 1983. The phrase "a constitution for the oceans" has become synonymous with the United Nations Convention for the Law of the Sea.

Straits Used for International Navigation

Negotiating the International Straits Regime

Straits have always been important to shipping. The Straits of Malacca and Singapore, to take one example, have been used by ships for thousands of years. They were the most convenient route for ships going from the east to the west and from the west to the east. In ancient times, the two dangers that ships faced when traversing the straits were piracy and unpredictable storms. As long as coastal States were content to claim a three-mile territorial sea and in all cases where the strait was wider than six miles, there was a high seas corridor in such straits. Ships travelling along the high seas corridor were protected by the freedom of the high seas. The coastal States had to respect the right of passage of ships under international law and not interfere with it.

The end of the Second World War brought about many revolutionary changes in the world. The peoples of Asia and

Africa revolted against their colonial masters and demanded the right to self-determination and independence. Other countries, such as those in Latin America, which were already independent, began a campaign of questioning the existing international legal order. They led the revolt against the three-mile territorial sea.

Under the 1958 Territorial Sea Convention,[1] the width of the territorial sea was not specified. It was not specified because there was no consensus at the First and Second United Nations Conferences on the Law of the Sea. In 1958, 41 States claimed a territorial sea of three miles, 11 States claimed six miles, and another 6 States claimed twelve miles. By 1974, when the Third United Nations Conference on the Law of the Sea (UNCLOS III) held its second session, the situation had been reversed; 51 States claimed a territorial sea of twelve miles and 25 States claimed a territorial sea of three miles.

Given that prevailing trend, it was difficult, if not impossible, to resist the demand that the width of the territorial sea should be extended from the traditional 3 to 12 miles. There was, however, one major complication. The complication arose from the fact that there are 116 straits used for international navigation that are between 6 and 24 miles in width. There were high seas corridors in those straits when coastal States were allowed to claim a territorial sea of three miles. But, when coastal States extended their territorial seas to 12 miles, the high seas corridors disappeared and all the waters within those straits became territorial waters. This was the reason that led the United States, the USSR and other major maritime powers to demand that the extension of the territorial sea to 12 miles had to be balanced

---

[1] Convention on the Territorial Sea and Contiguous Zone, Geneva, 29 April 1958, 516 U.N.T.S. 206.

by either the preservation of a high seas corridor in straits used for international navigation or the establishment of a *sui generis* regime of passage through, over and under such straits.

In order to break the impasse, two Commonwealth delegations, Fiji and the United Kingdom, undertook a joint initiative at UNCLOS III. They convened a private group consisting of themselves as co-chairs and 13 other delegations (Argentina, Australia, Bahrain, Bulgaria, Denmark, Iceland, India, Italy, Kenya, Nigeria, Singapore, the United Arab Emirates and Venezuela). In composing the group, the co-chairs had excluded the two superpowers (US and USSR) as well as three major strait States, namely, Indonesia, Malaysia and Spain. The private group succeeded in producing, by consensus, a draft text on straits used for international navigation at the third session of the Conference in 1975. The draft text was submitted to the chair of the relevant committee who incorporated it into the Informal Single Negotiating Text. The draft text survived many attempts to amend it and is the text of Part III of the 1982 United Nations Convention on the Law of the Sea.[2] Having participated in the negotiating group, I can say with some immodesty that our consensus text survived because we had struck the right balance between the interests of the strait States and those of the international community.

The Straits Regime

For a strait to qualify as a strait used for international navigation, it must satisfy two criteria: a geographical criterion and a

---

[2] *United Nations Convention on the Law of the Sea*, Montego Bay, 10 December 1982, 1833 U.N.T.S. 397.

functional criterion. The geographical criterion is that the strait must connect:

i. one part of the high seas with another part of the high seas; or

ii. one part of the high seas with an exclusive economic zone; or

iii. an exclusive economic zone with another exclusive economic zone.

The second criterion is factual. The strait must be used for international navigation. The volume of traffic is not relevant. The litmus test is actual usage.

The Convention distinguishes between four different categories of straits used for international navigation. For the purpose of this essay, I will confine myself to the most important category of straits to which the regime of transit passage applies. Most of the 116 straits affected by the extension of the territorial sea, including such important straits as Gibraltar, Dover, Hormuz, Bab-Al-Mandeb, and Malacca–Singapore, fall into this category.

The term "transit passage" has no antecedent in international law. It was not used in the 1958 Territorial Sea Convention or in customary international law. It was invented by the British delegation to the Conference and contained in their draft articles on the territorial seas and straits.[3]

Transit passage means the exercise, in accordance with Part III of the Convention, of "the freedom of navigation and overflight solely for the purpose of continuous and expeditious

---

[3] United Kingdom, "Draft articles on the territorial sea and straits," Doc. A/Conf. 621 (c. 2) L. 3, 3 July 1974, in Third United Nations Conference on the Law of the Sea. *Official Records*, Vol. III (New York, 1975), 183–186.

transit of the strait...."[4] The phrase "freedom of navigation and overflight" is legally significant because it is language normally used in connection with the high seas and therefore connotes a regime superior to "non-suspendable" innocent passage and innocent passage *simpliciter*. The limitation is that the transit must be continuous and it must be expeditious. There is, however, a "Singapore exception".[5] A ship or aircraft transiting the Straits of Malacca and Singapore may stop at Singapore and still enjoy the regime of transit passage.

The regime of transit passage has the following characteristics:

i. it is applicable to all ships including warships;
ii. submarines may remain submerged during their passage; and
iii. a ship, submarine and aircraft enjoys unimpeded passage through, under and over a strait used for international navigation.

What are the duties of a ship or aircraft during transit passage? The following four duties are applicable to both ships and aircraft:

i. the duty to proceed without delay through or over the strait;
ii. the duty to refrain from any threat or use of force against the sovereignty, territorial integrity, or political independence of States bordering the strait;
iii. the duty to refrain from any activities other than those incident to their normal modes of continuous and expeditious transit unless rendered necessary by *force majeure* or by distress; and

---

[4] LOS Convention, *supra* note 2, Art. 38(2).
[5] *Ibid.*, Art. 38(2), second sentence.

iv. the duty to comply with other relevant provisions of Part III of the Convention.[6]

I interpret the relevant articles of Part III to mean that a warship in transit may not conduct naval exercises or arms practices. Also, a ship in transit passage may not carry out marine scientific research or hydrographic surveys without the prior consent of the strait State. A ship in transit passage is to respect the applicable sea lanes and traffic separation schemes. In addition, ships in transit passage have to comply with generally accepted international regulations, procedures and practices for safety at sea, including the International Regulations for Preventing Collisions at Sea.[7] Finally, ships in transit passage must comply with generally accepted international regulations, procedures and practices for the prevention, reduction and control of pollution from ships.

Under Part III of the Convention, strait States have the right to adopt laws and regulations in respect of four matters. It would appear that this is a closed list and strait States have no right to enact laws on anything which is not covered by the following four matters.

First, a strait State can adopt laws and regulations for the safety of navigation and the regulation of maritime traffic. This power has to be exercised in accordance with Article 41 of the Convention. Thus, for example, the strait States cannot designate sea lanes or prescribe traffic separation schemes until they have been adopted by the International Maritime Organization (IMO). In the case of the Straits of Malacca and Singapore, the three strait States, namely Indonesia, Malaysia and Singapore, have

---

[6] *Ibid.*, Art. 39(1).

[7] *Ibid.*, Art. 39(2)(a), *Convention on the International Regulations for Preventing Collisions at Sea*, London, 20 October 1972, as amended, 1050 U.N.T.S. 16.

cooperated with one another, and consulted with the IMO and major user States. As a result, the IMO has adopted the proposals of the strait States to maintain a single, under-keel clearance of 3.5 metres, to prescribe traffic separation schemes in three critical areas and to designate a sea lane in the Strait of Singapore for ships whose draught exceeds 15 metres.[8]

Second, a strait State can adopt laws and regulations for the prevention, reduction and control of pollution. This power has two limitations. The laws and regulations can only deal with "the discharge of oil, oily wastes and other noxious substances in the strait" and not other kinds of pollutants.[9] The second limitation is that the strait State cannot adopt laws and regulations if there are no applicable international standards and the laws and regulations must neither exceed nor be below the applicable international standards. The other two matters for which a strait State can adopt laws and regulations are respecting fishing vessels, the prevention of fishing, including the stowage of fishing gear, and the loading or unloading of any commodity, currency or person in contravention of the custom, fiscal, immigration or sanitary laws and regulations of strait States.[10]

Strait States have a number of duties and obligations, as follows:

    i. not to suspend, hamper or impede transit passage;

    ii. to give appropriate publicity to any danger to navigation or overflight within or over the strait of which they have knowledge;

    iii. to indicate clearly all sea lanes and traffic separation schemes designated or prescribed by them;

---

[8] See generally: IMO, *Ships' Routeing* (2010 ed.) (London: IMO, 2010), B.V. 1-1 to 9, C. III 2-3, F. 7-1, and G.1/14-1 to 14-6.

[9] LOS Convention, *supra* note 2, Art 42(1)(b).

[10] *Ibid.*, Art. 42(1)(c) and (d).

iv. not to discriminate among foreign ships, in form or in fact, in the adoption and application of the laws and regulations which would have the practical effect of denying, hampering or impairing the right of transit passage; and

v. to give due publicity to all the laws and regulations adopted.

The Convention has made a significant contribution to international law and to the rule of law in the world. The Convention has replaced legal uncertainty with legal certainty. It has put an end to conflicts between States over their respective powers and jurisdictions with respect to ocean space. It has also introduced a much welcome but grossly underutilised system of compulsory dispute settlement.

The Convention was negotiated and concluded by consensus and on the basis of a package deal. All parts of the Convention are inter-related. No party is allowed to pick what it likes and disregard what it does not like. For this reason, the Convention does not permit exceptions. It is not an exaggeration to say that there would have been no Convention if there were no agreement on the width of the territorial sea and no agreement on the territorial sea without agreements on straits used for international navigation and archipelagic sea lanes passage. Part III of the Convention was therefore an indispensable element of the grand bargain at the Conference.

Australia and the Torres Strait

The 1982 Convention came into force in 1994. Since then, the regime of transit passage has been observed both by the strait States and user States. There is, however, one current controversy relating to a strait used for international navigation. The country causing the controversy is a fellow Commonwealth country and, surprisingly, an original member of the private group on straits co-chaired by Fiji and the United Kingdom. That country is Australia and the strait in question is the Torres Strait. Let me try to present the two sides of the dispute as objectively as possible.

The Torres Strait is located between northern Australia and Papua New Guinea. Both Australia and Papua New Guinea acknowledge that the Torres Strait is a strait used for international navigation within the meaning of Part III of the Convention. The Torres Strait is a difficult strait for ships to navigate because at one point it has an under-keel clearance of only one metre, strong currents, narrow channel, and tidal difference, which means that the strait is navigable only during certain conditions.

The Torres Strait is also located near the Great Barrier Reef. There are indigenous people living on islands in the Torres Strait whose livelihood would be jeopardised in the event of a major oil spill in the Strait. For all these reasons, Australia argues that all ships transiting the Torres Strait should take on board experienced Australian pilots. I agree with this view. My difference with Australia is over the means to achieve this desired goal. In my view, a just end must still be pursued by just means. I wish that Australia had worked with the major shipping organisations and the major flag States to reach an agreement that all ships transiting the Torres Strait would take on board Australian pilots without being compelled to do so.

The following is a brief chronology of the key events relating to the Torres Strait.

- On 10 April 2003, Australia and Papua New Guinea submitted a proposal to the IMO to extend the Great Barrier Reef Particularly Sensitive Sea Area (PSSA) to the Torres

Strait and to extend the Great Barrier Reef compulsory pilotage system to the Torres Strait.

- On 22 July 2005, the Marine Environment Protection Committee (MEPC) of the IMO adopted Resolution MEPC.133(53).[11] The resolution approved the extension of the Great Barrier Reef PSSA to the Torres Strait. The Resolution also recommended that governments inform ships flying their flag that they should act in accordance with Australia's system of pilotage when navigating the Torres Strait. Following the adoption of the resolution, the US delegation stated that:

> ... this resolution was recommendatory and provided no international legal basis for mandatory pilotage for ships in transit in this or any other strait used for international navigation. The US could not support this resolution if this Committee took a contrary view.[12]

Several delegations supported the statement of the US. The delegation of Australia indicated that it did not object to the statement by the US.[13]

- On 16 May 2006, the Australian government issued Marine Notice 8/2006 entitled "Revised Pilotage Requirements for Torres Strait".[14] It advised shipowners and

---

[11] "Designation of the Torres Strait as an Extension of the Great Barrier Reef Particular by Sensitive Sea Area," Resolution MEPC.133(53), 22 July 2005, in IMO, "Report of the Marine Environment Protection Committee on its Fifty-Third Session," MEPC.53/24, 25 July 2005, Annex 21.

[12] *Ibid.*, para. 8.5.

[13] *Ibid.*, para 8.6.

[14] Australian Maritime Safety Authority, "Marine Notice 8/2006," 16 May 2006. http://www.amsa.gov.au/shipping_safety/marine_notices/2006/documents/0806.pdf (accessed 31 August 2011).

operators of a new compulsory pilotage area for the Torres Strait commencing on 6 October 2006. It advised that significant penalties would apply to a master or owner who failed to comply with the compulsory pilotage requirements. Australia cited IMO Resolution MEPC.133(53) as the justification.

- In July 2006, Singapore brought the matter up in the Sub-Committee on Safety of Navigation of the IMO. Fourteen other States supported Singapore's concern. Australia, however, refused to engage, arguing that the matter had been settled by previous meetings of the Maritime Safety Committee (MSC) and MEPC.

- In July 2006, the US sent Australia a diplomatic note of protest. Singapore followed suit in August 2006. Singapore sent Australia a second diplomatic note on 6 October 2006.

- On 3 October 2006, Australia issued Marine Notice 16/2006 entitled "Further Information on Revised Pilotage Requirements for the Torres Strait."[15] The first point of the notice is to exempt warships. The second point is to clarify that Australia does not intend to intercept ships exercising transit passage through the Torres Strait if they fail to take on a pilot. However, it will prosecute such vessels upon their next entry to an Australian port even if the ship is en route to a destination outside Australia.

- The MEPC met from 9 to 13 October 2006. The major shipping organisations had submitted a joint statement

---

[15] Australian Maritime Safety Authority. "Marine Notice 16/2006," 30 October 2006. http://www.amsa.gov.au/shipping_safety/marine_notices/2006/Documents/16_06.pdf (accessed 25 October 2011).

on the Torres Strait.[16] It requested the MEPC to reaffirm its understanding that Resolution MEPC.133(53) was recommendatory in nature. At the request of the Chair, the Committee confirmed that Resolution MEPC.133(53) was of a recommendatory nature.[17] Following the decision of the Committee, Australia stated that it agreed with the Chair's view.[18] With the support of 21 other delegations, Singapore urged Australia to review its two marine notices and to bring them into line with the MEPC's understanding of its resolution. In response, Australia, with the support of Papua New Guinea and New Zealand, made a statement,[19] prepared in advance, which ignored the implication of the Committee's decision. Australia contended that the MEPC was not empowered to decide whether Australia's action was in conformity with the Convention. The Statement argued that only the Legal Committee of the IMO was empowered to decide on the legality of Australia's measure and since it was unable to reach a consensus on the legal issues, no committee of the IMO would be able to consider whether Australia had acted contrary to international law.

• In February 2007, the US sent Australia a second diplomatic note setting out in detail why the Australian system

---

[16] International Chamber of Shipping, BIMCO, INTERCARGO and INTERTANKO, "Identification and Protection of Special Areas and Particularly Sensitive Sea Areas: Torres Strait," MEPC.55/8/3, 10 August 2006.

[17] IMO, "Report of the Marine Environment Protection Committee on Its Fifty-Fifth Session," MEPC.55/23, 16 October 2006, para. 8.10.

[18] *Ibid.*, para. 8.11.

[19] "Statement by the Delegation of Australia concerning Pilotage in the Torres Strait PSSA," *ibid.*, Annex 23.

of pilotage was inconsistent with international law and the Convention.

- On 17 April 2009, Australia issued Marine Notice 7/2009, entitled "Bridge Resource Management and the Torres Strait Pilotage".[20] The new notice sought to justify the compulsory pilotage system on the bases of both the IMO Resolution MEPC.133(53) and as a port entry requirement. The Marine Notice was amended on 21 April 2009.
- On 17 April 2009, Singapore sent Australia a third diplomatic note, rejecting the new marine notice on the grounds that the IMO Resolution does not authorise the Australian system of compulsory pilotage and there is no international legal basis for Australia's imposition of penalties, non-custodial or otherwise, on vessels exercising their right of transit passage through the Torres Strait.

I think Australia's actions are questionable on three grounds. First, as explained above, the power of strait States to make laws and regulations is strictly limited to four areas. Compulsory pilotage does not fall within any of the four. I would argue that Australia, as a strait State, has no power to enact a law imposing compulsory pilotage on ships transiting the Torres Strait. Australia's action creates a very unfortunate precedent that could undermine the integrity of the regime of transit passage. Australia has argued that the Torres Strait is *sui generis* and cannot constitute a precedent. This is a slippery argument because there is nothing to stop another strait State from making a similar argument.

---

[20] Australian Maritime Safety Authority. "Marine Notice 7/2009", 17 April 2009. http://www.amsa.gov.au/Shipping_Safety/Marine_Notices/2009/0709.pdf (accessed 25 October 2011).

Second, it is unacceptable for Australia to continue to insist that its action has been endorsed by the IMO through Resolution MEPC.133(53). On the contrary, the IMO Resolution is recommendatory in nature. As noted above, in response to the concerns of the major shipping organisations, the MEPC reaffirmed, at its meeting in October 2006, that Resolution MEPC.133(53) does not support Australia's imposition of compulsory pilotage.

Third, Australia's recent attempt to justify its system of compulsory pilotage is to invoke the power of a port State to prescribe requirements for entry to its ports. A port State may prescribe requirements for entry to its ports. This power is, however, not unfettered. A port State must act in accordance with international law and its treaty obligations. If Australia lacks the jurisdiction under the Convention to impose compulsory pilotage on ships transiting the Torres Strait, it cannot cure its lack of jurisdiction by purporting to characterise it as a port entry requirement.

Cooperation and the Straits of Malacca and Singapore

I do not want to conclude my essay on a contentious note. I want my essay to have a happy ending. I have spent many years of my life trying to get an agreement between Indonesia, Malaysia and Singapore, on the one hand, and the user States on the other hand, to implement Article 43. Together with the IMO, I convened two conferences in 1996 and 1999 in Singapore. Although the conferences were well attended and helped to clarify the issues, Indonesia was not ready to implement Article 43. So, I will refer to another recent development. This pertains to Article 43 of the Convention, which enjoins user States and States bordering a strait to agree to cooperate:

   i. in the establishment and maintenance in a strait of neces-
     sary navigational and safety aids, or other improvements
     in aid of international navigation; and

  ii. for the prevention, reduction and control of pollution
     from ships.

The Straits of Malacca and Singapore are probably the most important straits in the world. It has been estimated that 50 per cent of world trade, 50 per cent of the world's oil shipments, and two-thirds of the world's trade in liquefied natural gas, pass through the Straits of Malacca and Singapore. On average, 900 ships transit the Singapore Strait each day.

The three States bordering the Straits of Malacca and Singapore (Indonesia, Malaysia and Singapore) have behaved in an exemplary manner. They cooperate closely through a technical body known as the Tripartite Technical Experts Group (TTEG). The three strait States have also cooperated with the IMO and major user States. However, until 2007, among the user States, only Japan had been helping these strait States in undertaking hydrographic surveys, in maintaining navigational and safety aids, and in building the capacity to respond effectively to any oil spills resulting from accidents in the straits. The other user States were happy to be free riders. This caused considerable resentment on the part of the strait States.

At the request of the IMO, a Singapore think-tank, the Institute of Policy Studies, co-organised two international conferences on the Straits of Malacca and Singapore in 1996 and 1999. The objective of the two conferences was to achieve a consensus among the strait States and the user States to implement Article 43. However, the three littoral States were not able to reach a consensus on how Article 43 should be interpreted. At the same time, apart from Japan, the other user States were not willing to commit themselves to helping the strait States.

I must credit the former Secretary-General of the IMO, Admiral Mitropoulos, for launching a new initiative that led to a breakthrough. In 2005, he convened a workshop in Indonesia to discuss the Straits of Malacca and Singapore. The workshop was successful and led to a second workshop in 2006 in Malaysia. This paved the way for the convening, in Singapore in September 2007, of an IMO-Singapore meeting on the Straits of Malacca and Singapore. I was given the privilege of chairing that meeting, which adopted a cooperation mechanism for the Straits of Malacca and Singapore. It was the first occasion on which Article 43 of the Convention had been implemented.

The cooperation mechanism consists of a cooperation forum, a project coordination committee, and an Aids to Navigation Fund. Each of the three strait States has put forward two projects. China, South Korea, Australia, the US, India, Greece, Germany, and Norway have joined Japan in the cooperation mechanism and are assisting the strait States in implementing the projects with financial and technical assistance.

The Straits of Malacca and Singapore are the only straits used for international navigation that have successfully implemented Article 43 of the Convention. The time has surely come for other strait States and user States to emulate our good example. What we have achieved is a victory for international rule of law and for international cooperation.

Conclusion

We live in an increasingly globalised and interconnected world. International law is one important pillar of global governance. We should promote the study, research, and observance of international law. All countries, big and small, are better off in a world governed by international law and the rule of law than in a lawless world. I have discussed the importance of the 1982 Convention and shared two recent developments, one positive and another negative. Let me conclude with the hope that countries will eschew the temptation to achieve a desired and laudable goal by means which are contrary to the law. It is in no country's long-term interest to undermine the respect for and adherence to international law.

———⌘———

This essay consolidates Professor Tommy Koh's writings on the topic of straits used for international navigation under UNCLOS. It was originally written as a tribute to esteemed legal scholar Edgar Gold in *The Regulation of International Shipping: International and Comparative Perspectives – Essays in Honor of Edgar Gold*, ed. Chircop et al. (2012) and later delivered as a lecture "Straits used for International Navigation" by Professor Tommy Koh for the United Nations Audiovisual Library of International Law on 7 December 2016.

Negotiating a
New World Order
for the Sea

The United Nations Convention on the Law of the Sea of
1982 took almost nine years to negotiate. The opposition
of the present United States government notwithstanding, the
treaty represents one of the major achievements of the United
Nations during the past decade. For the last two years of the
Third United Nations Conference on the Law of the Sea, I
was privileged to serve as its President. In what follows, I shall
attempt to tell the remarkable story of negotiating a new world
order for a realm that encompasses more than two-thirds of the
surface of the earth.

First, I shall trace briefly the evolution of the traditional
law of the sea. Second, I shall discuss the different forces that
eroded and then finally brought about the collapse of the old
legal order, leading to the eventual convening of the Third United
Nations Conference in December 1973. Third, I shall give

selected examples of the subjects and issues that were negotiated at the Conference. In doing so, I shall discuss the nature of the competing interests that had to be reconciled and the mutual accommodations that had to be made in order to reach a successful result. Fourth, I shall discuss some of the more interesting, perhaps even unique, features of the negotiating process that we used. Finally, I shall answer the question: What is the long-range significance of the new legal order governing the uses and resources of the world's oceans, as embodied in the 1982 United Nations Convention?

First, we need to place our subject in its historical context. From the end of the fifteenth to the beginning of the nineteenth century, the law concerning the uses and resources of the sea was unsettled. There were two contending schools of thought. The first, *mare clausum* (Closed Sea), held that the sea and its resources were capable of being subject to appropriation and dominion. The second school of thought, called *mare liberum* (Free Sea), was brilliantly expounded by Hugo Grotius in the legal opinion he wrote for the Dutch East India Company. He argued that things which cannot be seized or enclosed cannot become property. According to Grotius, no one can claim dominion or exclusive fisheries rights or an exclusive right of navigation on the high seas.

In the course of the eighteenth century, the Grotian view came gradually to predominate over the opposing view. Coastal States were permitted to claim a narrow belt of the sea off their shores for the purpose of fishing, as well as for protecting their neutrality. Beyond that belt, the sea and its resources were *res communis*, no one's property, and subject to the freedom of the sea.

By the beginning of the nineteenth century, following the end of the Napoleonic Wars and the Congress of Vienna, the three-mile territorial sea became almost universally accepted. Great Britain, which emerged from the Napoleonic Wars as the world's greatest power, became the champion of the *mare liberum* idea. It was logical for it to adopt such a position. "In manufacture, in merchant marine, in foreign trade, in international finance, we had no rival," as the British diplomat and historian Lord Strang has explained. "As we came, by deliberate act of policy, to adopt the practice of free trade and to apply the principle of 'all seas freely open for all,' we moved towards the *Pax Britannica*, using the Royal Navy to keep the seas open for the common benefit, to suppress piracy and the slave trade, and to prepare and publish charts of every ocean."[1]

This British-dominated maritime legal order prevailed for over a hundred years. New forces, however, began to challenge it, as well as British supremacy. An American scholar, Sayre A Swarztrauber, has suggested that the old legal order began its decline in 1930.[2] In that year, the Hague Codification Conference was held under the auspices of the League of Nations. The objective of that conference was to codify the international law regarding the territorial sea. Forty-eight States attended the Hague conference; of these, only ten favoured a three-mile territorial sea, provided that a contiguous zone was added. (A contiguous zone enables a State to exercise the control necessary to prevent and to punish infringements of its customs, fiscal, immigration or sanitary laws and regulations within its territory or territorial sea.) Six States favoured a six-mile territorial sea, and six others

---

[1] Lord William Strang, *Britain in World Affairs: The Fluctuation in Power and Influence from Henry VIII to Elizabeth II* (New York: Frederick A Praeger, 1961), pp. 99–100.

[2] Sayre A Swarztrauber, *The Three-Mile Limit of Territorial Seas* (Annapolis: Naval Institute Press, 1972).

wanted a six-mile territorial sea together with a contiguous zone. Because the views expressed were so divergent, no formal vote was taken on any of the proposals. A possible compromise consisting of a three-mile territorial sea and a nine-mile contiguous zone was quashed by strong British opposition. The 1930 conference, therefore, ended in failure. Swarztrauber has argued that, by allowing the conference to fail, "the great maritime powers ended their oligarchical maintenance of the maxim *mare liberum*. The [c]onference suggested to all that the great powers were no longer committed to the enforcement of the three-mile limit."[3]

Ironically, the US struck a second blow to the traditional law of the sea following the Second World War. In 1945, President Harry S Truman issued two famous proclamations relating to the sea. In the first, the US asserted its jurisdiction and control over the natural resources of the subsoil and seabed of the continental shelf contiguous to the US coast. The term "continental shelf" defined generally that portion of the seabed extending from land to the point where the waters reached a depth of 600 feet, or 200 metres isobath.[4] In the second proclamation, the US declared that it "regards it as proper to establish conservation zones in those areas of the high seas contiguous to the coast of the US wherein fishing activities have been or in future may be developed and maintained on a substantial scale."[5] The proclamation

---

[3] *Ibid.*, p. 140.
[4] Proclamation No. 2667, "Policy of the United States with Respect to the Natural Resources of the Subsoil and Sea Bed of the Continental Shelf," September 28, 1945, 10 *Federal Register* 12303; also printed in S Houston Lay, Robin Churchill, Myron Nordquist, KR Simmonds, and Jane Welch, comps. and eds., *New Directions in the Law of the Sea, Documents*, 11 vols. (Dobbs Ferry, NY: Oceana Publications, 1973–1981), 1: 106–09.
[5] Proclamation No. 2668, "Policy of the United States with Respect to Coastal Fisheries in Certain Areas of the High Seas." September 28, 1945, 10 *Federal Register* 12304; also printed in Lay et al., *New Directions*, 1: 95–98.

provided that the conservation zones would be established and maintained through direct agreement with those States whose subjects traditionally had fished the areas in question.

These unilateral actions of the US were immediately emulated and exceeded by its regional neighbours. Mexico issued a similar proclamation one month after the US did. A year later, Argentina not only claimed sovereignty over its own continental shelf but also to the water column above the shelf. Between 1946 and 1957, ten other states claimed sovereignty over their continental shelves and the superjacent waters. Between 1947 and 1955, five Latin American states declared 200-mile limits for exclusive fishing rights.

It was in these circumstances of a rapidly eroding legal order that the United Nations held its First Conference on the Law of the Sea in 1958. That international gathering succeeded in adopting four conventions: the Convention on the Territorial Sea and the Contiguous Zone, the Convention on Fishing and Conservation of the Living Resources of the High Seas, the Convention on the High Seas, and the Convention on the Continental Shelf. The First United Nations Conference failed, however, to arrive at agreed limits on the territorial sea and on the coastal States' exclusive fishing rights. In the Convention on the Continental Shelf, the rights of the coastal States were to extend "to a depth of 200 metres or, beyond that limit, to where the depth of the superjacent waters admits the exploitation of the natural resources".[6] The second of these two criteria, the exploitability criterion, was imprecise and soon gave rise to trouble. In 1960, the United Nations held its Second Conference on the Law of

---

[6] Convention on the Continental Shelf, done at Geneva, April 29, 1958, in Lay et al., *New Directions*, 3: 101–05.

the Sea in order to find agreement on the limits of the territorial sea and the fishing zone. This conference also failed.

During the decade of the 1960s, the British, Dutch and French colonial empires, in decline for many years, largely disintegrated. The former colonies of the European states in Asia, Africa and the Caribbean acceded to independence, joined the United Nations, and became new members of the international community. Most of these newly independent countries had not participated in the 1958 and 1960 United Nations Conferences on the Law of the Sea and therefore took no proprietary interest in them. They also felt dissatisfied with the traditional law that they regarded as the product of European experience. Therefore, they wanted an opportunity to remould the international law of the sea to reflect their aspirations and interests.

In the fall of 1967, the then permanent representative of Malta to the United Nations, Dr Arvid Pardo, drew the attention of the world to the immense resources of the seabed and ocean floor, beyond the limits of national jurisdiction. He proposed that the seabed and ocean floor should be used exclusively for peaceful purposes and that the area and its resources should be considered the common heritage of mankind. He argued that neither the freedom of the sea nor claims of sovereignty then being asserted by coastal States could ban the spectre of pollution, exhaustion of marine life, and international political strife.[7] Pardo and others further urged that a constitution or charter be adopted that would deal with ocean space as an organic and ecological whole. This was a revolutionary concept, one that

---

[7] For a statement of his views, see Arvid Pardo, "Who Will Control the Seabed?" *Foreign Affairs* 47, no. 1 (October 1968): 123–37.

conditioned subsequent international discussion of the law of the sea problem. Unlike lawyers, who tend to favour dealing with issues in manageable packages, statesmen such as Pardo, influenced by scientific discoveries of the inter-relatedness of oceanographic matters, persuasively advocated a more unified treatment. The focus of this new vision and approach was the seabed. As a result, the United Nations established the Seabed Committee to examine the question and to elaborate a legal regime for the exploration and exploitation of the resources of the ocean floor area.

At about the same time, the USSR approached the US and other countries in order to discuss the idea of recognising a 12-mile territorial sea, provided that a high seas corridor was preserved in international straits. In 1968 and 1969, the US started ascertaining the views of its NATO partners, the USSR, and other countries about the desirability of conceding 12 miles as: the maximum permissible breadth of the territorial sea in return for free navigation of warships and overflight of military aircraft in and over straits used for international navigation.

By 1970, it was clear to all that the old maritime legal order had collapsed. Support for the convening of the Third United Nations Conference on the Law of the Sea seemed logical and timely. Such a meeting was needed to resolve the unfinished business of the First and Second United Nations Conferences: namely, the limit of the territorial sea, the limit of the fishing zone, and the replacement of the exploitability criterion by a more precise continental shelf definition. It was necessary to replace the chaos created by the unilateral and conflicting claims of coastal States. The great maritime powers, especially the two superpowers, felt the need for a new internationally agreed regime for the passage of ships and aircraft through and over straits. The newly independent countries of the Third World wanted a new conference in which they could participate. Such a conference would be a model for the New International Economic Order in which they were greatly interested. In addition, the world community would have to agree on rules, as well as institutions, for the exploitation of the mineral resources in the seabed and ocean floor beyond the limits of national jurisdiction. Finally, there was the pollution issue. The historic 1972 Stockholm Conference on the Human Environment and a series of accidents involving oil tankers had raised the world's consciousness regarding the threat to the marine environment. There was a consequent desire to adopt new rules to protect and preserve it.

The agenda of the Third United Nations Conference on the Law of the Sea (UNCLOS III)—which gathered initially in New York and then moved to Caracas, alternated between Geneva and New York, and concluded at Montego Bay in Jamaica—consisted of 25 subjects and issues. Although it is impossible for me to discuss all of these questions, I wish to elaborate on a number of especially significant examples and to explain what were the competing interests and how those competing interests were reconciled.

First of all, the maximum breadth of the territorial sea and the regime of passage through straits used for international navigation were related subjects. At the 1930 Hague conference, as well as at the 1958 and 1960 conferences, the international community was unable to agree on the maximum breadth of the territorial sea. By the time UNCLOS III convened in December 1973, only a minority of States, 27 out of 111 coastal States, claimed a 3-mile territorial sea. Nearly a majority, 52 out of these 111 States, claimed a territorial sea of 12 miles. The great powers could not accept 12 miles as the maximum permissible breadth of the territorial sea, however, unless it was also agreed that there would be a special regime for passage through and over straits used in international navigation. This was because there are 116 straits in the world whose breadths are between 6 and 24 miles. With the extension of the territorial sea from 3 to 12 miles, the waters in these straits would become territorial waters, and the high seas corridor would be lost.

The US and the USSR are, of course, global powers with allies and interests in areas far from their own shores. They require the use of the seas and the air space above them for the purpose of projecting their conventional military power. Freedom of navigation for their navies and of overflight for their military aircraft is a strategic imperative. The straits constitute choke points in the world's communications system, and the question of passage through them is critical. Each superpower also keeps part of its stockpile of ballistic missiles in submarines at sea. It is considered important by each superpower for its adversary not to know the precise location of its nuclear-armed submarines because this works as a deterrent against either of them launching a first strike against the other. As long as each superpower retains a second-strike capability, safe at sea, this acts as a deterrent against the temptation of launching a sneak attack. Because secrecy and mobility of their respective submarine fleets are critical, the two superpowers have demanded free and submerged passage for their submarines through straits.

The negotiators of the United Nations Convention sought to reconcile the competing interests of coastal States and of the great maritime powers. The outcome, embodied in the 1982 Convention, recognises 12 miles as the maximum permissible breadth of the territorial sea (Article 3) and, at the same time, prescribes a special regime, called "transit passage", for ships and aircraft through and over straits used for international navigation (Articles 37 to 44).[8] The text uses the words "freedom of navigation and overflight" to describe the nature of transit passage. Significantly, these are words normally used in connection with the high seas where the great maritime powers have always enjoyed freedom of movement.

A second issue is fisheries. There were at least four competing interests that the Conference had to reconcile. First, there was mankind's general interest in the conservation as well as the optimum use of fish resources, for many countries and peoples, the cheapest source of animal protein. The second interest was that of the coastal States, some 76 in all. In many countries, there are numerous communities that depend solely or mainly on fishing for their livelihoods Many of the coastal States, which for certain purposes operated as a group at UNCLOS III, complained that the traditional law was unfair to them. The developing coastal countries felt unable to compete with the technologically more advanced countries in catching the fish stocks lying off their own coasts. Because, under traditional law, fish stocks beyond the narrow belt of the territorial sea constitute a common property, many of the world's fish stocks have become dangerously depleted owing to overfishing. The regional fisheries commissions have not been given sufficient powers to enforce conservation measures. For these reasons, the coastal States claimed the right to establish "exclusive economic zones" (EEZs) of up to 200 miles. Within these EEZs, they would have sovereign rights to the resources. The third interest the Conference

---

[8] For the text of the articles of the 1982 convention, see United Nations, *The Law of the Sea: Official Text of the United Nations Convention on the Law of the Sea with Annexes and Index* (New York: United Nations, 1983).

had to take into account was that of the landlocked and geo-graphically disadvantaged States. These, numbering 55 altogether, would either have nothing to gain or would have something to lose if these EEZs were established by coastal States. Then there was a fourth interest: that of the distant-water fishing nations. These countries had large sums of money invested in their fishing industries and, in some cases, had been fishing in certain fishing grounds for a considerable length of time.

The provisions of the 1982 Convention dealing with the EEZs represent an attempt to reconcile these competing interests. Every coastal State is entitled to establish such a zone of up to 200 miles (Articles 55 and 57), within which it has sovereign rights to the living resources (Article 56). The coastal State is, however, under obligation to the international community to undertake conservation measures in order to ensure that these resources are not overexploited. At the same time, the coastal State is obliged to fix the total allowable catch of different species in order to ensure the optimum use of the resources (Article 61). If the State is unable to harvest the entire allowable catch, it is under an obligation to allocate the surplus to other States (Article 62). The first priority will go to landlocked and geographically disadvantaged States, the second priority to developing countries, and the third priority to other countries, including the traditional fishing nations (Articles 62, 69, 70). The arrangement is an intricately balanced one, with which most States are satisfied.

A third issue concerns the mineral resources of the seabed and ocean floor. The main form of these resources is polymetallic nodules, also known as manganese nodules. In 1967, Pardo called the world's attention to the existence of these resources and proposed that the seabed and ocean floor outside the then prevailing limits of national jurisdiction, as well as the resources themselves, be declared a common heritage of mankind. In 1970, the United

Nations General Assembly adopted a declaration of principles governing the seabed and ocean floor, and subsoil thereof, by a vote of 108 to 0, with 14 abstentions. (The US voted for the declaration.) Although the Soviet bloc abstained in the vote, its members subsequently stated their support for the declaration. That declaration says, *inter alia*, that the sea floor area shall not be subject to appropriation by States, or by other entities, and that no State shall claim or exercise sovereign rights over any part thereof. It also declares that no State, or other entity, shall have rights with respect to the Area or its resources incompatible with the international regime to be established. All activities regarding the exploration and exploitation of the resources of the Area shall be governed by that international regime.[9]

In the negotiations on this question, the Conference had to reconcile the following competing interests. There was the interest of the international community as a whole in promoting the development of the seabed's resources. There were also more special interests: those of potential consumers of the metals that could be extracted from the mid-ocean polymetallic nodules; those of the countries that had invested funds, or were planning to invest funds in mining the nodules; those of the developing countries that, as co-owners of the resource, wished to benefit not only as consumers but also as participants in its exploitation; and finally, those of the countries that produced in their land territories the same metals that are contained in the polymetallic nodules. It should be mentioned that owing to the high cost of

---

[9] United Nations, General Assembly. Declaration of Principles Governing the Sea-Bed and the Ocean Floor, and the Subsoil Thereof, beyond the Limits of National Jurisdiction, Resolution 2749, December 17, 1970, in Lay et al., *New Directions*, 2: 740–41.

the necessary technology as well as the fact of existing surpluses, the future profitability of seabed mining was highly uncertain.

The provisions of Part XI of the Convention, Annex III and Resolution II, taken together, contain compromises that seek to accommodate these prospectively competing interests. In view of the continuing controversy over the seabed settlement, these provisions merit close consideration. Under Resolution II, the consortia and States that have already invested research and development funds in the exploration of specific mine sites have been recognised as "pioneer investors." If the State to which a consortium belongs, signs and ratifies the Law of the Sea Convention, that consortium may be formally registered as a pioneer investor. In the case of a consortium that is unincorporated and that consists of partners from a number of different countries, the consortium may be registered as a pioneer investor if only one of those countries accepts the Convention. Upon being registered as a pioneer investor, the consortium acquires the exclusive right to explore a specific mine site. When the Convention comes into force, following completion of the ratification process, the registered pioneer investor gains an automatic right to actually mine that specific mine site, so long as it complies with the requirements of the Convention and so long as its sponsoring State is a party to the Convention. Thus, the troublesome question about guaranteed access to the resources of the deep seabed has been largely resolved by Resolution II.

In order to give land-based producers some protection against the possible adverse economic consequences of seabed exploitation, the Convention contains a formula for limiting the amounts of metals which can be produced from the seabed for a period of 25 years (Article 151). Resolution II states that the pioneer investors shall have priority in the allocation of the production authorisation calculated under the formula. According to the experts, the production limitation in the Convention poses more of an ideological than a pragmatic problem for the seabed miners. This is because, given the economic prospects of the mining industry in the foreseeable future and the limited number of actors that are likely to enter the industry, any reasonable projection will give us a number of mine sites adequate to accommodate all those who are likely to want to enter this arena.

Consistent with the concept of the common heritage of mankind, a seabed miner will have to pay to the International Seabed Authority (ISA) either a royalty payment, or a combination of a royalty payment and a share of his profits (Annex III, Article 13). The seabed miner may choose either one of the two schemes. If he chooses the latter, he will find a tax structure that is more progressive than any to be found in land-based mining contracts. The tax that a seabed miner pays to the ISA will vary, depending upon the profitability of his project, calculated annually, as well as over the life span of the project. The tax system uses the internal rate of return as the measurement of the project's profitability.

Under the terms of the Convention, a seabed miner may be required by the ISA to sell his technology to the authority (Annex III, Article 5). This transfer-of-technology provision has caused great concern to industrialised countries. It should be borne in mind, however, that this obligation can not be invoked by the authority unless the same or equivalent technology is not available in the open market. An internal study carried out by the US Department of Commerce shows that, for every component of seabed mining technology, there are at least four sellers on the market. If this is true, then the pre-condition cannot be met, and the objectionable obligation can never be invoked. Moreover, it should be noted that the Convention contains elaborate provision for the resolution of disputes over its terms.

These examples, the territorial sea and straits questions, the fisheries issue and creation of the EEZ, and the problem of access to the resources of the seabed and ocean floors, all illustrate how the Law of the Sea Conference managed to reach agreement. The procedures followed by UNCLOS III and its negotiating process also contain many interesting, even unique, features. The Conference committed itself from the very start to work by the procedure, pioneered over the years in committee meetings at the United Nations, of "consensus." Progress was made by this method, which puts a premium on skilful and scrupulously fair chairmanship, because delegates could tacitly consent by waiving their right of disagreement. Typically, a chairman would declare, "If there are no objections, the proposal is adopted." An appendix to the Rules of Procedure states, "The Conference should make every effort to reach agreement on substantive matters by way of consensus and there should be no voting on such matters until all efforts at consensus have been exhausted."[10] The Conference placed such an emphasis on consensus for two major reasons: it wanted to adopt a Convention that would enjoy the widest possible support in the international community, and the consensus procedure was intended to protect the interests and views of minorities at the Conference.

The commitment of the Conference to consensus was strongly buttressed by its formal rules of procedure. The rules made it very difficult to vote on a proposal or an amendment; they also make it difficult for such a proposal or amendment to be adopted by a vote. For example, when a matter of substance

---

[10] United Nations, *Law of the Sea*, p. 165.

came up for voting for the first time, either the President or 15 delegations could request a deferment for a period not exceeding ten days (Rule 37, 2a). During this period, the President was obliged to make every effort to facilitate the achievement of general agreement (Rule 37, 2c). At the end of the period, the President was to inform the Conference of the results of his efforts. A vote on a proposal could be taken only after the Conference had determined that all efforts at reaching agreement were exhausted (Rule 37, 2d). During the first eight years of UNCLOS III, not a single vote was taken, either by roll call or by ballot, on any of the substantive issues it had been initially called to resolve.

At the last session of the Conference, 33 amendments were submitted to the draft Convention. I ordered a cooling-off period of ten days. During this time, I found that there was general support for only one of the amendments. It was adopted by the Conference without a vote. I managed to persuade the proposers of all but three of the remaining amendments to withdraw. All three amendments were put to the vote and rejected by the Conference. One of them obtained the required two-thirds majority of those present and voting but failed to satisfy the second requirement of a majority of the delegations attending the Conference.

There were two other important procedural understandings that advanced the work of the Conference. The Conference agreed to work on the "package deal" principle. This meant that the Conference would adopt one comprehensive convention instead of several conventions, as happened at the 1958 conference. The instrument of this integrating, balancing process was the Informal Single Negotiating Text, which, after going through a number of transformations, became the formal Convention on the Law of the Sea. The other understanding that reinforced the building of consensus was the rule that the Convention would permit no reservations (Article 309).

Another interesting and important feature of the Conference was the emergence of new interest groups. The traditional ones, such as regional groups, played a very minor role in the work of the Law of the Sea Conference. Instead, groups were formed by countries that had kindred interests, such as coastal States, landlocked and geographically disadvantaged States, strait States, archipelagic States, broad-continental-shelfed States (the "margin-eers"), and many others. One particularly important group, the Group of Five (irreverently dubbed the "Gang of Five" by a Canadian representative), was composed of the industrialised states of the UK, France, Japan, the US, and the USSR.

The group system played both a positive and a negative role at the Conference. On the positive side, it enabled countries to join forces with other countries with which they shared a common interest. In this way, a country could acquire a bargaining leverage that it would not have had if it had operated alone. It proved to be impossible to conduct serious negotiations at UNCLOS III until these special interest groups were formed. It was only after their formation that the competing groups were able to formulate their positions in concrete texts and to appoint representatives to engage in negotiations. On the negative side, it must be admitted that once a group had adopted a common position, it was often difficult for the group to modify its position. This meant that the negotiators were given a mandate and had little or no flexibility.

Yet another feature of our negotiating process was the fact that there were two parallel structures of negotiations at the Conference. On the one hand, there were the officially established committees and negotiating groups. Because these were generally forums of the whole, they were too large to function effectively for negotiations. The need for small but representative negotiating bodies was filled by the establishment of informal and unofficial negotiating groups. Most of these groups were established on the initiative of individuals; for example, the Evensen Group of juridical experts was set up at the personal initiative of Jens Evensen, leader of the Norwegian delegation. The Evensen Group did extremely valuable work on the EEZ. The Castañeda Group, convened by the leader of the Mexican delegation, Jorge Castañeda, succeeded in resolving the controversial question of the legal status of the EEZ and its related issues. There was also a private group on dispute settlement, convened on the initiative of Professor Louis B Sohn of the US. Sometimes, an unofficial negotiating group was even formed on the initiative of two competing ones. This happened when the group of coastal States and the group of landlocked and geographically disadvantaged States agreed to establish a negotiating body comprising ten representatives from each group and approached Ambassador Satya Nandan of Fiji to be its chairman. Personal leadership at UNCLOS III did not always coincide with the size of the country of the individual who offered it or was asked to give it. Sometimes it did, however, as in the noteworthy case of Elliot L Richardson, the effective chairman of the US delegation.

Toward the later stages of the Conference, the other presiding officers and I gradually miniaturised the size of the negotiating groups. It was absolutely essential to transform a large, unwieldy conference of approximately 140 delegations into small, representative, and efficient negotiating groups. Although the efforts to miniaturise the official negotiating forums inevitably encountered resistance, they were essential and ultimately successful.

Another lesson I have learned is that a Conference needs the full range of formal, informal, and even privately convened negotiating groups. As a general rule, the more informal the nature of the group, the easier it is to resolve a problem. However, secrecy must be scrupulously avoided. In addition, if the results of a negotiating group are to have any chance of winning the support of the Conference, then the group must include all those who have a real interest at stake, as well as the acknowledged conference leaders.

What is the significance of the new Convention on the Law of the Sea? I would draw attention to the fact that it is the first comprehensive convention governing all aspects of the uses and resources of the world's oceans. Unlike the four Geneva conventions of 1958, the 1982 Convention represents an attempt to respect the inter-relationships between different aspects of the law of the sea. We also tried very hard to live up to Pardo's exhortation to view ocean space as an ecological whole.

The new Convention on the Law of the Sea is also important because it will contribute to the promotion of international peace, by replacing a plethora of conflicting claims by coastal States with universally agreed limits for the territorial sea, the contiguous zone, the exclusive economic zone, and the continental shelf. The Convention represents a victory for the rule of law. It is the first major multilateral treaty which contains mandatory provisions for the settlement of disputes. Moreover, the Convention affirms the possibility for countries of north and south, and east and west, to cooperate for their mutual benefit. Finally, the successful outcome of UNCLOS III vindicates the United Nations as an institution that, given the necessary exercise of political will by its member states, can be used to conduct serious negotiations on matters of vital importance to the world.

—— ⚬⚬⚬ ——

This essay was first published in *Negotiating World Order: The Artisanship and Architecture of Global Diplomacy*, ed. Alan K Henrikson (Scholarly Resources Inc: 1986).

Negotiating the United Nations Convention on the Law of the Sea

A Practitioner's Reflection

The United Nations Convention on the Law of the Sea or UNCLOS is an extremely important treaty. It applies to 70 per cent of the earth's surface. It is the embodiment of the modern law of the sea. It creates a legal order for the world's oceans. It promotes peace and cooperation. It supports the peaceful settlement of disputes and the rule of law.

The President of the Third United Nations Conference on the Law of the Sea (1973–1980) was Ambassador Hamilton Shirley Amerasinghe of Sri Lanka. He passed away in December 1980. In March 1981, I was elected to succeed him. In this regard, I will give a practitioner's account of the negotiating process that led to the adoption of the UNCLOS.

Preparing for the Conference

The first point I wish to make is that the Third United Nations Conference on the Law of the Sea did not follow the negotiating process of the First (1958) and Second (1960) United Nations Conferences on the Law of the Sea. The preparatory work for the first two conferences was undertaken by the International Law Commission and, later, by a Group of Experts.

In the case of the Third Conference, the preparatory work was entrusted to the United Nations Seabed Committee. Inexplicably, the Conference began in December 1973 without a draft text. This is just one of the many unusual, if not unique features of the negotiating process of the Third Conference. I shall identify and discuss the most important of these features.

Second, the Conference had an extremely broad agenda—covering almost every aspect of the oceans, its resources, and its uses. The agenda covered 25 very broad issues. This, plus the fact that the Conference began without a draft text, accounted for its length. The whole process, beginning with the United Nations Seabed Committee in 1968, took 14 years. The Conference itself lasted nine years.

Third, the Conference agreed to work on the "package-deal" principle. The logic behind this principle is that many of the items on the agenda were inter-related. The ambition was to treat ocean space as an ecological whole. The second reason is that delegations were making trade-offs between their positions on different issues. They were willing to make a concession in one area in return for a gain in another area. The result was the consensus that delegations could not pick and choose. They had to accept the Convention as a whole.

Fourth, the rules of procedure contained two unusual features. First, the rules discouraged the taking of decisions by voting.

The objective was to adopt a Convention that would command the widest support. Hence, it was felt that it was necessary to incorporate into the rules of procedure safeguards against hasty voting and providing for a cooling-off period. The second feature was the agreement to have special rules concerning the majority of votes required for the taking of decisions. During the cooling-off period, the President would make every effort to achieve consensus.

Fifth, in November 1973, a month before the commencement of the Conference, the United Nations General Assembly adopted a resolution that included a so-called "Gentlemen's Agreement". The operational paragraph of this resolution states that "the conference shall make every effort to reach agreement on substantive matters by way of consensus and there should be no voting on such matters until all efforts at consensus have been exhausted." The agreement was observed in letter and spirit. No decision at the Conference, on a substantive matter, was taken by vote except the vote on the adoption of the Convention taken by the Conference on 30 April 1982.

The Conference Begins

My sixth point is that the politics of the Conference and the long duration of the negotiating process produced new groupings and alliances that both facilitated and hindered the negotiations. The usual United Nations regional groups existed in the Conference but they were less influential than the interest groups that emerged. These interest groups cut across geographical regions, ideology, and development status. Some of the most influential groups were the Coastal States Group, with 76 members; the Group of Landlocked and Geographically Disadvantaged States, with

55 members; the "Margineers Group" or Group of Broad Shelf States, with 13 members; the Strait States Group; the Group of Archipelagic States; the Group of Maritime States; and the Great Maritime Powers.

Of the traditional groups, the most influential was the Group of 77, to which the developing countries belonged. This group played a major role in the negotiations on Part XI of the Convention, which applies to the seabed and ocean floor beyond national jurisdiction. Of the regional groups, the one that was the most united and vocal was the Latin American Group.

The emergence of the interest groups had a profound impact on the negotiations. The Conference had to acknowledge their existence and allocate facilities for their meetings. On the positive side, they helped to identify and clarify the issues in dispute. On the negative side, the interest groups consumed a great deal of the Conference's time and resources. Also, once a group had adopted a common position, it was often rigid in the negotiations.

Seventh, there were two parallel systems of negotiations. There was the official negotiating structure, consisting of the Plenary, the three main committees, and the subsidiary groups. There was an unofficial negotiating process consisting of the interest groups and the informal private negotiating groups.

The role of the informal private negotiating groups was a unique feature of the Conference. They emerged to fulfil a need. The Conference had 151 participating States. It was extremely difficult to negotiate in such a large body. It was difficult to reduce the size of the negotiating groups because no State was willing to be left out. The informal private negotiating groups emerged in order to fulfil the need for small but representative negotiating groups. The convenors of these groups were individuals of stature at the Conference. They could choose which delegations to invite to join their respective groups.

The remarkable story is that some of the most important provisions of the Convention, for example, on the exclusive economic zone (EEZ), straits used for international navigation, and the legal status of the EEZ and dispute settlement, were the fruits of negotiations conducted in these informal private negotiating groups. The Group of Juridical Experts, convened and chaired by Jens Evensen of Norway, contributed to many of the texts in the chapter on the EEZ. The difficult issue of the status of the EEZ was resolved in the private negotiating group of 17 delegations, convened and chaired by Jorge Castañeda of Mexico. The Chapter on Straits Used for International Navigation was negotiated in a private group of 13 delegations co-convened by Fiji and the United Kingdom. The text of Chapter XV on dispute settlement emerged from a private group co-chaired by Australia, El Salvador and Kenya.

Eighth, the manner in which the Informal Single Negotiating Text came to be prepared was most unusual. The Conference had begun in December 1973 without a negotiating text. At the third session of the Conference in 1975, the delegation of Singapore proposed that it was time to prepare an Informal Single Negotiating Text. This was accepted by the Conference and the task was entrusted to the chairmen of the three main committees, namely, Ambassadors Paul Engo of Cameroon, Galindo Pohl of El Salvador, and Alexander Yankov of Bulgaria. Ambassador Pohl had met with an accident and he delegated the task to his rapporteur, Ambassador Satya Nandan of Fiji. It was extraordinary, to say the least, to entrust so much power and responsibility to three men. In retrospect, we can say that, fortunately for the Conference, two of the three did their job well but one did not. The subsequent difficulties experienced by the Conference in negotiating a balanced and acceptable text of Part XI of the Convention could be traced back to this source.

Although President Amerasinghe had no mandate from the Conference, he took it upon himself to offer a text on dispute settlement. He enlisted the help of Professor Louis Sohn of the US delegation and two members of the Secretariat, namely Hugo Caminos and Gitakumar Chitty. The team relied heavily on the paper that had been prepared by the private group on dispute settlement. Professor Sohn had served as the rapporteur of that group.

Ninth, the Conference leadership consisted of the President, the chairmen of the three main committees, the Chairman of the Drafting Committee, and the Rapporteur-General. They constituted the Collegium that played a pivotal role in the management of the Conference. When I succeeded Amerasinghe as the President, I consolidated the Collegium and tried to inject it with a greater sense of unity and *esprit de corps*. The ability of the six principal officers of the Conference to work as a team was important to its success because the team provided leadership, good management and direction.

Tenth, the Secretariat made an enormous contribution to the success of the Conference. I entrusted the Head of the Secretariat, Undersecretary-General Bernardo Zuleta, on several occasions, with the responsibility to undertake consultations on my behalf, on some procedural questions. Some members of the Secretariat helped the various chairmen of the main committees and negotiating groups with the preparation of texts. At its best, there was a symbiotic relationship between the Conference leaders and the Secretariat.

Eleventh, the non-governmental organisations played a very constructive role at the Conference. They provided the Conference with three valuable services. They brought in independent experts to brief the delegates, especially on the highly technical issues. They helped the delegates of the developing countries to narrow the knowledge gap between them and their colleagues from the developed countries. They also provided the Conference with opportunities to meet at informal settings and to brainstorm on some of the most difficult issues.

Conclusion

The negotiating process of the Third United Nations Conference on the Law of the Sea had several unique features. First, it was most unusual for a treaty-making conference to begin without a draft text. The subsequent decision to request the chairmen of the three main committees to prepare the Informal Single Negotiating Text was a leap of faith. The second unique feature was the role of the unofficial private negotiating groups. The third unique feature was the deep commitment to finding consensus on all substantive matters and to avoid voting.

The Third United Nations Conference on the Law of the Sea must be considered as one of the most important treaty-making conferences ever convened by the United Nations. The stakes for the member States of the United Nations and, indeed, for the entire global community, were very high. Only the United Nations, with universal membership, could convene such a conference.

—⟨∞⟩—

This essay is republished with kind permission from Oxford University Press. It is originally published in *The Oxford Handbook of United Nations Treaties*, eds. Chesterman et al. (OUP: 2019).

For a detailed account of the negotiating process and dynamics, see "The Negotiating Process of the Third UN Conference on the Law of the Sea", TTB Koh and S Jayakumar in *United Nations Convention on the Law of the Sea 1982: A Commentary*, ed. Myron Nordquist, (Center for Oceans Law and Policy: 1985).

Celebrating the
20th Anniversary
of the International
Seabed Authority

The International Seabed Authority (ISA) is one of the three institutions created by the 1982 United Nations Convention on the Law of the Sea (UNCLOS). The other two institutions are International Tribunal for the Law of the Sea (ITLOS) and the Commission on the Limits of the Continental Shelf. I am happy to report that all three institutions are working effectively.

In celebrating the 20th anniversary of the ISA, we are also commemorating the 32nd anniversary of the 1982 UNCLOS, which is the fulfilment of our quest for an authoritative and comprehensive law to govern all aspects of the ocean. It is the modern law of the sea. Speaking at the final session of the Conference in Montego Bay in December 1982, I described the

UNCLOS as, "a constitution for the oceans", a term which has come to be universally accepted.

I would like to thank the distinguished Secretary-General, my good friend Nii Odunton, for inviting me to deliver the keynote speech on this auspicious occasion. I feel less deserving of this honour than some of my friends who will be speaking after me. Let me, therefore, pay a brief tribute to each of them.

My brother from Fiji, Ambassador Satya Nandan, has made many outstanding contributions. He played a leadership role in the Third United Nations Conference of the Law of the Sea. He was instrumental in negotiating the 1994 Agreement relating to the implementation of Part XI of the Convention. He then served for 12 years as the founding Secretary-General of the ISA. His legacy is both substantial and enduring.

Judge José Luis Jesus of the ITLOS made an important contribution as the chairman of the Preparatory Commission for the ISA from 1987 to 1994. A few years ago, I had the pleasure of representing my country in a case before him at the ITLOS.

My brother from Indonesia, Professor Hasjim Djalal, an esteemed expert on the law of the sea, was the first President of the Assembly in 1996. He has devoted many years of his life to promoting peace and cooperation in the South China Sea. The Seabed Disputes Chamber of the ITLOS has made an important contribution to our work by way of its advisory opinion.

Judge Vladimir Golitsyn is with us in his capacity as the President of said chamber, as well as the representative of the President of the ITLOS, Judge Shunji Yanai.

The UNCLOS enjoys near universal acceptance with 166 State parties. Countries that have not yet become parties to the UNCLOS have nevertheless acknowledged it as the authoritative law. The UNCLOS has promoted cooperation among States. It has replaced legal chaos with legal certainty. It has strengthened the rule of law and the principle of the peaceful settlement of disputes. Conflicts at sea are avoidable if the parties involved would strictly abide by the law and are willing to settle their disputes by peaceful means. The UNCLOS has, therefore, served the world well. It is a good answer to those who denigrate the United Nations, dismissing it as a mere talk shop which is incapable of solving the problems of the real world.

I would like to congratulate the ISA on the occasion of its 20th birthday. During the past 20 years, the ISA has methodically developed the rules, regulations, and procedures governing contracts for the exploration of the Area.[1] It has taken an evolutionary approach in its work. Regulations have been formulated to deal with polymetallic nodules, polymetallic sulphides, and cobalt-rich ferromanganese crusts. The legal regime governing contracts of exploration has rightly emphasised the protection of the marine environment, the promotion of scientific research, safety, and the training of personnel from developing countries.

The success of the ISA's work can be seen in the numbers: 16 contracts of exploration are in force; 3 are in the process of conclusion; and 7 plans of work were approved by the Council yesterday. This brings the total to 26.

I would like to commend the Secretariat for having accomplished so much with so little. I wish to thank the Secretary-General, the Legal Counsel, and the other members of their small team for their hard work. The ISA must be one of the United Nations' leanest and most cost-efficient institutions. However, as the workload of the Secretariat continues to increase, we must be fair and enhance its capacity in a commensurate way.

---

[1] The Area refers to the international seabed consisting of the Clarion-Clipperton Fracture Zone, the Indian Ocean, the Mid Atlantic Ridge, the Pacific Ocean and the South Atlantic Ocean.

I would like to make one other comment about the ISA. We should help to raise its visibility and inform the world about its important mission. The ISA should enhance its outreach programme. It should, for example, encourage the leading law schools of the world to teach a module on Part XI of the Convention. It should also reach out to the students and researchers in the fields of oceanography and ocean engineering. It should continue to organise seminars and co-organise workshops in different regions of the world. When financial resources are available, it should proceed to build a museum in order to showcase the results of research on, including new discoveries of, the flora, fauna, and mineral resources of our last frontier, which covers an area of 160 million square kilometres. It is ironic that we seem to know more about outer space than we do about the seabed and ocean floor.

We must prepare now for the next stage of the ISA's work. The first generation of contracts for exploration will be coming to an end in the next few years. Our regulations assume that most, if not all, of the contractors will apply for contracts for exploitation.

We must, therefore, begin formulating the rules, regulations and procedures applicable to contracts for exploitation. One important issue is the financial regime. Our approach should be that we are dealing with an industry at a nascent stage. We should encourage those with contracts for exploration to proceed to the next stage of exploitation.

The industry faces several challenges. It will have to invest substantial funds in order to develop and perfect the technology to mine in very deep waters, and to do it without damaging the environment. It would have to cope with the vagaries of the world metal market and competition from land-based sources.

Based on the ISA's track record, I am confident that we will succeed in adopting a legal regime for contracts for exploitation which is both business-friendly and, at the same time, fair to all stakeholders. I am also confident that the ISA will succeed in establishing a standardised taxonomy regime, on seabed flora, fauna, and minerals.

I shall conclude. As a young man, I had a dream. I dreamt of a world ruled by law and not by might. I dreamt of a world in which big countries and small countries, developed countries and developing countries cooperated with one another as equals and with mutual respect. I dreamt that we were good stewards of the oceans that give us life. I dreamt that we would succeed in negotiating a new legal order to govern all activities in the oceans. I dreamt that the mineral wealth of the deep seabed and ocean floor would be shared by all countries, including landlocked countries, as the common heritage of mankind. I dreamt that one day seabed mining would become a reality. I believe that the time for seabed mining has come. It is now within our power to turn the ideal of the common heritage of mankind into reality. The future is in our hands.

―――∞∞∞―――

Adapted from a keynote address given at the commemoration of the International Seabed Authority's 20th Anniversary at Kingston, Jamaica on 22 July 2014. As at March 2019, the ISA continues to engage with all State parties on ideas on operationalizing the Enterprise, an organ foreseen in the United Nations Convention on the Law of the Sea as the ISA's mining arm.

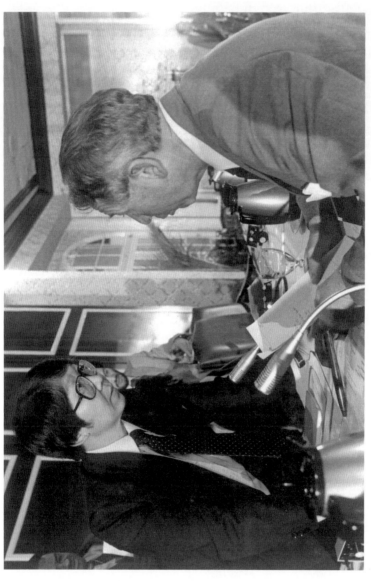

Ambassador Tommy Koh with Ambassador Jens Evensen just prior to the beginning of the signing session of the Conference of the Law of the Sea in Montego Bay on 6 December 1982. Ambassador Evensen was later appointed as Judge of the International Court. Credit: UN Photo 266302 by UN Photo.

At the United Nations on the day Tommy Koh was elected President of UNCLOS III (13 March 1981). Left to right: Bernardo Zuleta, Tommy Koh, David Hall. Credit: UN Photo 145796 by Saw Lwin.

Press briefing by Tommy Koh, President of Law of Sea Conference (24 March 1981). Credit: UN Photo 258094 by Yutaka Nagata.

Professor Tommy Koh with judges outside ITLOS at Hamburg during Singapore's Land Reclamation Case (2003). Left to right: Judge Mohamed Mouldi Marsit (Tunisia), Professor Bernie Oxman, S Jayakumar, S Tiwari, Judge Alexander Yankov (Bulgaria), unidentified Judge, Judge Tullio Treves (Italy), Judge Hugo Caminos (Argentina), Judge Akl Joseph (Lebanon), Tommy Koh, Judge Rudiger Wolfrum (Germany), unidentified Judge and Judge Paul Bamela Engo (Cameroon). Credit: Author's own.

The 20th anniversary of the establishment of the International Seabed Authority (ISA). Left to right: Ambassador Hasjim Djalal of Indonesia, founding President of the ISA (1996); Tommy Koh, President of the 3rd UN Conference on the Law of the Sea; and Ambassador Satya Nandan, former Secretary-General of the ISA. Credit: Author's own.

Tommy Koh introducing the draft resolution (document A/38/L.18/Rev.1) before the vote (14 December 1983). Credit: UN Photo 267947 by Saw Lwin.

Tommy Koh addresses the General Assembly at the 30th anniversary of the launch of UNCLOS (10 December 2012). Credit: UN Photo 537401 by Devra Berkowitz.

Exploring the Last Frontier on Earth

Seventy per cent of the Earth's surface is covered by sea and ocean. However, we seem to know less about ocean space than we do about outer space. On 26 March 2012, the award-winning American movie director, James Cameron, descended alone in a submersible called the *Deepsea Challenger* to the bottom of the Mariana Trench. It is the deepest part of the ocean floor at 11 kilometres below the surface. He took pictures and collected samples from the ocean floor, and said the ocean was "the last frontier for science and exploration on this planet".

One of the surprising discoveries is the life on the ocean floor. In spite of the darkness and the pressure, scientists have discovered many forms of life such as the shrimp-like crustaceans known as amphipods; gelatinous animals called holothurians; and other strange life forms. Scientists have isolated a compound from one of the amphipods, called scyllo-inositol. It is being investigated for its potential to treat Alzheimer's disease. Scientists are also studying the rocks from ocean trenches in their quest to better understand the earthquakes that create the powerful tsunamis around the Pacific Rim.

Minerals Below

I agree with Cameron that the ocean space is our last frontier. One of the mysteries of the deep seabed and ocean floor is the discovery of deposits of polymetallic nodules, polymetallic sulphides, and cobalt-rich ferromanganese crusts. The polymetallic nodules contain precious metals such as manganese, cobalt, nickel, copper and other rare earth elements.

As the supply of these precious metals on land begins to diminish, demand continues to increase, and as metal prices remain high, interest in recovering the nodules and exploiting the sulphides and crusts has increased.

There are, however, many challenges. The polymetallic nodules, which are black in colour and resemble potatoes and golf balls, lie on the floor of the seabed in very deep waters. The depth ranges from 4,000 to 5,000 metres. Technology has not yet been perfected to harvest them in a way that is commercially viable and environmentally benign. The good thing is that as the nodules lie on the seabed, they need only to be recovered. There is no need for digging or dredging like conventional mining on land. The three methods being considered are to use nets, claws and suction to raise them to the surface.

Whether deep sea mining will become feasible will partly depend on technology, and partly on whether the costs of recovering the metals from ocean space can compete with the costs of recovering them from mines on land. The industry is, however, optimistic about the future. It believes the technological problems will be solved by leveraging on established offshore drilling technology in the oil and gas industry, which has ventured into very deep waters. Given our insatiable demand for these precious metals, the industry believes it is a matter of time before deep sea mining becomes a reality.

Ownership of Resources

This leads us to the legal question: To whom do these resources belong? The answer is that it depends on where the resources are located. The Papua New Guinea government has granted a concession to a private company to recover the polymetallic nodules located within its territorial sea. The Cook Islands government announced it has rich deposits of polymetallic nodules within its exclusive economic zone and continental shelf and intends to tender out exploration licences. These resources belong to the Cook Islands. If the resources are located within a coastal country's territorial sea, contiguous zone, exclusive economic zone or continental shelf, they belong to the coastal country.

What about the resources at the bottom of the seabed and ocean floor beyond the national jurisdiction of coastal states? The answer is that they belong to all of us. The 1982 United Nations Convention on the Law of the Sea calls them "the common heritage of mankind".

The Convention has established an institution to act on behalf of mankind to regulate seabed mining—it is the International Seabed Authority (ISA) in Kingston, Jamaica. Any state or company that wishes to mine the seabed has to apply to the ISA for a contract to do so.

In the case of an application by a company, it must be sponsored by a State that is a party to the Convention. Without this contract, it would be difficult to raise the financing for a seabed mining project.

To date, the ISA has signed thirteen contracts of exploration for polymetallic nodules, four contracts of exploration for polymetallic sulphides, and will sign two contracts of exploration for cobalt-rich ferromanganese crusts.

Keppel's Venture

A Singapore company with a sterling reputation and track record in the offshore and marine sector, Keppel Corporation, has incorporated a subsidiary company called Ocean Mineral Singapore (OMS) to venture into deep seabed mining. The Singapore government is sponsoring the application of OMS because it has the resources, relevant technology and expertise. OMS is 78.1 per cent owned by Keppel, while UK Seabed Resources Limited (UKSRL) and Lion City Capital Partners hold the remaining shares. OMS is effectively controlled by Keppel.

In July 2013, I led a Singapore delegation to the 19th annual session of the ISA. The delegation consisted of the representatives of the Ministries of Foreign Affairs, Trade and Industry, the Attorney-General's Chambers, and Keppel. We submitted an application to the Legal and Technical Commission for a contract of exploration for a mine site which is located in the deep seabed, east of Hawaii and west of Mexico. It is between the Clarion Fracture Zone in the north, and the Clipperton Fracture Zone in the south. The Clarion-Clipperton Fracture Zone contains one of the richest known deposits of polymetallic nodules.

The mine site that OMS applied for was originally half of a larger mine site that UKSRL had applied for. Under the Convention, UKSRL was obliged to give up half the mine site to the ISA as a "reserved area" for the benefit of developing countries. As a developing country, Singapore is therefore entitled to apply for a "reserved area".

Potential Prospects

The Legal and Technical Commission unfortunately ran out of time at its meeting in July 2013. As a result, the applications of Russia, Britain, India and Singapore were deferred to its next meeting in February 2014. If the applications are approved, the Commission's recommendations will be considered by the council of the ISA at its next meeting in July 2014.

I am optimistic that the application of OMS will be successful. The contract of exploration will give the company 15 years to conduct its research and prospecting. There is an opportunity for Singapore's oceanographers, marine biologists and marine geologists to participate in the research.

At the same time, the ISA is starting work to develop an exploitation code for deep sea mining. If everything turns out well, Singapore through OMS, will join four other Asian countries— China, India, Japan and South Korea—in exploring the deep seabed and ocean floor.

Exciting new job opportunities will be created for our young engineers, marine scientists and lawyers. A new era is about to begin.

This essay was originally published in *The Straits Times* as an opinion editorial "The Last Frontier: Singapore may soon be diving deep into the unexplored riches of our ocean floors" on 24 August 2013.

The International Seabed Authority awarded a 15-year exploration contract to OMS in January 2015. Under the contract, OMS has exclusive rights for the exploration of polymetallic nodules in the eastern part of the Clarion-Clipperton Fracture Zone in the Pacific Ocean.

To date, the ISA has awarded a total of 29 exploration contracts that allow contractors to explore parts of the international seabed and ocean floors beyond national jurisdictions.

Peace at Sea

Singapore is an island nation. However, most Singaporeans take the sea for granted. On weekends, we will find more Singaporeans in our shopping malls than on the beaches.

I would therefore like to begin my essay by reminding Singaporeans that modern Singapore was founded in 1819 because of its deep natural harbour, its strategic location at the southern end of the Straits of Malacca and the need to service international shipping and maritime trade.

Today, 198 years later, the sea continues to be of great salience to Singapore. It is the world's busiest port. The Singapore flag is carried by the fifth largest merchant fleet in the world. Singapore has become an important international maritime centre. The maritime sector contributes 7 per cent to Singapore's GDP and provides 170,000 jobs in the nation.

Chaotic versus Orderly World

No country, big or small, benefits from a chaotic world, a world without laws, rules and conventions. Every country, including the major powers, prefers a world governed by universally accepted rules. International law fulfils this need.

For many centuries, the world's oceans were governed by customary international law. For example, customary international law prescribed that a coastal State may claim a territorial sea of three miles.

Customary international law came under challenge in the 1950s and 1960s. Several coastal States in Latin America challenged the three-mile territorial sea rule and made claims of between 12 to 200 miles. Other newly independent countries in Asia and Africa emulated them.

What ensued was a period of chaos. Countries used to quarrel and, sometimes, even fight over the width of the territorial sea, fishing rights, and so on. I recall that a dispute over fishing rights led to a brief shooting war between Iceland and the United Kingdom.

The United Nations and the Rule of Law

It took the Third United Nations Conference on the Law of the Sea nine arduous years of negotiations to arrive at a consensus on all the contentious issues, such as the width of the territorial sea, the width of the contiguous zone and the limits of the continental shelf. The Conference also created new concepts of international law, such as the exclusive economic zone, archipelagic sea lanes passage, transit passage and the common heritage of mankind. I served as the President of the Conference in its final two years.

The United Nations Convention on the Law of the Sea (UNCLOS) is a comprehensive and authoritative statement of the modern law of the sea. This is why I have called it a constitution for the world's oceans.

The Convention has 168 State parties, including the European Union. Although the United States is not a party, it recognises most of the Convention as customary international law. It seeks to conform to the Convention and expects other countries to do the same. Many of the Convention's provisions have been accepted by tribunals and courts as customary international law.

The UNCLOS and Peace at Sea

How does the UNCLOS promote peace at sea? It does so in three ways: first, by establishing a new, fair and equitable world order for the oceans; second, by promoting the rule of law; and third, by promoting the peaceful settlement of disputes. A unique feature of the Convention is that the settlement of disputes is mandatory and not optional. In other words, a State party cannot opt out of the dispute settlement system contained in the Convention.

The UNCLOS and Dispute Settlement

The UNCLOS has promoted peace through the peaceful settlement of disputes. When negotiations fail to resolve differences, it is better for the parties involved to try to settle the dispute through conciliation, arbitration or adjudication than to let the dispute fester and contaminate the overall health of the bilateral relationship.

Singapore and Malaysia have resolved several of their disputes peacefully and in accordance with international law. In the case of Pedra Branca, an island that sits at the eastern entrance of the Singapore Strait, the two countries agreed to refer their dispute over its ownership to the International Court of Justice.

In the case of the dispute over Singapore's land reclamation activities near the Johor Strait, the legal process involved arbitration, adjudication, fact-finding by a group of independent experts, and negotiations.

The dispute between Indonesia and Malaysia over two islands, Sipadan and Ligitan, was referred to the International Court of Justice. The dispute between Bangladesh and Myanmar over their maritime boundaries was referred to the International Tribunal for the Law of the Sea. The dispute between Bangladesh and India over their maritime boundaries was referred to arbitration. All of them were resolved peacefully and the results accepted by the parties.

Threats to Peace at Sea

What are the threats to peace at sea?

I can think of the following four threats:

    i. piracy and other international crimes against shipping;
    ii. unfaithful interpretation and application of the UNCLOS;
    iii. resorting to force or unilateral action to enforce one's claims instead of relying on the UNCLOS system of compulsory dispute settlement; and
    iv. illegal, unreported and unregulated fishing.

Piracy and Armed Robbery

Piracy and armed robbery of ships pose a serious threat to international shipping and to peace at sea. Until a few years ago, the biggest threat to international shipping was posed by Somali pirates. In 2011, they were responsible for 237 out of a total of 439 attacks against ships worldwide. In 2015, out of 246 attacks against ships worldwide, none was carried out by Somali pirates.

Instead, the largest number of attacks took place in Indonesian waters. Over half of the attacks took place in Southeast Asia. This is a stain on the good name of ASEAN. It is incumbent upon Southeast Asia to clean up its act or it will be known as the piracy capital of the world.

I am happy to report that the number of attacks has dropped remarkably this year as a result of enhanced vigilance and cooperation. Singapore is a founder member and host of the Regional Cooperation Agreement on Combating Piracy and Armed Robbery against ships in Asia, or ReCAAP, the first regional government-to-government agreement to enhance counter-piracy cooperation. Singapore also hosts the ReCAAP Information Sharing Centre, an intergovernmental network for the prompt sharing of alerts and information on piracy incidents, and a platform for broader cooperation and capacity-building.

Role of the Singapore Navy

The Singapore Navy has played three roles. The first role is to defend Singapore against any seaborne attack. The second role is to protect international shipping and the sea lines of communication. The third is to foster practical cooperation on issues of common concern between navies at sea in support of a rules-based international order.

In contributing to the protection of international shipping and the sea lines of communication, the Singapore Navy has deployed forces to the Gulf of Aden, in support of the international anti-piracy operations since 2009.

Singapore is a signatory to regional cooperation initiatives to deal with piracy and armed robbery of ships in our region. The Information Fusion Centre (IFC) in the Changi Command and Control Centre was established in 2009 to facilitate the exchange of information and cooperation, and to enhance maritime security. It has contributed to effective regional responses to numerous maritime security threats, a recent example being the successful apprehension in February 2016 of FV *Viking*, a vessel on Interpol's Purple Notice and wanted by 13 countries for illegal fishing.

To keep the Straits of Malacca and Singapore safe, the four littoral States, Indonesia, Malaysia, Singapore and Thailand, conduct joint sea and air patrols. The Singapore Navy has participated actively in such patrols. The Malacca Straits Patrol has been highly effective in reducing the incidence of piracy and armed robbery and has been cited as a successful model of collaboration among States.

The Singapore Navy and other regional navies regularly conduct joint exercises for the interdiction of suspicious vessels, under the United Nations-inspired Proliferation Security Initiative. In 2014, the Singapore Navy, together with 20 other regional navies, adopted a Code for Unplanned Encounters at Sea (CUES).

The above are some examples of how the Singapore Navy contributes to peace at sea and to upholding the rule of law at sea.

Unfaithful Interpretation

The second threat is posed by the unfaithful interpretation and application of the UNCLOS. The tendency to cheat is a failing of States as well as humans. There are many examples of States which have made claims or asserted rights which are not consistent with the Convention. There is a proliferation of excessive claims by coastal States. In my view, such claims should be challenged and, if possible, the courts or arbitral tribunals should be asked to rule on them.

Acting Unilaterally

The third threat is posed by the behaviour of some States that seem to have rejected the UNCLOS system of compulsory dispute settlement in favour of acting unilaterally. In the case of maritime disputes, States are obliged to settle their disputes in accordance with international law, including the UNCLOS. Under the UNCLOS, disputes could be resolved through negotiation, conciliation, arbitration and adjudication.

Parties to a dispute may also wish to put aside their competing sovereignty claims and enter into a win-win arrangement to jointly develop the resources in the disputed area and share in their benefits. Given goodwill on both sides, there are many ways in which a dispute can be resolved or managed peacefully.

Illegal, Unreported and Unregulated Fishing

The fourth threat is posed by illegal, unreported and unregulated fishing. The United Nations Food and Agricultural Organization (FAO) has repeatedly warned that that the world's fisheries are in a state of crisis. This crisis is caused by illegal fishing activities as well as overfishing and the use of destructive and unsustainable methods of fishing. The FAO's code of conduct for responsible fisheries should be strengthened. In the case of the South China Sea, regional countries urgently need to establish a regional fishery management organisation. In the absence of such a mechanism, no one is looking after the marine environment and the biodiversity of the South China Sea.

Conclusion

The quest for peace at sea is achievable, provided everyone is prepared to do the following three things. First, all should uphold the rule of law. This means abiding by international law, including the UNCLOS, the IMO and FAO conventions. Second, all should settle disputes peacefully and in accordance with recognised international diplomatic and legal processes. Third, political will and a spirit of give and take are needed. Without political will, nothing can be achieved. With political will, almost every problem has a solution.

This essay was originally published in *A Maritime Force for a Maritime Nation: Celebrating 50 Years of the Navy* (Straits Times Press: 2017).

South China Sea

An Overview

During the past two years, tension has been rising in the South China Sea. As a result of a deadline set by a United Nations body for coastal States to submit their claims to extended continental shelves, there was a flurry of claims and counterclaims in 2009, including a joint submission by Malaysia and Vietnam and a response by China.

There have also been several incidents at sea, between China and Vietnam, over fisheries; and between China, on the one hand, and the Philippines and Vietnam, on the other, over the collection of seismic data and exploration for hydrocarbons by oil companies.

At the ASEAN Regional Forum held in Hanoi in July 2010, there was a sharp exchange of words between the foreign ministers of China and the United States.

Much has been written about the South China Sea, but the salient questions of law and fact involved remain unclear.

What and where is the South China Sea?

The South China Sea is a semi-enclosed sea, bounded by China in the north, the Philippines in the east, Vietnam in the west, East Malaysia and Brunei in the southeast, and Indonesia and West Malaysia in the southwest. This body of water is about 3.5 million square kilometres. It forms part of the Pacific Ocean, one of the global commons.

What is the significance of the South China Sea?

First, it is the highway for trade, shipping and telecommunications. Eighty per cent of world trade is seaborne. One-third of world trade and half of the world's traffic in oil and gas pass through the South China Sea. Freedom of navigation in the South China Sea is, therefore, of critical importance to China, Japan, South Korea, ASEAN and other trading nations and maritime powers.

Second, it is rich in fish and other living resources. Fish is a principal source of protein and fishing is a source of employment for millions of Asians who live in coastal communities.

Third, it is presumed that there are significant deposits of oil and gas in the continental shelves underneath the South China Sea.

Is there a law governing the South China Sea?

It is governed by international law, particularly the United Nations Convention on the Law of the Sea (UNCLOS), which was adopted in 1982 and came into force in 1994. China, Japan, South Korea and all the ten ASEAN countries are parties to this Convention and thus bound by its provisions.

Which are the claimant countries and what have they claimed?

Two groups of geographic features located in the South China Sea are subject to competing claims of sovereignty, namely the Paracel Islands, located in the northern part of the South China Sea, and the Spratly Islands, located in the central part of the South China Sea. In particular, the sovereignty dispute over the Spratly Islands is a continual source of conflict and tension in the region.

China, Brunei, Malaysia, the Philippines and Vietnam are the claimant States. Taiwan is also a claimant but not recognised by the international community as a sovereign and independent State. It is, therefore, not a party to the UNCLOS.

Brunei reportedly claims part of the area of waters in the Spratly Islands adjacent to it, including two maritime features, namely Louisa Bank and Rifleman Bank, as part of its continental shelf.

The Philippines reportedly claims 53 of the maritime features in the Spratly Islands, which the country calls the Kalayaan Island Group, as well as Scarborough Shoal.

Malaysia reportedly claims sovereignty over 11 maritime features in the Spratly Islands.

Vietnam claims sovereignty over all the maritime features in the Paracel Islands and the Spratly Islands.

China claims sovereignty over all the maritime features in the South China Sea.

Taiwan's claims are identical to those of China. Taiwan is, however, in physical possession of the largest maritime feature in the South China Sea, namely Itu Aba or Taiping.

Are the claims consistent with the UNCLOS?

The Convention does not contain any new law on how to determine a State's claim to sovereignty over territory. The question has to be determined by customary international law.

Disputes over sovereignty can be resolved by negotiation, conciliation, arbitration or adjudication. It is, thus, not possible for one to say whether the sovereignty claims by the five claimant States are valid or not. They have not been tested in a court of law or arbitral tribunal.

The Chinese claim is not clear. The ambiguity is caused by a map that was attached to a Chinese official note to the United Nations on the outer limits of its continental shelf under the UNCLOS in May 2009. The map contains nine-dashed lines forming a U, enclosing most of the waters of the South China Sea. The map was first published in 1947 by the Republic of China under the Kuomintang, prior to the founding of the People's Republic of China.

What is not clear is whether China is claiming sovereignty over the maritime features enclosed by the lines or to both the features and the waters so enclosed. If the former, this is consistent with the Convention. However, if the latter, then China's assertion of rights, based upon history, to the waters, is not consistent with the Convention. The Convention does not recognise such rights.

When China acceded to the Convention, it agreed to be bound by the new legal order set out in the Convention. Under the law of treaties, when a State becomes a party to a treaty,

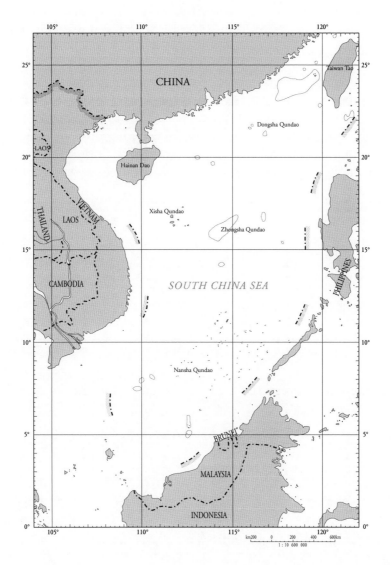

China's map of the South China Sea attached to China's note verbale to the United Nations Secretary-General Nos CML/17/2009 and CML/18/2009.

Source: *The South China Sea Arbitration (The Republic of Philippines v The People's Republic of China)* Award on Jurisdiction and Admissibility (29 October 2015) PCA 2013-19, 5. Reprinted with permission of the Permanent Court of Arbitration (copyright holder).

it is under a legal obligation to bring its laws and conduct into conformity with the treaty.

What maritime zones are the features entitled to?

There is considerable confusion about the answer to this question. First, there is no authoritative study of the different maritime features which make up the Spratly Islands group. Such a study should classify them into the following: islands, rocks, low-tide elevations and artificial islands.

Second, under the Convention, artificial islands are not entitled to any maritime zones except for a 500 metre safety zone. A low-tide elevation is not entitled to any maritime zone but can be used as a base point in measuring the territorial sea. A low-tide elevation is submerged at high tide. A rock is entitled to a 12-nautical mile (22 kilometres) territorial sea. An island is entitled to a territorial sea, a 200-nautical mile exclusive economic zone and a continental shelf. Under Article 121 of the Convention, the difference between a rock and an island is that an island is capable of sustaining human habitation or economic life.

Third, the policies and pronouncements of the claimant States show little regard for the law and are self-serving. To put it crudely, they seem to be saying, "My rock is an island and your island is only a rock." In its submission to the United Nations in 2009, Indonesia contends that all the features in the South China Sea are rocks and not islands.

What is ASEAN's position on the South China Sea?

ASEAN, as a group, does not support or oppose the claims of the four ASEAN claimant States. The group has also not taken a position on the merits of the disputes between China and ASEAN claimant States. Therefore, any perception that the claims of Brunei, Malaysia, the Philippines and Vietnam are backed by ASEAN is incorrect.

ASEAN is, however, a stakeholder in the South China Sea. First, it wishes to maintain peace in the region. Second, it wishes to promote good relations with China. Third, it is committed to the peaceful settlement of disputes. Fourth, it wishes to ensure that all interested parties act strictly in accordance with international law, especially the UNCLOS.

In 2002, when tensions were high, ASEAN drafted a Declaration on the Conduct of Parties in the South China Sea (DOC). The DOC was signed by ASEAN and China. In July 2011, the ASEAN Regional Forum adopted a set of implementing guidelines. Both the DOC and the guidelines are non-binding.

Although they are not unimportant, the fact is that some claimant States have violated both the letter and spirit of the DOC by acting unilaterally to expand and fortify the features they occupy.

ASEAN and China should work together to formulate and adopt a binding code of conduct as their next goal.

What is the United States' position on the South China Sea?

The US is neither a claimant nor a littoral State. It is, however, a stakeholder. Why? First, the US is a major trading nation and maritime power. It has a legitimate interest in ensuring that the freedom of navigation and other lawful uses of the sea are respected by both the claimant States and littoral States.

Second, the US has an interest in ensuring that the claimant States act strictly in accordance with international law, including the UNCLOS, of which it is, unfortunately, not a State party to.

Third, while the US has not endorsed the claims of the Philippines and Vietnam, it is concerned that the disputes should be resolved peacefully, without resort to force.

Fourth, the US is concerned about the Chinese map and would oppose any attempt by China to assert rights to the waters enclosed by the nine-dash line.

Fifth, the US has a treaty alliance with the Philippines but it has been ambiguous over whether and under what conditions that alliance might apply to an armed conflict in the South China Sea involving the Philippines and another claimant State.

What could China and the ASEAN claimant States do to bring about an amicable settlement to their disputes?

They have two fundamental choices. The first option is to try to resolve their sovereignty disputes through negotiations, both bilaterally and multilaterally. However, if the negotiations prove to be fruitless, the parties should consider whether to resort to other modalities of dispute settlement, such as conciliation, arbitration and adjudication.

It must be noted, however, that sovereignty disputes cannot be referred to any form of third-party dispute settlement without the consent of the parties.

Also, China has exercised its right, under Article 298, to opt out of compulsory binding dispute settlement, for disputes concerning its maritime boundary delimitation. So, a claimant State, such as the Philippines, cannot refer maritime boundary delimitation disputes with China to arbitration under Annex VII of the UNCLOS, or adjudication before the International Tribunal for the Law of the Sea.

However, the Philippines could, for example, frame the issue as one relating to other UNCLOS provisions, such as its rights to explore and exploit the natural resources in its exclusive economic zone or to determine whether certain disputed features are rocks or islands.

The second choice is for the parties to put aside their sovereignty disputes and to apply the concept of joint development to the disputed areas. Joint development has worked in other cases, for example, between Malaysia and Thailand (1979–1990), between Malaysia and Vietnam (1992) and between Australia and Timor-Leste (2002).

However, there is a major obstacle. The concept of joint development must be applied in the context of a disputed area. But, until China is prepared to clarify its claims, we will not be able to determine what are the disputed areas.

What is Singapore's position?

Singapore is not a claimant State. It does not support the position of any of the claimant States. On the merits of the various claims, Singapore is neutral.

Singapore is, however, not neutral on the need for all the claimant States to strictly adhere to international law, in general, and to the UNCLOS in particular. Singapore is also insistent that the disputes must be resolved peacefully. Any threat or use of force would be unacceptable. Singapore shares ASEAN's aspiration to maintain peace in the region and to promote good relations between ASEAN and China.

Pending the resolution of the dispute, Singapore supports the effort by ASEAN and China to implement the DOC that would serve as a guide for the behaviour of the claimant States in order to avoid confrontation and reduce tensions.

As a neutral party, trusted by all the claimants, Singapore seeks to play a helpful role, especially through the National University of Singapore's Centre for International Law, to bring the parties together, to elucidate the issues, research the facts and the law, and to help the parties find ways to achieve an amicable settlement to their disputes.

Published originally as "Mapping out rival claims to the South China Sea" in *The Straits Times* on 13 September 2011. The Philippines initiated compulsory arbitration against China under Annex VII of the UNCLOS in January 2013 with regard their disputes in the South China Sea. For an in-depth reading on the South China Sea disputes and the subsequent arbitration brought by the Philippines, refer to *The South China Sea Disputes and Law of the Sea*, eds. Jayakumar, Koh and Beckman (Edward Elgar: 2014) and *The South China Sea Arbitration: The Legal Dimension*, eds. Jayakumar et al. (Edward Elgar: 2018).

Maritime Boundary Conciliation between Timor-Leste and Australia

We live in a very troubled world. There are conflicts and disputes between and among States in every region of the world. One category of disputes that is hard to resolve is disputes between States over their land and sea boundaries. The recent tension between China and India is a reminder that their land boundaries have not yet been resolved. In the South China Sea, there are disputes between China and several ASEAN countries on their competing sovereignty and maritime claims.

Viewed against this background, the announcement by the Conciliation Commission in Copenhagen on 1 September 2017, that there had been a breakthrough in the conciliation proceedings on maritime boundaries between Timor-Leste and Australia, was happy news. I wish to explain the facts of the case, the nature of the conciliation proceedings, the elements of the package deal agreed upon by the two parties and some lessons learnt.

Peaceful Settlement of Disputes

There is a lot of confusion in the media and in the minds of the public about the peaceful settlement of disputes. The United Nations Charter refers to the following modalities for the peaceful settlement of disputes: negotiation, fact-finding, mediation, conciliation, arbitration and judicial settlement. When a country becomes a party to the United Nations Convention on the Law of the Sea (UNCLOS), it can make a declaration that its preferred mode of dispute settlement is arbitration or the International Court of Justice or the International Tribunal for the Law of the Sea. If it fails to make a choice, it is deemed to have chosen arbitration. Dispute settlement under the UNCLOS is compulsory. This is why Malaysia was able to institute arbitral proceedings against Singapore in 2003 without our consent. Malaysia did not need Singapore's consent because our consent was given when we became a party to the Convention.

Background of the Case

Australia and Timor-Leste are neighbouring States, separated by the Timor Sea at a distance of approximately 300 nautical miles. Timor-Leste (East Timor) was a Portuguese colony from the 16th century until 1975. On 28 November 1975, a political party, FRETILIN (Revolutionary Front for an Independent East Timor), declared the territory's independence. Nine days later, it was invaded and occupied by Indonesia. In 1976, Indonesia declared East Timor as its 27th province. In 1999, the people of East Timor voted overwhelmingly for independence. From 1999 to 2002, it was administered by the United Nations Transitional Administration in East Timor (UNTAET). It became independent on 20 May 2002.

Main Issues in the Dispute

There are several issues in the dispute between Timor-Leste and Australia. The first main issue concerns boundaries: the boundaries of the two countries' exclusive economic zones and their continental shelves. Timor-Leste had, from 2003, requested that Australia negotiate those boundaries but to no avail. The second main issue concerns the development arrangements in a field called Greater Sunrise which, in Timor-Leste's view, belonged to Timor-Leste and not Australia.

Compulsory Conciliation

While dispute settlement under the UNCLOS is compulsory, States can make a declaration to exclude from the UNCLOS arbitral or judicial proceedings certain categories of disputes, including maritime boundary disputes. However, these disputes are subject to compulsory conciliation. On 22 March 2002, about two months before Timor-Leste became independent, Australia made a declaration to exclude from the UNCLOS arbitral and judicial proceedings disputes concerning its exclusive economic zone and continental shelf boundaries. Timor-Leste is therefore unable to initiate arbitral or judicial proceedings against Australia on their sea boundaries.

On 11 April 2016, Timor-Leste surprised Australia by notifying Canberra that it was initiating compulsory conciliation proceedings against Australia. Timor-Leste also informed Australia that it was appointing Judge Abdul Koroma and Judge Rüdiger Wolfrum to the commission of conciliators. On 2 May 2016, Australia informed Timor-Leste that it had appointed Dr Rosalie Balkin and Professor Donald McRae as its conciliators. The four conciliators, with the consent of the two countries, chose

Ambassador Peter Taksøe-Jensen as the commission's fifth conciliator and chairman.

Australia objected to the commission's competence. In response, the commission held a special hearing on competence from 29 to 31 August 2016. On 19 September 2016, the commission decided unanimously that it had competence. It also decided that it would aim to conclude its work 12 months from 19 September 2016, as prescribed by Article 7 of Annex V of the UNCLOS.

This was the first occasion that Annex V of the UNCLOS had been invoked. It may therefore be useful to find out more about conciliation under the UNCLOS. My first point is that under the UNCLOS, we have voluntary conciliation and compulsory conciliation. My second point is that the conciliation commission is not a court of law. It is not the commission's job to rule on the legal rights of the two parties. The function of the commission is to "hear the parties, examine their claims and objectives, and make proposals to the parties with a view to reaching an amicable settlement."

Package Deal

At their meeting in Copenhagen on 30 August 2017, the two parties accepted a package deal proposed by the commission. The package agreement addressed their maritime boundary in the Timor Sea, the legal status of the Greater Sunrise gas field, the establishment of a special regime for Greater Sunrise, the development of the oil and gas resources, and the sharing of the resulting revenue.

It is the intention of the commission and the two parties to embody the agreement in a legally binding treaty. The two parties will meet at the Hague in October 2017 to sign an agreement on the text of the treaty. The treaty itself will be signed subsequently, possibly at the United Nations, and witnessed by Secretary-General António Guterres.

Lessons Learnt

What lessons can we learn from this case? There are several. First, countries that have disputes about their sea boundaries or have competing claims about territorial sovereignty, should seriously consider using conciliation to solve their disputes. Unlike arbitration and judicial settlement, conciliation is non-adversarial and the outcome is consensual and win-win.

Second, conciliators should be chosen wisely. In this case, there were five excellent conciliators. The chairman of the commission, Ambassador Peter Taksøe-Jensen, drove the process with energy, determination and fairness. The UNCLOS deadline for the commission to produce a report within 12 months helped to put pressure on everyone.

Third, the two countries were very well represented. Timor-Leste's Chief Negotiator is Xanana Gusmão, the father of the nation. Their agent, Minister Agio Pereira, is cool, wise and solid. Their legal team included two top legal minds, Professor Vaughan Lowe and Sir Michael Wood. The same is true on the Australian side. Gary Quinlan, the Deputy Secretary of the Department of Foreign Affairs and Trade, made an important contribution. Sir Daniel Bethlehem and Professor Chester Brown are a good match for Lowe and Wood.

Finally, and perhaps, the most important factor, is that there was the political will on both sides to find a just and durable compromise. Both sides were willing to give and take. Without the requisite political will, the case would not have succeeded. We must congratulate the governments of Timor-Leste and Australia for setting a good example for the world.

———∞∞∞———

Originally published as "A success story in resolving sea boundary disputes" in *The Straits Times* on 28 September 2017. For an in-depth reading on the conciliation case, refer to *The Timor-Leste/Australia Conciliation: A Victory for UNCLOS and Peaceful Settlement of Disputes* (World Scientific: 2019).

SECTION THREE

ACADEMIC ESSAYS

The Origins of the 1982 Convention on the Law of the Sea[1]

The Birth of the Old Legal Order

On 30 April 1982, the Third United Nations Conference on the Law of the Sea adopted the world's first comprehensive treaty dealing with all aspects of the seas and its resources. The treaty is called the United Nations Convention on the Law of the Sea. It was opened for signature in Montego Bay, Jamaica, on 10 December 1982 and was signed by 119 countries on that first day.

How will the Convention affect the multifaceted activities of man in ocean space? Will the Convention safeguard the world community's interest in commercial navigation? How does the Convention resolve the conflict between coastal fishermen and distant-water fishermen? Will the Convention lead to the better

---

[1] The author thanks Mr RC Beckman for his help in editing.

management and more equitable utilisation of the world's fish stocks? This article and the two to follow will attempt to answer these and other questions concerning the new treaty.

To begin, a brief retrospective look at the history of this branch of international law may be helpful. In 1493, Pope Alexander VI promulgated a Papal Bull, "Inter Caetera", in which a line was drawn down the Atlantic Ocean.[2] Under the Papal Bull, the ocean space and territories west of that line discovered by Spain belonged to her. The ocean space and territories discovered by Portugal, east of that line, belonged to her. The two powers, Spain and Portugal, concluded a bilateral treaty at Tordesillas on 7 June 1494, in line with the Papal Bull.[3] England, followed by Holland, protested against this agreement.

When the Spanish ambassador to England complained against the voyage of Sir Francis Drake to the Pacific, Queen Elizabeth I replied: "The use of the sea and air is common to all; neither can any title to the ocean belong to any people or private man, for as much as neither nature nor regard of the public use permitteth any possession thereof."[4]

The view of Spain and Portugal, often referred to as *mare clausum*, was that the sea was capable of being subject to dominion and sovereignty. Spain claimed exclusive dominion over the Pacific Ocean and the Gulf of Mexico. Portugal claimed exclusive dominion over the Atlantic Ocean, south of Morocco, and the Indian

---

[2] For a history of these early developments, see R Lapidoth, "Freedom of Navigation – its Legal History and its Normative Basis" (1975) 6 J. Mar. & Comm. 259 at 261–268; W Fulton, *The Sovereignty of the Sea* (1911), pp. 105–107. The Papal Bull is reprinted in (1973) 4 *Annals of International Studies*, p. 309.

[3] (1973) 4 *Annals of International Studies*, p. 317.

[4] Fulton, *supra* note 1, p. 107.

Ocean. The opposing view of the English Queen, Elizabeth I, commonly referred to as *mare liberum* was that the sea was incapable of appropriation as it was a *res communis*, belonging to all nations. The struggle between these two schools of thought was to continue for 300 years, from the 15th to the 18th century before the law was settled in favour of *mare liberum*.

In 1601, a naval commander of the Dutch East India Company captured a Portuguese galleon loaded with a valuable cargo of spices in the Strait of Malacca. At that time Portugal was under the dominion of Spain and Spain was at war with Holland. The ship, *Santa Catarina*, was brought to Amsterdam to be sold as prize. Some shareholders of the Dutch East India Company objected to the sale. The company retained a young Dutch lawyer, Hugo Grotius, to prepare an opinion on the question. Grotius completed his legal brief, entitled "De Jure Praedae" (on the Law of Spoils) in 1604. Chapter XII of the brief was entitled "*Mare Liberum*" (The Free Sea). This chapter was published anonymously in 1609.[5] Grotius later included it as part of a larger work entitled *Re Jure Belli ac Pacis*, which was published in 1625. According to RP Anand,[6] Grotius was aware of and influenced by the then prevailing Asian maritime practices of free navigation and trade in writing "*Mare Liberum*".

Ruth Lapidoth summarises the Grotian thesis as follows:

> Grotius bases the freedom of the high seas on two principles: one, things that can neither be seized nor enclosed cannot become property—they are common to all and their use pertains to the whole human race; two, things which have been created by nature in such a state that their usage by

---

[5] H Grotius, *Mare Liberum* (1608) (English translation by RVD Magoffin, 1916).

[6] RP Anand, *Origin and Development of the Law of the Sea* (1983).

one does not preclude or prejudice their use by others, are common, and their use belongs to all men. According to Grotius, on the high seas nobody can claim dominion or exclusive fisheries rights nor an exclusive right of navigation. The sea is under no one's dominion except God's; it cannot by its very nature be appropriated; it is common to all, and its use, by the general consent of mankind, is common, and what belongs to all cannot be appropriated by one; nor can prescription or custom justify any claim of the kind, because no one has the power to grant a privilege adverse to mankind in general.[7]

Meanwhile the view of the English government had moved from the *mare liberum* of Queen Elizabeth I to the *mare clausum* of the Scottish kings, the Stuarts. Perhaps mindful of Scotland's dependence on coastal fisheries and envious of the rise of Holland as a great maritime and trading power, King James I and his successors laid claim to the seas surrounding the British Isles. In 1609, King James I issued a proclamation under which foreigners who wished to fish within view of the British coast, fixed at 14 miles, had to obtain a licence. Under the reign of Charles I and II, Britain asserted sovereignty over all the seas surrounding the British Isles.

During the rule of the Stuarts in Britain, numerous legal scholars sought to refute the Grotian thesis of *mare liberum*. The most important of these scholars was John Selden who published in 1635, *Mare Clauseum sive De Dominio Maris*. Ruth Lapidoth summarises Selden's thesis as follows:

Selden maintains that the ancient law on the community of things has become modified in certain respects and that

---

[7] Lapidoth, *supra* note 1, p. 264.

according to practice and custom, the sea was capable of appropriation. He cites many precedents from history to support this statement. Selden admits that to prohibit innocent navigation would be contrary to the dictates of humanity, but in his view the permitting of such innocent navigation does not derogate from the dominion of the sea—it is comparable to the free passage on a road across another's land—and it cannot always be claimed as a right. With respect to the argument that the sea cannot be appropriated because of its physical properties, he points to the example of rivers, lakes and springs, which even by Roman law could be appropriated. It is not true that the sea had no banks or limits—it is clearly bounded by the shores, and limits may be set in the open sea by nautical science. Selden denies that the sea is inexhaustible, and he maintains that its usage—for example, fishing, navigation, commerce and the extraction of pearls and corals and the like—by others, may diminish its abundance and prejudice its use by its owner.[8]

The British claims to the seas around the British Isles were maintained, in whole or in part, through most of the 17th century. They were discontinued at the beginning of the 18th century when Britain achieved naval supremacy. *Mare liberum* was obviously more advantageous to her once she became the supreme naval power. Gradually, the balance tilted in favour of the doctrine of the freedom of the seas. However, as Lucius Caflisch has pointed out:

> The doctrine was not, of course, carried to its extreme logical conclusion, namely, that no part whatever of the sea is susceptible of being placed under coastal state jurisdiction. Such a conclusion would have been a practical absurdity,

---

[8] *Ibid.*, p. 266.

for states have a vital interest in the protection of their laws, their security and, possibly, their neutrality within a strip of the seas adjacent to their coasts.[9]

The Evolution of the Concept of the Territorial Sea

According to Caflisch, the idea of a narrow belt of the sea placed under coastal State jurisdiction in matters of piracy and of offences committed in that area can be traced back to Bartolus (1314–1357), Baldus (1327–1400) and Jean Bodin (1530–1596). Alberto Gentili (1552–1608) was apparently the first scholar to use the expression "territorium" to describe the relationship between the coastal State and the sea adjacent to its coast. What was the nature of the coastal State's jurisdiction in this belt of the sea? It was limited to matters of capture at sea and of neutrality.

How broad a band of the sea off its coast could a State claim for this purpose? It was not originally conceived as a belt of uniform breadth following the coastline of a State. It existed only in those waters which fell under the range of guns effectively placed on the coast, the so-called canon-shot rule. The canon-shot rule had two defects. First, it was applicable only in those areas where guns had actually been placed on the coast. This meant that where there were no guns, the coastal State could make no claim. Secondly, the canon-shot rule did not produce territorial seas of uniform breadth because the range of canons varied greatly.

---

[9] L Caflisch, "The Doctrine of 'Mare Clauseum' and the Third United Nations Conference on the Law of the Sea," in R Blackhurst et al., *International Relations in a Changing World* (Geneva: Graduate Institute of International Studies; Sijthoff, 1977), p. 201.

A second criterion was developed as a result of the practice of States such as Spain, England, Denmark and Norway. This was the line-of-sight rule. Under this rule, a coastal State could claim a band of the sea from its coast to as far as the human eye could see, within which the coastal State could exercise powers to protect its security, to enforce its customs regulations and to protect the coastal population and its economic interests, for example, in fisheries. Like the canon-shot rule, the line-of-sight rule was imprecise and a coastal State could claim anything from three to twenty miles.

A third criterion emerged, largely as a result of the practice of the Scandinavians. According to Sayre A Swarztrauber,[10] Spain was the first country to apply the line-of-sight doctrine in 1565. The Dutch were the first to invoke the canon-shot rule in 1610. In the intervening period, the Danes instituted the use of an exactly fixed extent of territorial seas measured in marine leagues. The term "marine league" when used by Scandinavian publicists or by others referring to Scandinavian territorial waters, generally refers to a distance of four nautical miles. Otherwise, the term usually means three nautical miles. A Danish ordinance of 1598 ordered the seizure of any English ship hovering or fishing within two leagues of the coast. Thereafter, the Scandinavian states consistently measured their territorial sea boundaries in leagues. By the middle of the 18th century, the Scandinavians had evolved the common practice of claiming one marine league (four nautical miles) as the limit of their territorial seas, for the purposes of fishing as well as for neutrality.

The interesting story of how the three criteria, the canon-shot rule, the line-of-sight rule and the marine-league rule gradually merged to become the three-mile territorial sea has been

---

[10] S Swarztrauber, *The Three Mile Limit of Territorial Seas* (1972).

recounted by Swarztrauber.[11] The first step was taken in 1761 by France when it equated the canon-shot rule with three miles. At that time, England and France were at war. A French privateer had seized two British ships off Jutland, in waters claimed by Denmark as her territorial seas. Denmark claimed one marine league or four nautical miles as the extent of her territorial seas. France recognised the canon-shot rule for the purpose of neutrality. The British complained on behalf of the owners of the two ships to the Dano-Norwegian government. The latter, in turn, protested the seizures to the French. In the French memorial to the Danish government, France asserted that the seizures were legal and went on to state that it was prepared to depart from its previous position and recognise the Scandinavians' claim to a continuous belt of territorial sea, provided it was three and not four miles.

The second step was the publication in 1782 of a monograph entitled *The Duties of Neutral Princes towards Belligerent Princes* by Abbe Ferdinando Galiani. He wrote:

> It would appear reasonable to me, however, that without waiting to see if the territorial sovereign actually erects some fortifications, and what calibre of guns he might mount therein, we should fix, finally, and all along the coast, the distance of three miles, as that which surely is the utmost range that a shell might be projected with hitherto known gun powder.

The third step was the actions of the then newly independent United States of America, in embracing the three-mile rule. In response to a French request to fix the limit of the US territorial

---

[11] *Ibid.*, pp. 51–63. English translation from Italian contained in Swartztrauber, *ibid.*, p. 55.

sea, the then Secretary of State, Thomas Jefferson, informed the British and the French on 8 November 1793 that the US was provisionally fixing its territorial sea at three miles. This became formalised by an Act of Congress in 1794.[12] According to Swarztrauber, the US became the first State to incorporate the three-mile limit into its domestic laws.

Gradually, the three-mile territorial sea was incorporated into domestic laws, upheld by courts and advocated by publicists. The next important development occurred in 1818 when the three-mile rule was, for the first time, incorporated into a treaty between States. In the "Convention Respecting Fisheries, Boundary, and the Restoration of Slaves, October 20, 1818", concluded between Britain and the US, a key sentence read:

> And the United States hereby renounces, for ever, any liberty heretofore enjoyed or claimed by the inhabitants thereof to take, any, or cure fish on or within three marine miles of any of the coasts, bays, creeks, or harbours of His Britannic Majesty's dominions in America.[13]

In the course of the 19th century, the three-mile rule became almost universally accepted. Great Britain was its champion. It will be recalled that England, under Queen Elizabeth I, had challenged Spain's claim to exclusive dominion over the Pacific Ocean and the Gulf of Mexico and Portugal's claim to exclusive dominion over the Atlantic Ocean, south of Morocco, and the Indian Ocean. Under the reign of the Stuarts, the Scottish

---

[12] An act in addition to the act for the punishment of certain crimes against the United States, 5 June 1974, Ch. 50, 1 United States Statutes at Large, p. 384.

[13] Convention with Great Britain of 20 Oct. 1818, 8 United States Statutes at Large, p. 248.

kings, the British pendulum had swung from *mare liberum* to *mare clausum*. At the beginning of the 19th century, with the defeat of Napoleon and the Congress of Vienna, Britain emerged as the world's greatest power, on land as well as at sea. It was logical for Britain, as the world's supreme naval power, to advocate the universal adoption of the three-mile territorial sea. As Lord Strang explained:

> In manufacture, in merchant marine, in foreign trade, in international finance, we had no rival.... As we came, by deliberate act of policy, to adopt the practice of free trade and to apply the principle of "all seas freely open to all," we moved towards Pax Britannica, using the Royal Navy to keep the seas open for the common benefit, to suppress piracy and the slave trade, and to prepare and publish charts of every ocean.[14]

The three-mile territorial sea was accepted by all the great powers and most of the medium and small powers during the 19th century. There were, however, some exceptions to the general rule. The Scandinavians continued to claim a limit of one marine league or four nautical miles. Spain and Portugal claimed a limit of six miles; Mexico claimed a limit of nine miles; and Uruguay claimed a limit of five miles.

Aftermath of First World War

The First World War brought about important changes to the political geography of the world. The four defeated empires,

---

[14] Lord W Strang, *Britain in World Affairs* (1961), pp. 99–100, as quoted in Swarztrauber, *supra* note 10, pp. 64–65.

Russian, Ottoman, Austro-Hungarian and German, were broken up and new nations were born. Finland, Latvia, Estonia, Lithuania, Poland, Arabia, Egypt, Yemen, Czechoslovakia and Yugoslavia became independent. A new international organisation, the League of Nations, was established. One of the tasks of the League was the codification of the law of nations. The Assembly of the League requested the Council to convene a committee of experts to determine subjects of international law that should be considered for codification. In April 1925, the Council established the Committee of Experts for the Progressive Codification of International Law. The Committee selected 11 subjects for investigation and appointed a sub-committee to look into each subject. One of the 11 subjects was the territorial sea. The sub-committee on the territorial sea was chaired by Walter Schuckling of Germany and consisted of two other members, Barbosa de Magalhães of Portugal and George W Wickersham of the US. The three members of the sub-committee were unable to agree. Wickersham was for the three-mile territorial sea. Schuckling favoured a six-mile territorial sea with a customs and sanitary zone beyond. Barbosa de Magalhães proposed one single zone of twelve miles in order to satisfy all the needs of States.

The Committee of Experts decided to send questionnaires on seven of the eleven subjects to various governments. Attached to the second questionnaire was a draft article which read as follows:

Article 2

Extent of the rights of the riparian State. The zone of the coastal sea shall extend for three marine miles (60 to the degree of latitude) from low-water mark along the whole of the coast. Beyond the zone of sovereignty, States may

exercise administrative rights on the ground of either custom or of vital necessity....[15]

The dissenting views of Schuckling and de Magalhães were
appended to the questionnaire. In reply to the question whether
the law of the territorial sea should be made the subject of an
international convention, 25 States replied that a convention to
codify the law of the territorial waters would be possible and
desirable. Only three States, France, Italy and Poland replied
that the time was inopportune for such a convention. Spain
objected to the questionnaire because the proposal was contrary
to Spanish law. Austria and Switzerland abstained.[16]

On the question of whether it is possible to establish by way
of international agreement rules regarding the exploitation of the
products of the sea, 22 States, including France, Italy and the US,
favoured a convention. Six States, including the United Kingdom
and Japan, replied in the negative. Austria and Switzerland again
abstained.[17]

After examining the replies, the Committee of Experts
reported to the League's Council that seven subjects were ripe
for codification. The League decided to convene conferences to
examine three subjects, including the territorial sea, beginning
in 1929. A Preparatory Committee was appointed to prepare
detailed bases of discussion for the conferences. The Preparatory
Committee drew up, *inter alia*, the following bases of discussion:

---

[15] League of Nations, Second Session of the Committee of Experts for the
Progressive Codification of International Law, Official Records (1926), 20
Amer. J. Int'l L. (Spec. Supp), Report of the Sub-Committee on Territorial
Waters, p. 141; S Rosenne, *Committee of Experts for the Progressive Development of International Law* [1925–1928] (2 Vols. Oceana, 1972), Vol. 2, p. 98.
[16] Swartztrauber, *supra* note 10, p. 134.
[17] *Ibid.*

Basis of Discussion No. 3

The breadth of the territorial waters under the sovereignty of the coastal State is three nautical miles....

Basis of Discussion No. 5

On the high seas adjacent to its territorial waters, the coastal State may exercise the control necessary to prevent, within its territory or territorial waters, the infringement of its customs or sanitary regulations or interference with its security by foreign ships.

Such control may not be exercised more than twelve miles from the coast.[18]

The Hague Codification Conference of 1930

The Conference was held at the Hague in March 1930 and was attended by the representatives of 48 governments. The rules of procedure of the conference provided that drafts would be approved by a two-thirds majority of the delegates voting in the committee, although only a simple majority would be required in the plenary for final approval. The positions of the various delegations were as follows: ten States, South Africa, the US, Great Britain, Australia, Canada, China, Denmark, India, Japan and the Netherlands, favoured the three-mile limit. Two States, Greece and the Irish Free State, also supported the three-mile limit but they could accept a contiguous zone. Seven States, Germany, Belgium, Chile, Egypt, Estonia, France and Poland

---

[18] S Rosenne, *League of Nations Conference for the Codification of International Law* (1930) (4 Vols, Oceania, 1970), Bases of Discussion II—Territorial Waters, Vol. 2, pp. 251–252. Document C.74.M.39.1929.V.

would support the three-mile territorial sea, provided a contiguous zone was added. Three States, Iceland, Norway and Sweden, favoured a four-mile territorial sea. Finland also supported a four-mile territorial sea but wanted a contiguous zone as well. Six States, Brazil, Colombia, Italy, Romania, Uruguay and Yugoslavia favoured a six-mile territorial sea. Six others, Cuba, Spain, Latvia, Persia, Portugal and Turkey wanted a six-mile territorial sea together with a contiguous zone.

Because views were so divergent, no formal vote was taken on any of the proposals in the committee. A possible compromise consisting of a three-mile territorial sea and a nine-mile contiguous zone was squashed by strong British opposition. The conference therefore ended in failure. Swarztrauber has expressed the view that by allowing the conference to fail, "the great maritime powers ended their oligarchical maintenance of the maxim *mare liberum*. The Conference suggested to all that the great powers were no longer committed to enforcement of the three-mile limit. From 1930 on, the rule was subjected to increasing criticism, and its significance became diminished by the rapid development of the concept of the contiguous zone."[19]

The Contiguous Zone

What is the contiguous zone? The concept is that beyond the territorial sea, however limited, there would be a zone of the sea in which the coastal State would not have sovereignty but would exercise certain functional jurisdiction. Although the name "contiguous zone" was not used until the Hague Conference of 1930, the idea had a long history. For example, in the early 19th century, Britain asserted customs jurisdiction to a distance

---

[19] Swartztrauber, *supra* note 10, p. 140.

of 300 miles from its shores.[20] The US had always claimed exclusive customs jurisdiction inside a 12-mile limit.[21]

A proposal was made in the 1930 Hague Codification Conference to create a contiguous zone beyond the territorial sea. In this zone, the coastal State would be empowered to prevent or punish infringements by foreign vessels, in its territorial sea, of the coastal State's regulations regarding customs, sanitation and national security.[22] Although the proposal was not adopted, due mainly to British opposition, the concept was increasingly reflected in the practice of States. Between 1930 and 1940, the following contiguous zone claims were made:[23]

State	Extent	Purpose of Claim	Means & Date of Implementation
China	12 miles	Customs	Customs Preventive Law of 19 June 1934
Colombia	20 km	Customs	Customs Law of 19 June 1931
Cuba	5 miles	Sanitation	General Law on Fisheries of 28 March 1936
Czechoslovakia	12 miles	Anti-smuggling	Treaty with Finland, 21 March 1936

continue overleaf

---

[20] Act for the More Effectual Prevention of Smuggling, 12 July 1805, 45 Geo. III, c. 121, and the Act for the More Effectual Prevention of Smuggling, 13 Aug. 1807, 47 Geo. III (Sess. 2), c. 66.

[21] Sec. 27 & 54, Act to Regulate the Collection of Duties on Imports and Tonnage, 2 Mar. 1799, Ch. 22, 1 United States Statutes at Large 627 at 648 and 668; Sec. 581, Tariff Act of 1922, 21 Sep. 1922. Ch. 356, 42 United States Statutes at Large 858 at 979.

[22] League of Nations Conference, *supra* note 18, Vol. II, p. 34.

[23] Swartztrauber, *supra* note 10, p. 148.

Continued

State	Extent	Purpose of Claim	Means & Date of Implementation
Denmark	12 miles	Anti-smuggling	Act No. 316 of 28 November 1935
Dominican Republic	3 leagues	Naval security area	Law No. 55 of 27 December 1938
Ecuador	15 miles	Fishing	Decree No. 607 of 29 August 1934
El Salvador	12 miles	Police and Fishing	Law of Navigation and Marine of 23 October 1933
Finland	6 miles	Customs	Customs Regulation of 8 September 1939
France	20 km	Fishing	Presidential Decree of September 1936
Guatemala	12 miles	Port authority jurisdiction	Regulations of 21 April 1939
Hungary	12 miles	Anti-smuggling	Treaty with Finland of 23 November 1932
Iran	12 miles	Marine supervision	Act of 19 July 1934
Italy	12 miles	Customs	Customs Law No. 1424 of 25 September 1940
Lebanon	20 km	Customs	Order No. 137/LR of 15 June 1935
Norway	10 miles	Customs	Royal Resolution of 28 October 1932
Poland	12 miles	Customs	Customs Law of 27 October 1933
Syria	20 km	Customs	Customs Code of 15 June 1935
Venezuela	12 miles	Security, customs, sanitation	Presidential Decree of 15 September 1939

Developments After the Second World War

After the Second World war, the US eclipsed Great Britain in both naval and land power. The burden of defending the principle of the freedom of the seas, in general, and the three-mile territorial sea, in particular, was therefore transferred from the British to the Americans. For over a hundred years, the British had single-handedly enforced the three-mile territorial sea by precept, by example and, where necessary, by force. American policy was less consistent.

The point that, unlike the British, American behaviour was less consistent and coherent is well brought out by what the US did in 1945. In that year, President Truman issued two proclamations relating to the sea. In the first proclamation, the US asserted its jurisdiction and control over the natural resources of the subsoil and seabed of the continental shelf contiguous to the US coast.[24] The term "continental shelf" was described in an accompanying press release as generally extending to the point where the waters reached a depth of 600 feet or 200 metres isobath. In the second proclamation, the US "regards it as proper to establish conservation zones in those areas of the high seas contiguous to the coasts of the US wherein fishing activities have been or in the future may be developed and maintained on a substantial scale…".[25] The proclamation provided that the

---

[24] Proclamation No. 2667, "Policy of the United States With Respect to the Natural Resources of the Subsoil and Sea Bed of the Continental Shelf," 28 Sep. 1945, (1946) 40 Am. J. Int'l L. (Supp) 45; Whiteman, (1965) 4 Digest of International Law 756.

[25] Proclamation No. 2668, "Policy of the United States With Respect to Coastal Fisheries in Ceratain Areas of the High Seas," 28 Sep. 1945, (1946) 40 Am. J. Int'l L. (Supp) 46; Whiteman, (1965) 4 Digest of International Law 956.

conservation zones would be established and maintained through agreement with those States whose subjects traditionally fished in the areas in question.

The actions of the US were immediately emulated and exceeded by her regional neighbours. Mexico issued a similar proclamation one month after the US.[26] A year later, Argentina not only claimed sovereignty over her continental shelf but also to the water column above the shelf.[27] Between 1946 and 1957, ten other States claimed sovereignty over their continental shelves and the superjacent water.[28] Between 1947 and 1955, five Latin American States: Chile,[29] Peru,[30] Costa Rica,[31] Ecuador[32] and El Salvador[33] declared 200-mile limits for exclusive fishing rights. On 19 August 1952, the representatives of Chile, Ecuador and Peru issued a joint declaration, the Santiago Declaration on the Maritime Zone. The declaration specified its purpose as the conservation and preservation "for their respective peoples, the natural riches of the zones of the sea which bathed their coasts".

---

[26] Swartztrauber, *supra* note 10, pp. 162–165. This national legislation on law of the sea can be found in United Nations, *Laws and Regulations on the Regime of the High Seas*, Vol. I (1951) (UN Legislative Series, Document No. ST/LEG/SER.B/5lv.2).

[27] "Decree No. 14708 concerning National Sovereignty over Epicontinental Sea and the Argentine Continental Shelf, 11 October 1946," in United Nations, *Laws and Regulations on the High Seas*, pp. 4–5.

[28] Panama in 1946, Chile and Peru in 1947, Costa Rica in 1949, Nicaragua and El Salvador in 1950, South Korea in 1952, and Cambodia in 1957.

[29] Chilean Presidential Declaration of 23 June 1947.

[30] Peruvian Presidential Decree No. 781 of 1 Aug. 1947.

[31] Costa Rican Regulation No. 363 of 11 Jan. 1949 as amended by Decree No. 739 of 4 Oct. 1949.

[32] Ecuadorian Decree No. 1085 of 14 May 1955.

[33] El Salvadorian Decree No. 1961 of 25 Oct. 1955.

In order to achieve this purpose, the three governments "proclaim as the standard of their international maritime policy, that to each one of them belongs the sovereignty and exclusive jurisdiction over the sea that washes their respective coasts, up to the minimum distance of 200 nautical miles from the said coasts."

Swarztrauber blamed the Truman proclamations for providing the basis for the Latin American claims. He reasoned thus: "The Latin Americans had become concerned about the modern US fishing vessels seen off their coasts. Whether or not their concern was well-founded, they feared that their waters might be 'overfished' by foreigners and they wished to extend their exclusive fishing boundaries to eliminate outside competition. But such a bold departure from customary law would require a suitable pretext: it was fortuitous for them that the Truman Proclamations came when they did."[34]

Russia had, in 1927, claimed a 12-mile territorial sea. This had reflected the fact that Russia had traditionally been a land power rather than a sea power. This was still true in the period immediately after the Second World War when the Soviet navy was relatively small. During this period, the Soviet objective was to keep the ships and aircraft of her adversaries as far from her coasts as possible. The USSR's Warsaw Pact Allies followed her lead by declaring 12-mile territorial seas.[35]

Many new States were born between 1945 and 1960, as a result of the dissolution of the British, Dutch and French colonial empires. One of the questions which each new State had to consider was the extent of its territorial sea. Some opted for the three-mile rule but most have claimed territorial seas of more than three miles, especially twelve miles.

---

[34] Swartztrauber, *supra* note 10, p. 169.
[35] *Ibid.*, pp. 169–174.

First United Nations Conference on the Law of the Sea

At the end of the Second World War, a new international organisation, the United Nations, was created to take the place of the League of Nations. One of the purposes of the United Nations is to encourage the progressive development of international law and its codification. Pursuant to this purpose, the General Assembly of the United Nations established the International Law Commission. The Commission is mandated to select topics of international law for codification. The Commission began its work in 1949 and chose 14 topics including "the high seas" and "territorial waters". In 1954, the Commission submitted to the General Assembly provisional articles concerning the regime of the territorial sea. Article 3, on the breadth of the territorial sea was, however, left blank.[36] The General Assembly, in turn, circulated the draft articles to member governments and asked for their comments. Only 18 replies were received. Three States, the US, UK and the Netherlands favoured three miles; one State, Sweden, favoured four miles; four States, Egypt, Haiti, South Africa and Yugoslavia favoured six miles; one State, Mexico, favoured nine miles; one State, India, favoured twelve miles; El Salvador favoured 200 miles; Philippines favoured the archipelagic principle and six others, Australia, Belgium, Brazil, Iceland, Norway and Thailand reserved their positions.[37]

In 1955, the International Law Commission again submitted draft articles to the General Assembly and requested the views of member States. This time, Article 3 was not left blank. It read:

---

[36] [1954] 2 Y.B. Int'l L. Comm., pp. 153–162.
[37] [1955] 2 Y.B. Int'l L. Comm., pp. 19–41.

Article 3
Breadth of the territorial sea

1. The Commission recognises that international practice is not uniform as regards the traditional limitation of the territorial sea to three miles.

2. The Commission considers that international law does not justify an extension of the territorial sea beyond 12 miles.

3. The Commission, without taking any decisions as to the breadth of the territorial sea within that limit, considers that international law does not require States to recognise a breadth beyond three miles.[38]

Twenty-five replies were received but most of the replies were noncommittal. The Commission took the replies into account in drawing up a draft convention which was submitted to the General Assembly in 1956. Article 3 was revised to read:

Article 3
Breadth of the territorial sea

1. The Commission recognises that international practice is not uniform as regards the delimitation of the territorial sea.

2. The Commission considers that international law does not permit an extension of the territorial sea beyond 12 miles.

3. The Commission without taking any decision as to the breadth the territorial sea within that limit notes, on the one hand, that many States have fixed a breadth greater than three miles, and on the other hand, that many States

---

[38] *Ibid.*, p. 35.

do not recognise such a breadth when that of their own territorial sea is less.

4. The Commission considers that the breadth of the territorial sea should be fixed by an international conference.[39]

The General Assembly decided in 1957 to convene a conference of plenipotentiaries to consider the draft convention prepared by the Commission.[40] The First United Nations Conference on the Law of the Sea opened in February 1958, in Geneva. The Conference was confronted with a plethora of proposals on the limit of the territorial sea, ranging from three to 200 miles. The US initially proposed a three-mile limit with an exclusive fishing zone out to twelve miles.[41] Ceylon, Italy and Sweden[42] proposed six miles. Variations of the twelve-mile limit were proposed by Colombia, the USSR, India, Mexico, Burma, Indonesia, Morocco, Saudi Arabia, Egypt and Venezuela.[43] Realising

---

[39] *Ibid.*, p. 256.

[40] G.A. Res. 1105 of 21 Feb. 1957, UN. Gen. Ass. Off. Rec., 11th Sess. (1957), Supp. No. 17, p. 156 (A/3572).

[41] First United Nations Conference on the Law of the Sea. Off. Rec. (1958), United States proposal, Vol. III, p. 249, Document A/CONF.13/C.1/L.140 of 1 Apr. 1958.

[42] *Ibid.*, Ceylon proposal, Vol. III, p. 244, Document A/CONF.13/C.1/L.118 of 1 Apr. 1958; Italy proposal, Vol. III p. 248, Document A/CONF.13/C.1/L.137 of 1 Apr. 1958; Sweden proposal, Vol. III, p. 212. Document A/CONF.13/C.1/L.4 of 10 Mar. 1958.

[43] *Ibid.*, Colombia proposal, Vol. III, p. 233, Document A/CONF.13/C.1/L.82 and Corr. 1 of 31 Mar. 1958; USSR proposal, Vol. III, p. 233, Document A/CONF.13/C.1/L.80 of 31 Mar. 1958; India and Mexico proposal, Vol. III, p. 233, Document A/CONF.13/C.1/L.79 of 29 Mar. 1958; Burma, Colombia, Indonesia, Mexico, Morocco, Saudi Arabia, United Arab Republic and Venezuela proposal, Vol. III, p. 123, Document A/CONF.13/C.1/L.34 of 25 Apr. 1958.

the futility of pressing the three-mile limit, the US and UK attempted to reach a compromise at six miles. The British proposed a six-mile limit with a right of innocent passage for aircraft and vessels, including warships, between three and six miles.[44] The US proposed a territorial sea of six miles and exclusive fishing rights for another six miles, with the proviso that foreign States whose nationals had traditionally fished those coastal waters (for at least five years) could continue to do so in the outer six-mile belt.[45] None of the proposals obtained the necessary two-thirds majority vote.

Unlike the Hague Codification Conference of 1930, which ended without any achievement, the First United Nations Conference on the Law of the Sea of 1958 adopted four conventions: the Convention on the Territorial Sea and the Contiguous Zone;[46] the Convention on Fishing and Conservation of the Living Resources of the High Seas;[47] the Convention on the High Seas;[48] and the Convention on the Continental Shelf.[49] Although the Convention on the Territorial Sea and the Contiguous Zone did not contain an agreed limit on the maximum permissible breadth of the territorial sea, it did contain a comprehensive codification of the rules concerning the right

---

[44] *Ibid.*, United Kingdom revised proposal, Vol. III, pp. 247–248, Document A/CONF.13/C.1/L.134 of 1 Apr. 1958.

[45] *Ibid.*, United States revised proposal, Vol. III, pp. 253–254, Document A/CONF.13/C.1/L.159/Rev.2 of 19 Apr. 1958.

[46] *Ibid.*, Vol. II, pp. 132, Document A/CONF.13/L.52; 516 U.N.T.S. 205.

[47] *Ibid.*, Vol. II, pp. 135–139, Document A/CONF.13/L.53; 559 U.N.T.S. 285.

[48] *Ibid.*, Vol. II, pp. 139–141, Document A/CONF.13/L.54; 450 U.N.T.S. 11.

[49] *Ibid.*, Vol. II, pp. 142–143, Document A/CONF.13/L.55; 499 U.N.T.S. 311.

of innocent passage.[50] It also contained an agreed article on the contiguous zone.[51]

The Convention on Fishing and Conservation of the Living Resources of the High Seas did not contain an agreed limit on the coastal State's exclusive fishing rights. The Convention prescribed that conservation programmes should be undertaken on a multilateral basis and should extend over the whole of the fishery. It did permit unilateral conservation action in cases where negotiations were unsuccessful and provided for the settlement of conservation disputes by a special commission.

The Convention on the Continental Shelf provided for the exploitation of the natural resources of the seabed and subsoil and the sedentary species on the seabed beyond the territorial sea "to a depth of 200 metres or, beyond that limit, to where the depth of the superjacent waters admits of the exploitation of the natural resources."[52] Article 3 of the Convention ruled out any claims of sovereignty over the shelf's superjacent waters or air space.

Second United Nations Conference on the Law of the Sea

Before the 1958 Conference adjourned, it adopted a resolution requesting the General Assembly to study the possibility of calling a second conference to consider the questions left unsettled, that is the limits of the territorial sea and fishing zone.[53] The

---

[50] Convention on the Territorial Sea and Contiguous Zone, *supra* note 47A, Articles 16–23.

[51] *Ibid.*, Article 24.

[52] Convention on the Continental Shelf, *supra* note 47D, Article 1.

[53] First United Nations Conference on the Law of the Sea, Off. Rec (1958) Resolutions adopted by the Conference, Resolution VIII, Vol. I, p. 145.

General Assembly decided in 1958 to call a second conference in 1960.[54]

The second United Nations Conference on the Law of the Sea opened in Geneva in March 1960. The USSR introduced an optional three to twelve-mile limit combined with exclusive fishing rights to twelve miles. Mexico proposed an optional three to twelve-mile territorial sea combined with a sliding scale fishery limit. The idea was that if a State chose a narrow territorial sea, it would be rewarded with a greater exclusive fishing zone. The contest at the Conference was between a proposal submitted by 18 developing countries[55] and a proposal jointly submitted by Canada and the US.[56] The 18-power proposal contained two points. First, every State is entitled to fix the breadth of its territorial sea up to a limit of 12 miles. Second, when the breadth of the territorial sea is less than 12 miles, a State is entitled to establish a fishing zone up to a limit of 12 miles. This proposal was rejected by 39 votes to 36 votes with 13 abstentions.

The joint Canada–US proposal contained three points. First, a State is entitled to fix the breadth of its territorial sea up to a maximum of six miles. Second, a State is entitled to establish a fishing zone contiguous to its territorial sea extending to a maximum limit of 12 miles. Third, any State whose vessels have made a practice of fishing in the outer six miles of the fishing zone for five years may continue to do so for ten years. This proposal was adopted at the committee level of the conference by a vote of 43 to 33 with 12 abstentions. Under the rules of

---

[54] G.A. Res. 1307 of 10 Dec. 1958, U.N. Gen. Ass. Off. Rec., 13th Sess. (1958), Supp. No. 18, p. 148.

[55] Second United Nations Conference on the Law of the Sea, Off. Rec. (1960), pp. 165–166, Document A/CONF.19/C.1/L.2/Rev.1 of 11 Apr. 1960.

[56] *Ibid.*, p. 169, Document A/CONF.19/C.1/L.10 of 8 Apr. 1960.

procedure of the conference, substantive decisions required a two-thirds majority of the representatives present and voting in the plenary of the Conference In order to gain the additional support needed. Canada and the US accepted an amendment proposed by Brazil, Cuba and Uruguay which provided that:

> the coastal State has the faculty of claiming preferential fishing rights in any area of the high seas adjacent to its exclusive fishing zone when it is scientifically established that a special situation or condition makes the exploitation of the living resources of the high seas in that area of fundamental importance to the economic development of the coastal state or the feeding of its population.[57]

When the joint Canada–US proposal, as amended, was put to the vote in the plenary, it received 54 votes in favour, 28 against, with 5 abstentions, 1 vote short of the required majority. According to the leader of the US delegation, Arthur Dean,[58] the failure was due to a last-minute withdrawal of support by Chile, Ecuador and Japan. Thus, for the third time in 30 years, the representatives of the international community had been unable to agree on the maximum permissible breadth of the territorial sea.

The Death of the Old Legal Order

What led to the breakdown of the old legal order governing the seas? The old legal order collapsed under the weight of three causes: first, the progress of technology; second, the failure of the

---

[57] *Ibid.*, p. 169, Document A/CONF.19/L.12 of 22 Apr. 1960.
[58] A Dean, "The Second Geneva Conference on the Law of the Sea: The Fight for Freedom of the Seas," (1960) 54 Amer. J. Int'l L. 751.

traditional law to deal adequately with the concerns of coastal States regarding the utilisation of oceanic resources; and third, the emergence of the developing countries.

The combination of a narrow territorial sea and the freedom to fish in the high seas served the interests of the world community as long as there were plenty of fish for all. The progress in shipbuilding technology and fishing-gear technology, and in electronics produced factory fishing vessels and vessels equipped with electronic tracking gear had led to overfishing and to the depletion of certain fish stocks. The possession of such advanced technology by a few distant-water fishing States had naturally led the developing coastal States, dependent on coastal fisheries, to perceive the situation as being inequitable. Developing coastal States, which depend upon coastal fisheries for their economic survival and welfare, claim that they have a greater equity to such resources than the developed distant-water fishing States.

The statistics showing the impact of technology on the harvest of fish are revealing. In 1950, the world harvested a total of 16 million tonnes of fish. In 1979, the world's harvest of fish had increased to 71 million tonnes.

Progress in the field of shipbuilding technology had also had an impact on navigation and on the marine environment. The very large crude carriers or supertankers, nuclear-powered and nuclear-armed submarines are some examples of recent shipbuilding technology. There has been a vast increase in both the number and tonnage of vessels. In 1950, the world merchant tonnage was 76 million tonnes. By 1974, it had increased to 306 million tonnes. This vast increase had posed serious problems of congestion and navigational safety in important shipping lines.

The progress of technology has also led to new uses of the ocean. The exploitation of oil and gas in the continental shelf, at progressively greater depths, is such an example. Another is the development of technology to mine the polymetallic nodules that lie on the deep seabed and ocean floor under water 3,000 to 5,000 metres deep.

In the period since 1945, especially in the decades of the 1950s and 1960s, most of the colonial empires were liquidated and a great number of the former colonies acceded to independence. The developing countries generally felt that they had no part in the moulding of the traditional law and that it did not serve their interests. They, therefore, demanded that the traditional law of the sea should be remoulded in order to take their interests into account. A member of the small and middle-sized developed coastal States such as Canada, Norway, Australia, New Zealand and Iceland sought common cause with the developing coastal States. This coalition of forces brought about a historic movement for the expansion of the jurisdiction and resource rights of coastal States which one American expert on the law of the sea, Leigh Ratiner, has described as a "revolution".

Why didn't the major maritime powers oppose the expansionism of the coastal States? Why were the great maritime powers reluctant to use force in order to check the unilateral claims of the coastal States?

Initially, the great maritime powers of the west protested, by diplomatic means, all unilateral claims by coastal States. When these diplomatic protests failed to stem the tide of coastal States expansion, the great powers did not resort to force to check the tide. For example, the UK did not use its superior fire power against Iceland during the famous cod war.[59] The US

---

[59] In 1958, Iceland extended its fishing limit to 12 miles together with a set of 47 baselines surrounding the entire country and its fringe islands. British fishermen were the long-distance fisherman most affected, having fished those

did not send its navy to protect its tuna boats against seizure by Chile, Ecuador and Peru. Why didn't they do so?

They did not do so for four reasons. First, the US had itself been the first to make a unilateral claim in 1945 to the resources of the continental shelf. Its moral authority was therefore not impeccable. Second, most of the coastal States which had made unilateral claims were friends and allies of the great powers. Iceland and the UK are members of NATO. Chile, Ecuador, Peru and US are members of the Organization of American States. It is easier to use military force against an adversary than against a country that is an ally or friend. The use of force by a great power against an ally or friend would have serious repercussions on its alliance interests and its foreign policy. Third, the use of force is arguably unlawful under the United Nations Charter and is, in any case, impolitic. Great powers would be condemned by world public opinion for bullying small or militarily weak coastal States irrespective of the merit or demerit of the unilateral claims of the coastal States. Fourth, the developing States were often perceived to be claiming the resources of the sea in order to feed their hungry peoples and to augment their developing economies.

By the mid 1960s, the great powers and the coastal States both felt a need for a new legal order for the oceans. The four

---

waters up to the four-mile limit since 1836. As a result, there began the Anglo-Icelandic Fish War of eighteen and a half months during which British trawlers fished in groups under the protection of the British navy. In March 1960, the British declared a three-month truce and withdrew its forces in order not to spoil the atmosphere of the Second United Nations Conference on the Law of the Sea. The Conference failed to agree on the limit of a coastal State's exclusive fishing rights but the British in practice observed the Icelandic claim. Another dispute arose in 1971 following Iceland's notice of its intention to claim a 50-mile exclusive fishing zone.

Geneva Conventions of 1958 had been ratified by very few States and were being rapidly overtaken by State practice.[60] The great powers needed "a new consensus regarding the rules of ocean law that is compatible with the mobility, flexibility and credibility of a routine global deployment of forces". The coastal States wanted a new legal order to ratify the unilateral claims which they have made for oceanic jurisdiction, oceanic resources, for the protection of the marine environment, and for their security. The opportunity to build a new consensus on oceanic law was first presented in 1967 when then Ambassador of Malta to the United Nations, Dr Arvid Pardo, drew the attention of the world to the immense resources of the seabed and ocean floor, beyond the limits of national jurisdiction, and proposed that such resources be considered the common heritage of mankind.[61]

The coastal States immediately saw the advantage of broadening Pardo's proposal to include all aspects of the uses and resources of the sea. Their basic thought was that trade-offs could be made between the demand of the great powers for navigational and overflight rights and the demands of the coastal States for expanded resource rights.

---

[60] The Convention on the Territorial Sea and Contiguous Zones, *supra* note 46, came into force on 10 Sep. 1964 and has 46 parties as of 31 Dec. 1985. The Convention on the High Seas, *supra* note 48, came into force on 30 Sep. 1962 and has 57 parties as of 31 Dec. 1985. The Convention on Fishing and Conservation of the Living Resources of the High Seas, *supra* note 47, came into force on 20 Mar. 1966 and has 36 parties as of 31 Dec. 1985. The Convention on the Continental Shelf, *supra* note 49, came into force on 10 June 1964 and has 54 parties as of 31 Dec. 1985. United Nations, *Multilateral Treaties Deposited with the Secretary-General*, Status as of 31 Dec. 1985 (1986).

[61] UN Gen. Ass. Off. Rec., 22nd Sess. (1967) First Committee, 151th and 156th meetings on 1 Nov. 1967.

In 1967, the USSR approached the US and other countries on the idea of recognising a 12-mile territorial sea provided that a high seas corridor was preserved in international straits. In 1968 and 1969, the US started sounding out the views of some NATO countries, the USSR and others, on the idea of conceding 12 miles as the maximum permissible breadth of the territorial sea in return for free navigation of warship and overflight of military aircraft in straits used for international navigation.

The confluence of these three streams of thought led, in 1970, to the decision to convene the Third United Nations Conference on the Law of the Sea in December 1973.[62] The conference would attempt to reach agreement on the two questions left unresolved by the Hague Codification Conference of 1930 and the First and Second United Nations Conferences on the Law of the Sea, that is the limits of the territorial sea and exclusive fishing rights. In addition, the Conference would attempt a more precise definition of the continental shelf than the definition in the 1958 Convention on the Continental Shelf. The Conference would also deal with the contiguous zone, straits used for international navigation, archipelagos, resources of the high seas, the protection and preservation of the marine environment from pollution, marine scientific research and the regime and institutions for the exploration and exploitation of the resources of the international area of the seabed and ocean floor. In accordance with the exhortation of Pardo, the Conference would attempt to deal with the various subjects and issues as forming an integral whole and recognise that ocean space forms an ecological unity.

---

[62] G.A. Res. 2650C of 17 Dec. 1970, UN Gen. Ass. Off. Rec., 25th Sess. (1970) Supp. No. 28, p. 242.

⚬⚬⚬

The Territorial Sea, Contiguous Zone, Straits and Archipelagos Under the 1982 Convention on the Law of the Sea[1]

The Territorial Sea

The Maximum Permissible Breadth of the Territorial Sea

It will be recalled that the world community had made three fruitless attempts to reach an agreement on the maximum permissible breadth of the territorial sea at the Hague Codification

---

[1] This is the second in a series of three articles tracing the evolution of the Law of the Sea, by Prof. Tommy TB Koh. The first article was published in the July 1987 issue of this Review and the final article will be published in July 1988. We thank Mr RC Beckman for his help in editing this article. The Convention was adopted on 30 April 1982. The text is contained in UN Doc. A/CONF.62/122, 7 October 1982, and is reprinted in 21 I.L.M. 1245 (1982).

Conference of 1930, the First United Nations Conference on the Law of the Sea (1958) and the Second United Nations Conference on the Law of the Sea (1960).[2] At its fourth attempt, the world community agreed that every State has the right to establish the breadth of its territorial sea up to a limit not exceeding 12 nautical miles, measured from baselines determined in accordance with the 1982 Convention.[3] Since 12 miles is the maximum permissible breadth, it is not mandatory for every coastal State to claim the maximum. In 1981, 24 coastal States still claimed a territorial sea of only three miles.[4] The overwhelming majority, 78 out of the 137 independent coastal States, claimed 12 miles.[5] There were also 26 States that claimed a territorial sea of more than 12 miles.[6] If these 26 States choose to become parties to the 1982 Convention, they must alter their national laws in order to conform to the Convention.

Delimitation of the Territorial Sea

Article 3 of the 1982 Convention states that the territorial sea shall be measured from "baselines determined in accordance with this Convention". The provisions of the 1982 Convention on the drawing of baselines are taken from the 1958 Convention

---

[2] For the background of these conferences, see the first article in this series, "The Origins of the 1982 Convention on the Law of the Sea," (1987) 29 Mal. L.R. I at 7–14.

[3] 1982 Convention, *supra* note 1, Article 3.

[4] Choon-Ho Park, "Current Status of 200-Mile Claims in 'Exclusive Economic Zone'" in *Proceedings of the 7th International Ocean Symposium* (Tokyo: The Ocean Association of Japan, 1983), p. 31.

[5] *Ibid.*

[6] *Ibid.*

on the Territorial Sea and the Contiguous Zone.[7] In summary, they are:

First, the normal baseline for measuring the breadth of the territorial sea is the low-water line along the coast. The use of the low-water line as the normal baseline for delimiting the territorial sea emerged in the 19th century as a result of State practice.[8] The reason for using the low-water line rather than the high-water line is obviously intended to maximise the extent of the territorial sea for the coastal State. In most cases, the difference between the low-water line and the high-water line is not very great but in some cases, such as the Bay of Fundy in Canada, it can be more than a mile.

Second, Article 4 of the 1982 Convention states that the "outer limit of the territorial sea is the line every point of which is at a distance from the nearest point of the baseline equal to the breadth of the territorial sea." This provision is also reproduced from the 1958 Territorial Sea Convention.[9] What does it mean? Is a coastal State free to choose either the *trace parallele* method or the *courbe tangante* method in determining the outer limit of its territorial sea?

There are two methods for determining the outer limit of the territorial sea.[10] The first method is called the *trace parallele* method. The line drawn by this method is parallel to the general

---

[7] 1958 Convention on the Territorial Sea and Contiguous Zone, Articles 3–13, First United Nations Conference on the Law of the Sea, Off. Rec. (1958), Vol. II, pp. 132, Document A/CONF.13/L.52; 516 U.N.T.S. 205. (Hereinafter referred to as the 1958 Territorial Sea Convention.)

[8] S Swartztrauber, *The Three Mile Limit of Territorial Seas* (1972).

[9] 1958 Convention on the Territorial Sea and Contiguous Zone, *supra* note 7, Article 6.

[10] See Figure 1.

trend of the coast, following the sinuosities of the baseline. This method works well when the coast is straight or gently curving. It does not work so well when the coast is irregular or highly indented. The second method is called the *courbe tangante* method. Using this method, the line is constructed by drawing arcs of circles to seaward from every point on the baseline. The area enclosed by all the arcs of circles up to the baseline constitutes the territorial sea. Although the resulting line is not a

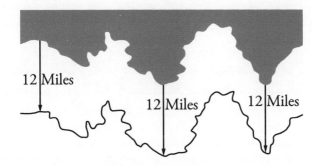

OUTER LIMIT OF
TERRITORIAL SEA
TRACE PARALLELE Application of Twelve-Mile Limit

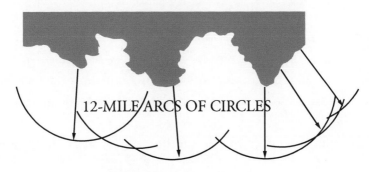

OUTER LIMIT OF
TERRITORIAL SEA
COURBE TANGANTE Application of Twelve-Mile Limit

Figure 1

straight line, neither does it follow the sinuosities of the coast-line. The *courbe tangante* method was proposed by the United States to the Hague Codification Conference of 1930. It was also recommended by the International Law Commission to the First United Nations Conference on the Law of the Sea. The language of Article 4, which is identical to Article 6 of the 1958 Territorial Sea Convention, is separately intended to sanction the use of the *courbe tangante* method[11] even though there is no reference to "arcs of circles". To conclude, it could be said that a coastal State could employ either the *trace parallele* method or the *courbe tangante* method in determining the outer limit of its territorial sea. Since the latter method is more advantageous to the coastal State than the former, it will probably be emp-loyed by most States except when the coastline is relatively straight, in which case, the two methods will produce roughly the same results.

Third, in the case of bays, the coasts of which belong to a single State, a straight line may be drawn across the mouth of the bay joining the low-water marks on each side of the mouth.[12] The territorial sea shall be measured from that line. The waters landward of that line are internal waters. The 1982 Convention reproduces two criteria from the 1958 Territorial Sea Convention[13] which must be complied with. The first criterion is that for an indentation of water to constitute a bay, its area must be equal to or larger than the area of the semicircle whose diameter is a line drawn across the mouth of that indentation.[14] The second criterion is that the line drawn across the mouth of

---

[11] See Swartztrauber, *supra* note 8, at pp. 220–222.

[12] 1982 Convention, *supra* note 1, Article 10, para. 4.

[13] 1958 Convention, *supra* note 7, Article 7.

[14] See Figure 2.

a bay must not exceed 24 miles. In a case where the mouth of a bay exceeds 24 miles, a straight baseline of 24 miles shall be drawn within the bay in such a manner as to enclose the maximum area of water. These provisions do not apply to "historic" bays or in any case where the system of straight baselines provided for in Article 7 of the 1982 Convention is applied.

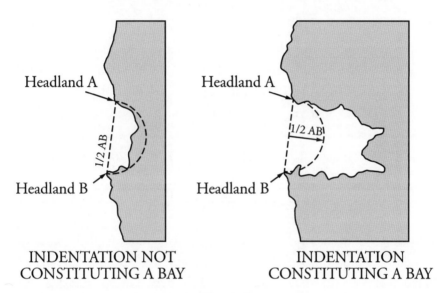

INDENTATION NOT CONSTITUTING A BAY

INDENTATION CONSTITUTING A BAY

Figure 2

Fourth, Article 7 of the 1982 Convention lays down the circumstances under which a coastal State may draw straight baselines instead of baselines that follow the contours of its coast. The system of drawing straight baselines may be applied where the coastline is deeply indented and cut into; there is a fringe of islands along the coast in its immediate vicinity; and the coastline is highly unstable because of the presence of a delta and other natural conditions. The use of straight baselines along irregular coastlines was introduced by Norway in 1935. This led to a dispute between Norway and the United Kingdom that was referred to the International Court of Justice.[15] The Court ruled that the straight baselines fixed by the Royal Norwegian Decree of 1935 were not contrary to international law. The Court explained that along rugged coastal areas, baselines need not necessarily follow the low-water mark but may be determined by lines reasonably drawn conforming to the general direction of the coast. This judicial precedent was accepted by the International Law Commission and incorporated into its recommendations and was adopted by the First United Nations Conference on the Law of the Sea.[16] Article 7 of the 1982 Convention is based upon Article 4 of the 1958 Territorial Sea Convention.

The 1982 Convention contains five provisos to the system of straight baselines. The drawing of straight baselines must not depart, to any appreciable extent, from the general direction of the coast and the sea areas lying within the lines must be sufficiently closely linked to the land domain to be subject to the regime of internal waters.[17] Straight baselines shall not be drawn to and from low-tide elevations, unless lighthouses or similar installations which are permanently above sea level have been built on them or except in instances where the drawing of baselines to and from such elevations has received general international recognition.[18] In the cases of a coastline that is deeply indented and where there is a fringe of islands along the coast, account may be taken, in determining particular baselines, of economic interests peculiar to the region concerned, the reality and the importance of which are clearly evidenced by

---

[15] *The Anglo-Norwegian Fisheries Case*, I.C.J. Rep. 1951, p. 119.

[16] *Supra*, note 2.

[17] 1982 Convention, *supra* note 1, Article 7, para. 3.

[18] *Ibid.*, Article 7, para. 4.

long usage.[19] The system of straight baselines may not be applied by a State in such a manner as to cut off the territorial sea of another State from the high seas or an exclusive economic zone.[20] Finally, where the establishment of a straight baseline has the effect of enclosing, as internal waters, areas which had not previously been so considered, a right of innocent passage shall exist in those waters.[21]

Innocent Passage in the Territorial Sea

The sovereignty that every coastal State enjoys over its land territory extends to its internal waters and its territorial sea.[22] The sovereignty of a coastal State over its territorial sea includes the air space over the territorial sea as well as the seabed and subsoil.[23] The sovereignty over the territorial sea is, however, "subject to this Convention and to other rules of international law".[24] One of the things that sovereignty is subject to is the right of innocent passage which ships of all States enjoy in the territorial sea.[25] Although the provisions of the 1982 Convention on innocent passage through the territorial sea are inspired by the provisions of the 1958 Territorial Sea Convention, the former are more extensive than the latter. The 1982 Convention contains new elements which are not found in the 1958 Territorial

---

[19] *Ibid.*, Article 7, para. 5.

[20] *Ibid.*, Article 7, para. 6.

[21] *Ibid.*, Article 8, para. 2.

[22] *Ibid.*, Article 2, para. 1.

[23] *Ibid.*, Article 2, para. 2.

[24] *Ibid.*, Article 2, para. 3.

[25] *Ibid.*, Article 17.

Sea Convention and which clarify and strengthen the regime of innocent passage in the territorial sea.

The term "innocent passage" is defined in two steps: first, what is passage and second, what is innocent passage. This two-step approach is based upon the scheme in the 1958 Territorial Sea Convention. "Passage" is defined as navigation through the territorial sea for two purposes.[26] The first purpose is traversing the territorial sea without entering internal waters or calling at a roadstead or port facility outside internal waters.[27] The second purpose is proceeding to or from internal waters, or a call at a roadstead or port facility outside internal waters.[28] The passage of a ship in the territorial sea "shall be continuous and expeditious".[29] Does this mean that a ship cannot stop or anchor under any circumstances? A ship may stop and anchor if stopping and anchoring are incidental to ordinary navigation.[30] For example, a ship may be forced to stop and anchor temporarily because of congestion in a shipping lane. A ship may also stop and anchor if it is rendered necessary by *force majeure* or distress, for example, as a result of a storm or accident.[31] A ship may also stop and anchor for the purpose of rendering assistance to persons, ships or aircraft in danger or distress.[32]

---

[26] *Ibid.*, Article 18, para. 1.

[27] *Ibid.*, Article 18, para. 1(a).

[28] *Ibid.*, Article 18, para. 1(b). The reference to a call at the roadstead or port facility outside internal waters is absent from Article 14 of the 1958 Convention.

[29] *Ibid.*, Article 18, para 2. This is implicit in Article 14, para. 3 of the 1958 Convention.

[30] *Ibid.*

[31] *Ibid.*

[32] *Ibid.*

Passage is said to be innocent "so long as it is not prejudicial to the peace, good order or security of the coastal State".[33] The 1958 Territorial Sea Convention states only one case of passage falling outside the scope of innocent passage: foreign fishing vessels fishing in the territorial sea, contrary to the laws and regulations of the coastal State.[34] In contrast, the 1982 Convention sets out 12 circumstances in which the passage of a foreign ship shall be considered to be prejudicial to the peace, good order or security of the coastal State and, therefore, to be not in innocent passage.[35] This list is probably intended to be exhaustive. Therefore, if the passage of a ship does not infringe against any of these 12 grounds, it must be presumed to be innocent.

What are the 12 circumstances in which the passage of a foreign ship shall be considered to be prejudicial to the peace, good order or security of the coastal State? First, if the ship engages in any threat or use of force against the sovereignty, territorial integrity or political independence of the coastal State or if the ship acts in any other manner contrary to the principles of international law contained in the United Nations Charter.[36] Second, if the ship engages in any exercise or practice with weapons of any kind.[37] Third, if the ship engages in any act aimed at collecting information to the prejudice of the defence or security of the coastal State.[38] Fourth, if the ship engages in

---

[33] *Ibid.*, Article 19, para. 1. This is identical to Article 14, para. 4 of the 1958 Convention.

[34] 1958 Convention, *supra* note 7, Article 14, para. 5.

[35] 1982 Convention, *supra* note 1, Article 19, para. 2.

[36] *Ibid.*, Article 19, para. 2(a).

[37] *Ibid.*, Article 19, para. 2(b).

[38] *Ibid.*, Article 19, para. 2(c).

any act of propaganda aimed at affecting the defence or security of the coastal State.[39] An example would be a ship making broadcasts urging the people of the coastal State to overthrow its government. Fifth, if the ship engages in the launching, landing or taking on board of any aircraft.[40] Sixth, if the ship engages in the launching, landing or taking on board of any military device.[41] Seventh, if the ship engages in the loading or unloading of any commodity, currency or person contrary to the customs, fiscal, immigration or sanitary laws and regulations of the coastal State.[42] Eighth, if the ship engages in any wilful and serious pollution contrary to the Convention.[43] An example would be a ship which deliberately discharges oil whilst traversing the territorial sea. Ninth, if a ship engages in any fishing activity.[44] Tenth, if a ship carries out research or survey activities.[45] Eleventh, if the ship interferes with any communications or any other facilities or installations of the coastal State.[46] An example would be a ship that attempts to jam the telecommunication system of the coastal State. The twelfth is the broadest category: if a ship engages in any activity not having a direct bearing on passage.[47] This category is vague and imprecise and could give rise to disputes over its interpretation and application.

---

[39] *Ibid.*, Article 19, para. 2(d).

[40] *Ibid.*, Article 19, para. 2(e).

[41] *Ibid.*, Article 19, para. 2(f).

[42] *Ibid.*, Article 19, para. 2(g).

[43] *Ibid.*, Article 19, para. 2(h).

[44] *Ibid.*, Article 19, para. 2(i).

[45] *Ibid.*, Article 19, para. 2(j).

[46] *Ibid.*, Article 19, para. 2(k).

[47] *Ibid.*, Article 19, para. 2(l).

What are the legal consequences of the distinction between passage that is innocent and passage that is not innocent? What rights does a ship in innocent passage enjoy that are denied to a ship which is not in innocent passage? A ship whose passage is not innocent has no right to traverse the territorial sea and a coastal State may take the necessary steps in its territorial sea to prevent the ship's passage.[48] *Per contra*, a ship in innocent passage has the right to traverse the territorial sea of a coastal State and the coastal State is under a duty not to hamper the innocent passage of such a ship.[49] In addition, the coastal State is under a duty not to impose requirements on foreign ships which have the practical effect of denying or impairing the right of innocent passage.[50] The coastal State is also under a duty not to discriminate against the ships of any State or any ships carrying cargoes to, from, or on behalf of any State.[51]

It does not mean that a coastal State is prohibited from adopting laws and regulations to regulate the innocent passage of ships in its territorial sea. The 1982 Convention empowers coastal States to adopt laws and regulations, relating to innocent passage through the territorial sea, in respect of eight matters[52] and foreign ships are under an obligation to comply with all such laws and regulations as well as all generally accepted international regulations relating to the prevention of collisions at sea.[53]

What are the eight matters on which a coastal State may adopt laws and regulations? First, the safety of navigation and

---

[48] *Ibid.*, Article 25, para. 1.

[49] *Ibid.*, Article 24, para. 1. Article 15, para of the 1958 Convention is similar.

[50] *Ibid.*, Article 24, para. 1(a).

[51] *Ibid.*, Article 24, para. 1(b).

[52] *Ibid.*, Article 21, para. 1.

[53] *Ibid.*, Article 21, para. 4.

the regulation of maritime traffic.[54] Can a coastal State adopt laws or regulations requiring ships in innocent passage through its territorial sea to use prescribed sea lanes and traffic separation schemes? The answer is yes, if the safety of navigation makes the adoption of such sea lanes and traffic separation schemes necessary.[55] However, in designating sea lanes or prescribing traffic separation schemes, the coastal State shall take into account the recommendations of the competent international organisation, such as the International Maritime Organization; any channels customarily used for international navigation; and the special characteristics of particular ships and channels and the density of traffic.[56] Can a coastal State adopt laws or regulations concerning the design, construction, manning or equipment of foreign ships? The answer is no, unless such laws and regulations are merely giving effect to generally accepted international rules or standards.[57]

Second, the protection of navigational aids and facilities and other facilities or installations.[58] Third, the protection of cables and pipelines.[59] Fourth, the conservation of the living resources of the sea.[60] This would, for example, enable a coastal State to divert traffic away from the spawning ground or nursery areas of a fish stock. Fifth, the prevention of infringement of the fisheries laws and regulations of the coastal State.[61] Sixth, the

---

[54] *Ibid.*, Article 21, para. 1(a).

[55] *Ibid.*, Article 22, para. 1.

[56] *Ibid.*, Article 22, para. 3.

[57] *Ibid.*, Article 21, para. 2.

[58] *Ibid.*, Article 21, para. 1(b).

[59] *Ibid.*, Article 21, para. 1(c).

[60] *Ibid.*, Article 21, para. 1(d).

[61] *Ibid.*, Article 21, para. 1(e).

preservation of the environment of the coastal State and the prevention, reduction and control of pollution thereof.[62] Seventh, regulations in respect of marine scientific research and hydrographic surveys.[63] Eighth, the prevention of infringement of the customs, fiscal, immigration or sanitary laws and regulations of the coastal State.[64]

The power of the coastal State to adopt laws and regulations on these eight matters is not unqualified. The power must be exercised, "in conformity with the provisions of this Convention and other rules of international law".[65] The coastal State must also give due publicity to all such laws and regulations.[66] A coastal State must give "appropriate publicity to any danger to navigation of which it has knowledge, within its territorial sea".[67]

Can a coastal State levy charges upon foreign ships for passing through its territorial sea? No, this is prohibited by the Convention.[68] The only kind of charges which a coastal State may levy upon foreign ships is payment for specific services rendered to the ship, for example, towage.[69] These charges must be non-discriminatory in nature.

Are there any circumstances under which a coastal State may suspend temporarily the innocent passage of ships in specified areas of its territorial sea? A coastal State may do so if such suspension is essential for the protection of its security, including

---

[62] *Ibid.*, Article 21, para. 1(f).

[63] *Ibid.*, Article 21, para. 1(g).

[64] *Ibid.*, Article 21, para. 1(h).

[65] *Ibid.*, Article 21, para. 1.

[66] *Ibid.*, Article 21, para. 3.

[67] *Ibid.*, Article 24, para. 2.

[68] *Ibid.*, Article 26, para. 1.

[69] *Ibid.*, Article 26, para. 2.

the carrying out of weapons exercises.[70] Such suspension must not discriminate among foreign ships and shall take effect only after having been duly published.[71]

Submarines

Do submarines and other underwater vehicles enjoy the right of innocent passage through the territorial sea? Submarines and other underwater vehicles do enjoy the right of innocent passage through the territorial sea but they must navigate on the surface and show their flag.[72]

Tankers, Nuclear-Powered Ships and Ships Carrying Dangerous Cargoes

There is one special rule applicable to tankers, nuclear-powered ships and ships carrying nuclear or other inherently dangerous or noxious substances. The first rule, which applies to all three categories of ships, is that a coastal State may require them to use only the designated sea lanes for passage through its territorial sea.[73] The second rule which is applicable to nuclear-powered ships and ships carrying nuclear or other inherently dangerous or noxious substances is that they must carry documents and observe special precautionary measures established for such ships by international agreements.[74]

---

[70] *Ibid.*, Article 25, para. 3.

[71] *Ibid.*

[72] *Ibid.*, Article 20.

[73] *Ibid.*, Article 22, para. 2.

[74] *Ibid.*, Article 23.

Warships

The 1982 Convention defines a warship as "a ship belonging to the armed forces of a State bearing the external marks distinguishing such ships of its nationality, under the command of an officer duly commissioned by the government of the State and whose name appears in the appropriate service list or its equivalent, and manned by a crew which is under regular armed forces discipline."[75]

Do warships enjoy the right of innocent passage in the territorial sea under the 1982 Convention? This question has always been controversial in international law. Equally eminent authorities on international law have come down on opposite sides of this question. After reviewing the practice of States, the decisions of international tribunals and the views of publicists, in 1977, Franciszek Przetacznik came to the conclusion that "the right of innocent passage of foreign warships through the territorial sea has yet to be established as a customary rule of international law."[76]

The question was hotly debated in the Third United Nations Conference on the Law of the Sea. Towards the end of the Conference, the delegation of Gabon submitted an amendment to Article 21, paragraph 1, of the Convention.[77] The amendment

---

[75] *Ibid.*, Article 29. This definition is similar to but not identical with the definition in Article 8, para. 2, of the 1958 Convention on the High Seas, First United Nations Conference on the Law of the Sea, Off. Rec., (1958), Vol. II, pp. 135–139, Document A/CONF.13/L.53; 559 U.N.T.S. 285.

[76] F Przetacznik, "Freedom of Navigation Through Territorial Seas and International Straits," (1977) 55 *Revue De Droit International De Sciences Diplomatiques et Politiques* 222–240, 299–319, at p. 309.

[77] Doc. A/CONF.62/L.97 of 13 April 1982, Third United Nations Conference on the Law of the Sea. Off. Rec., Vol. XVI, 11th Sess. (1982), p. 217.

would empower coastal States to adopt laws and regulations on the navigation of warships through the territorial sea, including the right to require prior authorisation and notification for the passage of warships through the territorial sea. Another amendment was jointly submitted by 28 delegations.[78] This would add the word "security" to Article 21, paragraph (1)(h). The effect of the amendment would be that a coastal State could make laws and regulations on the ground of its "security" even though such laws and regulations might impinge upon the innocent passage of ships in the territorial sea.

The two superpowers, working hand in hand, led the opposition to the two amendments. They could not accept Gabon's amendment because they held the firm view that warships must enjoy the right of innocent passage through the territorial sea. They could not accept the 28-power amendment because they feared that its adoption would confer extremely broad powers on coastal States over navigation in the territorial sea. The two superpowers threatened that if either amendment were adopted, it would alter their attitude towards the Convention as a whole. In view of the stand taken by them, the Conference could not afford to take the risk of putting the amendments to the vote for fear that either might be adopted.

The burden of persuading the co-sponsors of the two amendments not to insist on putting them to the vote fell on the

---

[78] Doc. A/CONF.62/L.117 of 13 April 1982 and Doc. A/CONF.62/L.117 of 14 April 1982, *Ibid.*, p. 225. The 28 co-sponsors were: Algeria, Bahrain, Benin, Cape Verde, China, Congo, Democratic People's Republic of Korea, Democratic Yemen, Djibouti, Egypt, Guinea-Bissai, Iran, Libyan Arab Jamahiriya, Malta, Morocco, Oman, Pakistan, Papua New Guinea, Philippines, Romania, Sao Tome and Principe, Sierra Leone, Somalia, Sudan, Suriname, Syria, Uruguay and Yemen.

Conference President.[79] He enlisted the help of his colleagues in the Collegium.[80] The delegation of Gabon agreed not to insist on putting its amendment to the vote. The 28 co-sponsors of the second amendment were, however, adamant and negotiations between them and the two superpowers continued into the dying hours of the Conference. On the afternoon of 30 April 1982, the 28 co-sponsors of the amendment were sequestered in one room, the two superpowers were in another, and the members of the Collegium were in a third. Negotiations were conducted by the Collegium between the US and the USSR and representatives of the co-sponsors.[81] Various texts were tried but none of them satisfied the two opposing sides. At the last moment, the Collegium succeeded in persuading the co-sponsors of the amendment not to insist on putting it to the vote on two conditions. First, the Conference President would read the agreed text of a statement into the record of the Conference. Second, no delegation would ask for the floor to interpret the President's statement or the provisions of the Convention affecting the question.

This is the statement which the Conference President read:

> Although the co-sponsors of the amendment contained in document L.117 had proposed the amendment with a view to clarifying the text of the Convention, in response to the President's appeal, they have agreed not to press it to a vote.

---

[79] Editor's note: The author of this article was the President of the Conference.

[80] The Collegium consisted of the President, the chairmen of the First, Second and Third Committees, the Chairman of the Drafting Committee and the Rapporteur-General.

[81] The 28 co-sponsors were represented in the negotiations by China, Malta, Morocco, Philippines, Romania and Sierra Leone.

They would, however, like to reaffirm that this is without prejudice to the right of coastal States to adopt measures to safeguard their security interests, in accordance with Articles 19 and 25 of this Convention.[82]

Although the Conference was saved from splitting over the question of the passage of warships through the territorial sea, it cannot be said that the position under the 1982 Convention is clear beyond dispute. Indeed, it is more than likely that the great maritime powers would argue that under the Convention, warships enjoy the same right of innocent passage through the territorial sea as other ships, whereas the 28 States that co-sponsored the amendment would argue that there is sufficient latitude under Articles 19 and 25 of the Convention to enable them to enact laws restricting the passage of warships through their territorial seas.

The proponents of the first view could point out that Article 17, which states that, "ships of all States, whether coastal or landlocked, enjoy the right of innocent passage through the territorial sea", makes no distinction between warships and other ships. Therefore, they could argue, the right of innocent passage is applicable to all ships, including warships. They could also state that the legislative history of the Conference on this question was consistent with their view because obviously the delegation of Gabon and the other 28 delegations would not have submitted their respective amendments if the Convention did not confer the right of innocent passage on warships. Those who uphold the opposing view could find support in the pre-existing law. They would have to argue that in view of the

---

[82] Plenary Meetings, 176th Meeting, Third United Nations Conference on the Law of the Sea, Off. Rec., Vol. XVI, 11th Sess. (1982), p. 132.

uncertainty surrounding the question, the provisions of the Convention should be read as merely codifying the pre-existing law and not as containing new law.

Contiguous Zone

There was very little discussion of the contiguous zone at the Third United Nations Conference on the Law of the Sea. Because of this, Article 24 of the 1958 Territorial Sea Convention has been incorporated into the 1982 Convention, as Article 33. The only change is that the maximum permissible breadth of the contiguous zone has been increased from 12 to 24 miles.[83]

It is a pity that the Third United Nations Conference did not seize the opportunity to reformulate the article in order to rid it of its ambiguity. Article 33, paragraph 1, of the 1982 Convention reads as follows:

1. In a zone contiguous to its territorial sea, described as the contiguous zone, the coastal State may exercise the control necessary to:

   (a) prevent infringement of its customs, fiscal, immigration or sanitary laws and regulations within its territory or territorial sea;

   (b) punish infringement of the above laws and regulations committed within its territory or territorial sea.

The ambiguity lies in the phrase, "within its territory or territorial sea" in sub-paragraphs (a) and (b). Because of the presence of this phrase, the text is capable of two interpretations. According

---

[83] 1982 Convention, *supra* note 1, Article 33, para. 2.

to the restrictive interpretation,[84] Article 33, paragraph 1(a), is applicable only to incoming ships, that is ships heading towards the territorial sea. When the ship is in the contiguous zone, heading towards the territorial sea, the power of the coastal State includes the conduct of necessary inquiries, investigation, examination and search. The coastal State does not, however, have the power to arrest the ship or to order or conduct it into port. The coastal State does not have such power because, at that point, the ship has not committed an offence "within its territory or territorial sea". According to this view, Article 33, paragraph 1(b), is applicable only to outgoing ships, that is to ships that are proceeding from the territorial sea into the contiguous zone. Such ships would already have committed offences "within the territory or territorial sea" of the coastal State. This, therefore, gives the coastal State the jurisdiction to punish such ships.

The restrictive interpretation, favoured by some British scholars and by the British government, represents a minority view of the law. The majority favours a more liberal interpretation of the text. Those who hold this view, for example, Shigeru Oda,[85] derive their support from State practice and from the legislative history of the text. According to this view, the coastal State may exercise, in its contiguous zone, the same powers in respect of customs, fiscal, immigration or sanitary control, as it does in its territorial sea. In other words, in respect of these four matters, the jurisdiction of the coastal State to enforce its laws is extended beyond its territory and territorial sea into its contiguous zone.

---

[84] G Fitzmaurice, "Some Results of the Geneva Conference on the Law of the Sea," (1959) 8 I.C.L.Q. 73.

[85] S Oda, "The Concept of the Contiguous Zone," (1962) 1 1 I.C.L.Q. 131.

Another point worth mentioning is that the text of Article 33 of the 1982 Convention, like the text of Article 24 of the 1958 Territorial Sea Convention, does not include the word "security". The story of the fight over the word "security" which took place at the First United Nations Conference is worth recalling. In its 1956 report, the International Law Commission (ILC) explained why it had omitted "security" from its recommendation. The report stated:

> The Commission did not recognise special security rights in the contiguous zone. It considered that the extreme vagueness of the term "security" would open the way for abuses and that the granting of such right was necessary. The enforcement of customs and sanitary regulations will be sufficient in most cases to safeguard the security of the State. In so far as measures for self-defence against an imminent and direct threat to the security of the State are concerned, the Commission refers to the general principles of international law and the Charter of the United Nations.[86]

At the First United Nations Conference, the text proposed by the ILC on the contiguous zone was referred to its First Committee. The delegations of the Philippines, Yugoslavia and Korea respectively submitted proposals to the effect that the concept of security should be included in the provision of the contiguous zone.[87] None of these were put to the vote. The delegation of

---

[86] Report of the International Law Commission to the General Assembly, Commentary 4 to article 66, (1956) 2 Y.B.I.L.C. pp. 294–295.

[87] A/CONF.13/C.1/L.13, L.54 and L.84, First United Nations Conference on the Law of the Sea, Off. Rec., (1958) Vol. III, pp. x, 226 and 234, UN Doc. A/CONF.13/39.

Poland proposed the following text in place of the text proposed by the ILC:

> In a zone of the high seas contiguous to its territorial sea, the coastal State may take the measures necessary to prevent and punish infringements of its customs, fiscal or sanitary regulations and violations of its security.[88]

The Polish proposal was adopted. It was adopted by the First Committee of the Whole by 50 votes in favour to 18 against, with 8 abstentions. The proposal was then transmitted to the Plenary. In the Plenary, in which a two-thirds majority was required, the First Committee's recommendation received only 40 votes in favour, 27 against, with 9 abstentions. The proposal therefore failed to be adopted. Instead, the Plenary adopted a US proposal to go back to the ILC's text, with the addition of the word "immigration". The defeat of the Polish proposal in the Plenary, after its easy passage in the First Committee, surprised the Conference. It was due largely to vigorous lobbying on the part of the US delegation which objected to the inclusion of "security".[89]

Straits Used for International Navigation

The nature of the regime for the passage of ships and aircraft through, over and under straits used for international navigation, was one of the most important and controversial questions faced by the Third United Nations Conference. Why was it such an important question? It was important to the strait States because

---

[88] A/CONF.13/C.1/L.78, *ibid.*, p. 232.

[89] Oda, *supra* note 85 at 148–153.

the question of sovereignty was involved. Some strait States felt strongly that insofar as the waters in a strait are territorial waters, the regime for the passage of ships must be innocent passage. They felt that any proposal to tilt the regime towards the high seas regime, including a *sui generis* regime, was an infringement against their sovereignty in their territorial sea and, therefore, unacceptable.

The question was important to the user States for two reasons. All States, whether east or west, north or south, have a common interest in the promotion of international trade. The bulk of international trade is seaborne. It is a truism that the seas constitute the highways of the world. This is why the freedom of navigation is not only of interest to the maritime powers but it is an interest shared by the entire international community. The straits are the chokepoints in the world's shipping lanes. The world community, therefore, has a strong interest in ensuring the safe and unimpeded passage of ships through these chokepoints without neglecting, at the same time, the environmental and other legitimate interests of the strait States.

The second reason has to do with the strategic importance of ocean space, in general and in straits, in particular, to the great military powers, especially to the two superpowers. The US and the USSR are global powers with allies and interests in areas far from their shores. They need to use the seas and the airspace above for the purpose of projecting their conventional military power. Freedom of navigation and overflight for their military aircraft are therefore strategic imperatives. Since the straits constitute chokepoints in the communication system, the question of passage through, over and under them, becomes even more critical. The nuclear arsenals of the two superpowers are based on land, aircraft and submarines. Each superpower keeps part of its stockpile of ballistic missiles in submarines at sea. It is important for each superpower not to know the precise locations of its adversary's submarines because this works as a deterrent against either of them launching a first strike against the other.[90] The theory is that if one superpower launches a first strike and succeeds in destroying all or substantially all of its adversary's land-based ballistic missiles, the victim will retaliate by launching its submarine-based ballistic missiles at the aggressor. As long as each superpower retains a second strike capability, this acts as a deterrence against the temptation of launching a sneak attack. Since secrecy and mobility of their respective submarine fleets are critical, the two superpowers have, therefore, demanded free and submerged passage for their submarines through straits.

The *Corfu Channel Case*

The pre-existing law can be found in the judgment of the International Court of Justice in the *Corfu Channel Case*[91] and in the 1958 Territorial Sea Convention. The Corfu Channel is a strait, bounded on the west by the island of Corfu, belonging to Greece, and on the east, by the mainland of Albania. The Corfu Chanel connects one part of the Mediterranean Sea with another part. The strait varies in width from one mile to six and a half miles. On 22 October 1946, two units of a Royal Navy squadron, HMS *Saumarez* and HMS *Voltage*, were proceeding through the North Corfu Channel. They struck mines

---

[90] M Reisman, "The Regime of Straits and National Security: An Appraisal of International Lawmaking," (1980) 74 A.J.I.L 48 at pp. 48–54; J Moore, "The Regime of Straits and the Third UN Conference on the Law of the Sea," (1980) 74 A.J.I.L 77 at pp. 78–85.

[91] I.C.J. Rep 1949, p. 1.

which had been laid in the fairway and as a result, 44 officers and men lost their lives and serious damage was caused to the two ships. The British government brought its complaint against the Albanian government to the United Nations Security Council. The Council recommended that the two governments should immediately refer the dispute to the International Court of Justice.

In its memorial to the Court, the British government argued, *inter alia,* that the North Corfu Channel, being a natural channel of navigation between two parts of the high sea, constituted an international highway, subject under international law to a right of innocent passage in favour of foreign shipping. In its counter-memorial, Albania argued that the Corfu Channel was not a strait but only a means of lateral traffic of secondary and limited importance. Albania recalled that it had informed the British government that it required to be notified of the passage of British warships. This had not been done in this case. Albania said that on that occasion, the British squadron entered Albanian waters without any warning or information whatever given to the Albanian authorities. In its reply the UK argued that, even though the Corfu Channel may not have been used by shipping on a large scale, its character as an international route depended on the fact that it connected two parts of the open sea, thus making it useful to navigation. It was true that no notice had been given to Albania of the intended passage of the British squadron on 22 October 1946 but no such notice was necessary.

On the question whether the Corfu Channel was a strait, the Court ruled that the test was not the volume of traffic passing through the strait or in its importance to international navigation. The decisive criterion, the Court said, was the geographical situation of the strait as connecting two parts of the high seas coupled with the fact that it was actually used for international navigation. To qualify as a strait, a channel need not be a necessary route. The fact that the Corfu Channel was a useful route for international maritime traffic was enough. Turning to the question of the legality of the Royal Navy's passage, the Court said that it was generally recognised, and in accordance with international custom, "that States in time of peace have a right to send their warships through straits used for international navigation between two parts of the high seas without the previous authorisation of a coastal State, provided that the passage is innocent. Unless otherwise prescribed in international convention, there is no right for a coastal State to prohibit such passage through straits in time of peace."[92]

The *Corfu Channel Case* may be viewed as having established two propositions. First, to qualify as a strait, a channel must satisfy two criteria: it must connect two parts of the high seas and it must actually be used for international navigation. Potential use is not enough. On the other hand, the volume of usage and its importance to international navigation is irrelevant. Second, warships have a right of innocent passage through straits in times of peace.

1958 Territorial Sea Convention

The judgement of the International Court of Justice in the *Corfu Channel Case* must have influenced the ILC and through it, the First United Nations Conference, which adopted the 1958 Territorial Sea Convention. In that Convention, the whole question of passage through straits used for international

---

[92] *Ibid.*, at p. 28.

navigation was disposed of in one paragraph. Article 16, paragraph 4 states:

> There shall be no suspension of the innocent passage of foreign ships through straits which are used for international navigation between one part of the high seas and another part of the high seas or the territorial sea of a foreign State.

The position under the 1958 Territorial Sea Convention can be summed up in the following propositions. First, a strait used for international navigation must satisfy two criteria: the one geographical, the other functional. The geographical criterion is that it must connect one part of the high seas with another part of the high seas or one part of the high seas with the territorial sea of a State. The functional criterion is that, as stated in the *Corfu Channel Case*, the strait must actually be used for international navigation. Second, all ships, including warships, enjoy the right of "non-suspendable" innocent passage through straits used for international navigation. Third, submarines do not have the right of submerged passage through straits used for international navigation but, as required by Article 14, paragraph 6 of the 1958 Territorial Sea Convention, must navigate on the surface and show their flag. Fourth, there is no right of overflight by aircraft over straits used for international navigation.

Were the great powers prepared to accept the mere repetition of the provisions of the 1958 Territorial Sea Convention in the new Convention? They were not. Why were they not prepared to do so? The answer lies in the progressive extension by coastal States of their territorial seas. The following table by William T Burke[93] will make the point clear:

---

[93] W Burke, "Submerged Passage Through Straits: Interpretations of the Proposed Law of the Sea Treaty," (1977) 52 Wash. L. Rev. 193 at p. 195.

Number of Territorial Sea Claims Over Time

Territorial Sea Claimed (Nautical Miles) Year	3	4	5	6	7	10	12	18	30	50	100	130	200
Before 1930	32	5		5			1						
1930	15	4		10			1						
1958	41	4	1	11	1	1	11						4
1960	40	4	1	12	1	1	16						4
1973	27	4		11		1	52	1	3	1	1	1	9
1974	25	4		13		1	51	1	4	3	1	1	10

In 1958, the majority of the international community, 41 out of 74 States, claimed a territorial sea of three miles. By 1974, the number of States claiming a territorial sea of three miles has declined to 25 and the number claiming more than three miles has increased to 89. The significance of this change lies in the fact that there are 116 straits used for international navigation which are between 6 and 24 miles in width. There were high sea corridors in these straits when the strait States claimed a territorial sea of three miles. But, when the strait States extended their territorial seas to 12 miles, the high sea corridors disappeared and all the waters within these straits became territorial waters. This was the reason which led the great powers to demand that the extension of the territorial sea to 12 miles must be balanced by either the preservation of a high sea corridor in straits used for international navigation or the establishment of a *sui generis* regime for passage through, over and under straits used for international navigation.[94]

---

[94] *Ibid.*

Position Under the 1982 Convention

Unlike the 1958 Territorial Sea Convention, which had only one paragraph of an article dealing with passage through straits used for international navigation, the 1982 Convention has 12 articles which deal directly with the question. The second significant fact is that these 12 articles are not located in Part II of the Convention, dealing with the territorial sea and the contiguous zone, but form a separate part of the Convention, Part III, entitled, "Straits Used for International Navigation". This is clear evidence of an intention to depart from the position under the 1958 Territorial Sea Convention.

Definition of Straits Used for International Navigation

How does the 1982 Convention define straits used for international navigation? Actually, the Convention does not define the term as such. What it does is that Article 37 states that Section 2 of Part III of the Convention, entitled "Transit Passage", applies to "straits used for international navigation between one part of the high seas or an exclusive economic zone and another part of the high seas or an exclusive zone." From Article 37, it is possible to infer that for a strait to qualify as a strait used for international navigation, it must satisfy two criteria: a geographical criterion and a functional criterion. The geographical criterion is that it must connect: (a) one part of the high seas with another part of the high seas or (b) one part of the high seas with an exclusive economic zone or (c) an exclusive economic zone with another exclusive economic zone. The functional criterion is that it is used for international navigation. How should the second criterion be interpreted? Does it require any volume of usage? Does the strait have to constitute an important route of international navigation?

The second criterion is borrowed from Article 16, paragraph 4, of the 1958 Territorial Sea Convention, which has never been the subject of an authoritative interpretation. This leaves us with no choice but to fall back on the judgement of the International Court of Justice in the *Corfu Channel Case*. In that case, it will be recalled that the Court said that evidence of actual usage of the strait for international navigation was sufficient. The Court rejected the idea that the usage of the strait must attain a certain volume. It also rejected the notion that the strait must achieve a requisite degree of importance to international navigation. If we accept the views of the Court on the meaning of the functional criterion, and there is no reason not to, it is relatively easy to apply. What we would be looking for is evidence that a strait is actually being used, the volume of such usage being irrelevant, for international navigation.

Arvid Pardo[95] has referred to the difficulties of identifying straits used for international navigation. In this respect, it should be pointed out that statements made by representatives of strait States are not necessarily correct or controlling. Pardo has suggested that the uncertainty surrounding the identification of straits used for international navigation could and should have been overcome by listing, in an annex to the Convention, all such straits. There is certainly some merit in such an approach but it also suffers from one defect. The defect is that it seeks to freeze what is essentially a dynamic situation. A strait which may not be used, at present, for international navigation may be so used in the future. Conversely, a strait which is being used for international navigation, at present, may cease to be so used in the future.

---

[95] A Pardo, "An Opportunity Lost," in Oxman, Carmon and Buderi (editors), *Law of the Sea: US Policy Dilemma* (1983), p. 17.

Nature of Regime Applicable to Straits Used for International Navigation

What is the nature of the regime or regimes applicable to straits used for international navigation? A careful reading of Part III of the 1982 Convention reveals four different kinds of regimes applicable to straits used for international navigation. To put it another way, one can say, along with John Norton Moore,[96] that the Convention distinguishes four different categories of straits used for international navigation. The four categories are as follows:

First, straits in respect of which there are long-standing conventions in force.[97] The legal regime for passage through, over and under such straits would, of course, be governed by their respective conventions. Examples of this category would be the Turkish Straits, *viz.* the Bosphorus, the Sea of Marmora and the Dardanelles, which are governed by the Montreux Convention of 1936,[98] and the Straits of Magellan.[99]

Second, straits used for international navigation in which a route through the high seas or an exclusive economic zone of similar convenience, with respect to navigational and hydrographical characteristics, exists. If such an alternative route exists, Article 36 seems to require international shipping and aviation to use the alternative route. Since the alternative route goes through the high seas or an exclusive economic zone, the regime

---

[96] Moore, *supra* note 90 at p. 111.

[97] 1982 Convention, *supra* note 1, Article 25, para. (c).

[98] 173 L.N.T.S. 213.

[99] Treaty concluded in 1881 between Chile and Argentina, in Martens, *Nouveau recueil general de traites*, 2nd ser., Vol 12, p. 491.

of passage will be governed by the relevant provisions of Parts VII and V respectively.

Third, the regime of "non-suspendable" innocent passage is applicable to the following two types of straits used for international navigation.[100] The first is a strait formed by an island of a State bordering the strait and its mainland and where there exists seaward of that island, a route through the high seas or through an exclusive economic zone of similar convenience with respect to navigational and hydrographical characteristics.[101] Two examples of such a strait would be the Strait of Pemba, formed by the island of Pemba (belonging to Tanzania) and the mainland of Tanzania and the Strait of Messina, formed by the island of Sicily (belonging to Italy) and the mainland of Italy. The second is a strait used for international navigation connecting one part of the high seas or an exclusive economic zone and the territorial sea of a foreign State.[102] Some examples of such a strait would be the Strait of Georgia and the Gulf of Honduras. What about the Strait of Tiran? The Strait of Tiran satisfies both the geographical and the functional criteria but Moore[103] has correctly pointed out that the passage regime applicable to the Strait of Tiran is contained in United Nations Security Council Resolutions 242[104] and 338[105] which override Article 45 of the

---

[100] 1982 Convention, *ante* note 1, Article 45.

[101] *Ibid.*, Article 45, para. 1(a) and Article 38, para. 1.

[102] *Ibid.*, Article 45, para 1(b).

[103] Moore, *supra* note 90, at p. 113.

[104] Security Council Res. 242 of 22 Nov. 1967, UN Security Council Off. Rec., 22nd year (1967).

[105] Security Council Res. 338 of 22 Oct. 1973, UN Security Council Off. Rec., 28th year (1973).

Convention. Those two United Nations Security Council Resolutions, *inter alia*, affirm "the necessity for guaranteeing freedom of navigation through international waterways in the area".

Fourth, the most important category is Article 37, straits to which the regime of transit passage applies. Most of the 116 straits affected by the extension of the territorial sea, including such important straits as Gibraltar, Dover, Hormuz, Bab-Al-Mandeb, Malacca-Singapore, fall within this category. The term "transit passage" has no antecedent. It was not used in the 1958 Territorial Sea Convention or in customary law. The concept of transit passage is new and represents one of the many creative innovations of the Third United Nations Conference.

Regime of Transit Passage

What is transit passage? Article 38, paragraph 2, states that transit passage means the exercise, in accordance with Part III of the Convention, of "the freedom of navigation and overflight solely for the purpose of continuous and expeditious transit of the strait…". The phrase "freedom of navigation and overflight" is normally used in connection with the high seas as in Article 87, paragraph 1(a) and (b). What is the significance of using this phrase in the definition of transit passage? The first significance could be to distinguish clearly the regime of transit passage from the inferior regimes of "non-suspendable" innocent passage and innocent passage *simpliciter*. The second and more important significance is to denote that transit passage is like the freedom of navigation and the freedom of overflight in the high seas except for the limitations on those freedoms imposed by Part III of the Convention. The most important of these limitations is that the freedom of navigation and overflight must be exercised "solely for the purpose of continuous and expeditious transit of the strait...".[106] In other words, the freedom of navigation and overflight must be exercised solely for the purpose of transit through the strait and that transit must be continuous and expeditious.

There is one exception to the requirement of continuous and expeditious transit. The exception covers the case of a ship or aircraft that is going through the strait for the purpose of entering, leaving or returning from a State bordering the strait.[107] An illustration of this exception would be the case of a ship going through the Straits of Malacca and Singapore from the Indian Ocean. The ship stops in Singapore to pick up cargoes and proceeds through the Strait of Singapore eastward into the South China Sea. Although the ship's passage is not "continuous" because of the stoppage in Singapore, it still enjoys the right of transit passage by virtue of the exception.

Aircraft, Warships and Submarines

Under the 1958 Territorial Sea Convention, the regime of non-suspendable innocent passage through straits used for international navigation does not extend to the overflight of such straits by aircraft. Under the 1982 Convention, transit passage applies to both ships and aircraft. Article 38, paragraph 1, states, "all ships and aircraft enjoy the right of transit passage". Article 39 lays down the rights and duties of ships and aircraft during transit passage. Article 42 paragraph 5, refers to "the state of registry of an aircraft" and Article 44 refers to "any danger to navigation or overflight".

---

[106] 1982 Convention, *ante* note 1, Article 38, para. 2.
[107] *Ibid.*

The fact that the regime of transit passage applies to warships is also clear beyond dispute. Article 38 states that "all ships" enjoy the right of transit passage. The clearest evidence is in Article 42, paragraph 5, which refers to ships entitled to sovereign immunity.

Under the 1958 Territorial Sea Convention, submarines must navigate on the surface and show their flag. Does the regime of transit passage include the submerged passage of submarines? An interesting and learned disputation on this question has taken place among four American legal scholars. William T Burke,[108] John Norton Moore[109] and Horace B Robertson Jr[110] have argued that transit passage includes the submerged passage of submarines, whereas Michael Reisman[111] has taken the position that the provisions of the Convention are ambiguous and can be interpreted to exclude such passage.

The conclusion that submarines may transit straits used for international navigation in submerged passage is not explicitly stated in the text but has to be derived from the text by way of interpretation. The conclusion was, however, agreed by the negotiators and the text was intended to convey that meaning. Article 38, paragraph 2 uses the term "freedom of navigation" when defining transit passage. The expression "freedom of navigation" is a term of art. It is used in Article 87 of the Convention dealing with the freedom of the high seas. The term was used in Article 2 of the 1958 Convention on the High Seas.[112]

---

[108] *Supra* note 93.

[109] *Supra* note 90.

[110] H Robertson, "Passage Through International Straits: A Right Preserved in the Third UN Conference on the Law of the Sea," (1980) 20 Va J. Int'l L. 801.

[111] *Supra* note 90.

[112] *Supra* note 75.

The term was deliberately chosen for use in the straits articles and none of the negotiators ever argued seriously that it was meant to exclude submerged transit. Secondly, the phrase "their normal modes of continuous and expeditious transit" in Article 39, paragraph 1(c) was also understood by the negotiators to cover submerged passage by submarines. It is, after all, undeniable that submerged transit is a "normal mode" of transit for submarines.

Rights and Duties of Strait States

What are the rights of strait States relating to transit passage? Subject to the provisions of Section 2 of Part III of the Convention, strait States have the right to adopt laws and regulations in respect of four matters. First, in respect of the safety of navigation and the regulation of maritime traffic. The power of strait States to adopt laws and regulations in respect of the safety of navigation and the regulation of maritime traffic is, however, severely circumscribed. It can only be exercised as provided in Article 41 of the Convention. Article 41 permits strait States to designate sea lanes and prescribe traffic separation schemes where it is necessary to promote the safe passage of ships. In doing this, strait States must observe two conditions. The sea lanes and traffic separation schemes must "conform to generally accepted international regulations".[113] The sea lanes and traffic separation schemes must be submitted to and adopted by the relevant international organisation which, in this case, is the International Maritime Organization (IMO), before the strait States can designate or prescribe them. The strait States, therefore, cannot designate sea lanes or prescribe traffic separation schemes until

---

[113] 1982 Convention, *ante* note 1, Article 41, para. 3.

they have been adopted by the IMO. On the other hand, the IMO cannot adopt sea lanes and traffic separation schemes without the agreement of the strait States. There is, therefore, a balance between the interests of the strait States and those of the international community which has been built into the decision-making process.

In the case of a strait where the sea lanes or traffic separation schemes pass through the waters of two or more strait States, they shall cooperate in formulating proposed sea lanes and traffic separation schemes in consultation with the IMO.[114] The Straits of Malacca and Singapore are examples of such a case. The three strait States, Indonesia, Malaysia and Singapore have acted in accordance with Article 41, paragraph 5, by cooperating with one another, by consulting IMO, and even, consulting the major user States. The IMO has adopted the proposals of the three strait States to maintain a single, under-keel clearance of 3.5 metres, to prescribe traffic separation schemes in three critical areas and to designate a sea lane in the Strait of Singapore for ships whose draught exceeds 15 metres.[115]

The second matter on which strait States may adopt laws and regulations is the prevention, reduction and control of pollution.[116] This power of the strait States is also limited. It is limited in two ways. The laws and regulations can only deal with "the discharge of oil, oily wastes and other noxious substances in the strait" and not other kinds of pollutants. The laws and regulations of the strait States must give effect to applicable international regulations. What this seems to say is that the strait State

---

[114] *Ibid.*, Article 41, para. 5.

[115] The relevant documents are contained in KL Koh, *Straits in International Navigation* (1982), Appendix A, B and C.

[116] 1982 Convention, *ante* note 1, Article 42, para. 1(b).

cannot adopt laws and regulations if there were no applicable international standards and the laws and regulations must neither exceed nor be below the applicable international standards.

If a foreign ship violates the laws and regulations, properly adopted by a strait State, on the safety of navigation and the regulation of maritime traffic or the prevention, reduction and control of pollution, can the strait State take enforcement measures against the foreign ship? According to Article 233, the strait State can only take enforcement action against the foreign ship if the violation of its laws and regulations causes or threatens to cause major damage to the marine environment of the strait. In taking appropriate enforcement measures against the foreign ship, the strait State must observe the safeguards contained in Section 7 of Part XII of the Convention on Protection and Preservation of the Marine Environment. No enforcement measures can be taken against warships and other ships which enjoy sovereign immunity.[117]

The third matter on which strait States may adopt laws and regulations is with respect to fishing vessels, the prevention of fishing, including the stowage of fishing gear.[118] The fourth matter is the loading or unloading of any commodity, currency or person in contravention of the custom, fiscal, immigration or sanitary laws and regulations of strait States.[119]

These are the only rights and powers which Part III of the Convention confers on strait States. What duties or obligations does the Convention impose on strait States?

---

[117] *Ibid.*, Article 233 and 236.

[118] *Ibid.*, Article 43, para. 1(c).

[119] *Ibid.*, Article 43, para. 1(d).

The first duty of strait States is not to suspend, hamper or impede transit passage.[120] The second duty of strait States is to give appropriate publicity to any danger to navigation or over-flight within or over the strait of which they have knowledge.[121] The third duty of strait States is to indicate clearly all sea lanes and traffic separation schemes designated or prescribed by them, pursuant to Articles 41 and 42, paragraph 1(a), on charts and to give due publicity to such charts.[122] The fourth duty of strait States is not to discriminate among foreign ships, in form or in fact, in the adoption and application of the laws and regulations referred to in Article 42, paragraph 1, which would have the practical effect of denying, hampering or impairing the right of transit passage.[123] The fifth duty of strait States is to give due publicity to all the laws and regulations adopted pursuant to Article 42, paragraph 1.[124]

Duties of Ships and Aircraft during Transit Passage

What are the duties of ships and aircraft during transit passage? Article 39 of the Convention imposes four duties common to ships and aircraft. In addition, the article imposes two duties on ships and two on aircraft. What are the four duties shared in common by ships and aircraft during transit passage? The first duty is to proceed without delay through or over the strait.[125] This duty flows logically from the requirement of continuous

---

[120] *Ibid.*, Article 44 and 38.

[121] *Ibid.*, Article 44.

[122] *Ibid.*, Article 41, para. 6.

[123] *Ibid.*, Article 42, para. 2.

[124] *Ibid.*, Article 42, para. 3.

[125] *Ibid.*, Article 39, para. 1(a)

and expeditious transit in the definition of transit passage.[126] The second duty is to "refrain from any threat or use of force against the sovereignty, territorial integrity or political independence of States bordering the strait, or in any other manner in violation of the principles of international law embodied in the Charter of the United Nations."[127] The second duty is a mere restatement of one of the duties which the United Nations Charter imposes on all member States. The third duty is to "refrain from any activities other than those incident to their normal modes of continuous and expeditious transit unless rendered necessary by *force majeure* or by distress."[128] Under this duty, the conduct of activities such as naval exercises or weapons practices would be forbidden.

The fourth duty of ships and aircraft in transit passage is to comply with other relevant provisions of Part III of the Convention. There do not appear to be other provisions in Part III which impose duties on aircraft. There are three provisions in Part III which are relevant to ships. Article 40 states that ships in transit passage may not carry out marine scientific research or hydrographic surveys without prior authorisation of the strait State. Article 41, paragraph 7, states that ships in transit passage shall respect applicable sea lanes and traffic separation schemes established in accordance with that article. Finally, Article 42, paragraph 4, requires ships in transit passage to comply with the laws and regulations adopted by strait States, pursuant to that article.

In addition to the four duties that Article 39 imposes on both ships and aircraft, the article imposes two separate duties

---

[126] *Ibid.*, Article 38, para. 2.

[127] *Ibid.*, Article 39, para. 1(b).

[128] *Ibid.*, Article 39, para. 1(c).

on ships and two others on aircraft. Therefore, the fifth duty of ships in transit passage is to comply with generally accepted international regulations, procedures and practices for safety at sea, including the International Regulations for Preventing Collisions at Sea.[129] The sixth duty of ships in transit passage is to comply with generally accepted international regulations, procedures and practices for the prevention, reduction and control of pollution from ships.[130]

The fifth duty of aircraft in transit passage is to observe the Rules of Air established by the International Civil Aviation Organization.[131] If the aircraft is a State aircraft, it will normally comply with such safety measures and will, at all times, operate with due regard for the safety of navigation. The sixth duty of aircraft in transit passage is to monitor, at all times, the radio frequency assigned by the competent internationally designated air traffic control authority or the appropriate international distress radio frequency.[132]

How the Straits Provisions were Negotiated

The negotiation on the regime for passage of ships and aircraft through, over and under straits used for international navigation began in 1971 during the preparatory stage in the United Nations Seabed Committee. During the summer 1971 session of the Committee's meeting, the US submitted draft articles on the breadth of the territorial sea, passage through straits and

---

[129] *Ibid.*, Article 39, para. 2(a).
[130] *Ibid.*, Article 39, para. 2(b).
[131] *Ibid.*, Article 39, para. 3(a).
[132] *Ibid.*, Article 39, para. 3(b).

fisheries.[133] In 1971, the USSR submitted its proposals which were rather similar to those of the US.[134] In 1973, the last year of the preparatory stage before the commencement of the Conference, about 50 proposals were submitted.[135] The two most important proposals were those submitted by Fiji,[136] and by a group of strait States, *viz.* Cyprus, Greece, Indonesia, Malaysia, Morocco, Philippines, Spain and Yemen.[137] Because of the contradictions between the various proposals, the Seabed Committee was unable to produce a single draft text for the consideration of the Third United Nations Conference. All that the Committee succeeded in doing was to reduce the number of variants to a more manageable number.

The second session of the Third United Nations Conference, held in Caracas in 1974, devoted six sessions to the discussion on the straits issue. A number of proposals were submitted to the Second Committee of the Conference. The most important of these were submitted by the UK,[138] the USSR and its East

---

[133] Report of the Committee on the Peaceful Uses of the Seabed and the Ocean Floor Beyond the Limits of National Jurisdiction, UN Gen. Ass Off. Rec., 26th Sess. (1971), Supp. No. 21, pp. 241–245 (UN Doc. A/8421).

[134] Report of the Committee on the Peaceful Uses of the Seabed and the Ocean Floor Beyond the Limits of National Jurisdiction, UN Gen. Ass. Off. Rec., 27th Sess. (1972), Supp. No. 21, pp. 161–163 (UN Doc. A/8721).

[135] Report of the Committee on the Peaceful Uses of the Seabed and the Ocean Floor Beyond the Limits of National Jurisdiction, UN Gen. Ass. Off. Rec., 28th Sess. (1973), Supp. No. 21, Vol. I, pp. 40, 61–66 (UN Doc. A/9021).

[136] *Ibid.*, Vol. III, p. 91.

[137] *Ibid.*, Vol. III, p. 3.

[138] UN Doc. A/CONF.62/C.2/L.3, Third UN Conference on the Law of the Sea, Off. Rec., Vol. III, (2nd Sess., 1974) p. 91.

European allies,[139] Denmark and Finland,[140] Oman,[141] Fiji,[142] and Algeria.[143] The British proposal was the one which contained the novel concept of "transit passage" through straits used for international navigation. Views were still too divergent at that stage and the session concluded without the adoption of any draft text. The Chairman of the Second Committee, in summing up the work of the session, stated that the idea of a territorial sea of 12 miles and an exclusive economic zone of up to 200 miles was a keystone of the compromise solution favoured by the majority of States, provided satisfactory solutions could be found to other issues, one of which being the issue of passage through straits used for international navigation.[144]

The straits issue was substantially resolved at the third session of the Conference, held in Geneva in 1975. It was one of the first, if not the first issue to be resolved. This was a remarkable feat given the intrinsic difficulty of the question, the divergent views held by different delegations and groups of delegations and the strong feelings held by the two superpowers, on the one hand, and some of the strait States on the other. How was this negotiating feat accomplished? It was accomplished as a result of an initiative taken jointly by Fiji and the UK. Those two delegations co-chaired a small, private and informal negotiating group on straits. They were not authorised by the Conference to convene such a group and the group's composition was

---

[139] UN Doc. A/CONF.62/C.2/L.11, *ibid.*, p. 183.
[140] UN Doc. A/CONF.62/C.2/L.15, *ibid.*, p. 191.
[141] UN Doc. A/CONF.62/C.2/L.16, *ibid.*, p. 192.
[142] UN Doc. A/CONF.62/C.2/L.19, *ibid.*, p. 196.
[143] UN Doc. A/CONF.62/C.2/L.20, *ibid.*, p. 198.
[144] UN Doc. A/CONF.62/C.2/L.86, *ibid.*, p. 243.

determined by the co-chairmen and not by the Conference. In addition to the two co-chairmen, the group consisted of the following 13 countries: Argentina, Australia, Bahrain, Bulgaria, Denmark, Iceland, India, Italy, Kenya, Nigeria, Singapore, United Arab Emirates and Venezuela.

On what bases did the co-chairmen compose the group? The co-chairmen excluded the two superpowers, on the one hand, and the radical strait States, on the other, probably on the ground that their views were too extreme. The British Chairman, Harry Dudgeon, no doubt, kept in touch with the US and the USSR, and the Fijian chairman, Satya Nandan, kept in touch with the strait States. Those invited to attend were probably selected because they held moderate views and because they were influential delegations in the politics of the Conference. When the existence of the group became known, the radical strait States criticised the composition of the group on the ground that the UK's interests on straits were identical to those of the US and USSR whereas the point of view of the radical strait States were not represented in the group. The group used the proposals of Fiji and the UK as the bases of their negotiations. Because the group had no official status in the Conference, it had no access to the Conference facilities. It is perhaps ironic that one of the most successful negotiating groups of the Conference held all its meetings in one of the delegates' lounges at the United Nations in Geneva!

The group succeeded in producing a consensus text on straits before the end of the 1975 Geneva session. The co-chairmen submitted the draft articles to the then Chairman of the Second Committee, Galindo Pohl. That was the session during which the Conference requested the chairmen of the three main committees to produce an Informal Single Negotiating Text. Galindo Pohl included, without any change, the draft articles on straits worked out in the private group on straits.[145] The draft articles initially received a cold reception by many of the strait States but the attitude of most of them changed with the passing years. Although the Informal Single Negotiating Text was to undergo six transformations before being adopted as the 1982 Convention, the articles on straits used for international navigation, prepared by the private group on straits in 1975, survived those transformations and repeated challenges by radical strait States, practically intact. The first successful use of a private group to negotiate a difficult issue created a procedural precedent which would be followed later.

Transit Passage Compared with the Pre-Existing Law

Under the pre-existing law, whether conventional law as contained in the 1958 Territorial Sea Convention or customary law as reflected in the judgement of the International Court of Justice in the *Corfu Channel Case*, the passage regime through straits used for international navigation, was non-suspendable innocent passage. Under the 1958 Territorial Sea Convention, the passage regime did not include overflight by aircraft and submarines had to navigate on the surface and show their flag.

Under the 1982 Convention, the regime for passage through, over and under straits used for international navigation has been clearly distinguished from the regime of innocent passage through the territorial sea. Transit passage includes overflight by aircraft and submerged passage by submarines. There is to be no discrimination against military vessels or aircraft. The strait States'

---

[145] A/CONF.62/WP.8/PART II, Third UN Conference on the Law of the Sea, Off. Rec., Vol. IV (1975), p. 152.

regulatory competence, to protect the safety of navigation, the marine environment and the security of the strait States, are carefully circumscribed and balanced against the world community's interest in the freedom of navigation. The right of transit passage is not subject to suspension, impairment or impediment by the strait State on the ground that the passage is not "innocent" or on the basis of any subjective criteria.

The Importance of Transit Passage to the Great Powers

The great military powers, especially the US and the USSR, have identical strategic interests in ocean space and the air space above it. Reflecting this fact, the delegations of the US and the USSR were able to work in unison, in pursuing their common strategic interests, on the straits issue. On the whole, representatives of the two superpowers are satisfied with the provisions of the 1982 Convention. Elliot Richardson, the leader of the US delegation from 1977 to 1980 has written that, "our fleet of missile ballistic submarines ... depend on complete mobility in the oceans and unimpeded passage through international straits. Only such freedom makes possible the secrecy on which their survival is based."[146] He has also said that, "the transit passage regime will satisfactorily protect and enhance the legal regime in straits that is essential for the continued mobility and flexibility of air and naval forces."[147]

---

[146] E Richardson, "Power, Mobility and the Law of the Sea," (1980) 58 Foreign Affairs 902 at p. 905.
[147] E Richardson, "Law of the Sea: Navigational and other Traditional National Security Considerations," (1982) Vol. 19, No. 3, San Diego L. Rev. 554 at pp. 565 & 566.

Archipelagic States

What is an archipelago? The 1982 Convention defines an archipelago as "a group of islands, including ports of islands, interconnecting waters and other natural features which are so closely inter-related that such islands, waters and other natural features form an intrinsic geographical, economic and political entity, or which historically have been regarded as such."[148] According to this definition, not every group of islands constitutes an archipelago. To qualify as an archipelago, a group of islands must satisfy one of two criteria. First, the islands and the interconnecting waters must be so closely inter-related as to form an intrinsic geographical, economic and political entity. Second, the islands have, historically, been regarded as constituting an archipelago.

What is an archipelagic State? The 1982 Convention defines an archipelagic State as "a State constituted wholly by one or more archipelagos and may include other islands".[149] It follows from this definition that whilst every archipelagic State is an archipelago, not every archipelago is an archipelagic State. An archipelago, such as Hawaii, which belongs to a continental State, the USA, is obviously not an archipelagic State.

Nature of Claim Made in Respect of Archipelagos

In the case of a single island, a territorial sea would be drawn around it. In the case of an archipelago, the claim made was to replace the normal method of drawing a territorial sea around

---

[148] 1982 Convention, *ante* note 1, Article 46, para. (b).

[149] *Ibid.*, Article 46, para. (a).

each island by applying the system of drawing straight baselines. The proposal was to draw straight baselines connecting the outermost points of the outermost islands of the archipelago. The territorial sea would be measured from such baselines. The claim made no distinction between archipelagic States and archipelagos belonging to continental States.

The Position of Archipelagos Under the Pre-Existing Law

What is the position of archipelagos under the pre-existing law? At the First United Nations Conference, the Philippines[150] and Yugoslavia[151] raised the question but the Conference did not take it up, arguing that it required more study. At the Second United Nations Conference, both the Philippines[152] and Indonesia[153] urged the Conference to recognise their status as archipelagic States. Because the Philippines based its case on historical grounds, the Conference decided it was inopportune to discuss the matter since the United Nations General Assembly had decided to embark upon a special study of historic waters.[154] The 1958 Territorial Sea Convention contains no provision which specifically refers to archipelagos or archipelagic States. There is, therefore, nothing in the pre-existing conventional law on archipelagos.

---

[150] UN Doc. A/CONF.13/C.1/L.98, First UN Conference on the Law of the Sea, Off. Rec., Vol. III, (1958) p. 239.

[151] UN Doc. A/CONF.13/C.1/L.59, *ibid.*, p. 227.

[152] Second UN Conference on the Law of the Sea, Off. Rec., Vol. III (1960), pp. 51–52.

[153] *Ibid.*, pp. 93–94.

[154] *Ibid.*, p. 151.

The position under customary law is less clear. The trend towards the recognition of the concept of archipelagic States was spearheaded by Indonesia and the Philippines. In 1955, the Philippines sent a note verbale to the Secretary-General of the United Nations,[155] claiming exclusive rights over the waters within the coordinates of the Treaty of Paris of 1898. By the Treaty of Paris and another treaty concluded in 1900, Spain ceded the Philippines to the US. The said treaties defined the Philippines by reference to geographical coordinates which, according to the Filipino view, involved the cession of maritime, as well as land territory. The note verbale was followed by the enactment of national legislation in 1961,[156] which described the waters enclosed by the strait baselines as inland waters. This legislation was protested against by the UK, US, Japan and Australia. In 1968, the Philippines required prior authorisation for the passage of warships through its inland waters, a move which met with further protests.

Indonesia followed the Philippines in adopting archipelagic baselines in 1957. On 14 December 1957, the Indonesian government issued a Declaration[157] stating that the geographical form of Indonesia, as a country composed of 13,000 islands, was unique; that in view of the territorial integrity and of the need to preserve the wealth of the Indonesian State, it was necessary to consider all the islands and seas between them as a

---

[155] Doc. A/CN.4/99 (1956) 2 Y.B.I.L.C. 69–70.

[156] Republic Act No. 3046, which was amended in 1968 by Act No. 5446.

[157] An English translation of the Indonesian text was published in the *Hukum* (Indonesian Law Journal) (1958), Nos. 5–6, Annex I. This text is reprinted in JJG Syatauw, *Some Newly Established Asian States and the Development of International Law* (1961) at pp. 173–174.

unit. The Declaration guaranteed the peaceful passage of foreign vessels through the waters enclosed by the islands so long as the passage was not contrary or harmful to the sovereignty of Indonesia. The 12-mile territorial sea would be measured from the straight baselines connecting the outermost parts of the islands. In spite of protests by Australia, France, the US, UK, Japan, New Zealand and the Netherlands, the Indonesian government enacted national legislation[158] on 18 February 1960, to strengthen its claim. Under Indonesian law, foreign warships are required to give notice unless they follow the normal shipping routes and submarines are required to navigate on the surface.

Why were the major maritime nations opposed to the claims of Indonesia and the Philippines? They were opposed because in some cases, the waters over which archipelagic status was claimed, for example the Java Sea, was not only vast in area but covered important straits and navigation and overflight routes, for example, the Sunda strait and the Lombok strait, critical to the movement of their military forces.

How was the Question Successfully Negotiated?

There were two groups of claimant States at the Third United Nations Conference on this question. There were, first of all, the archipelagic States, such as, Indonesia, Philippines, Fiji, Mauritius and Bahamas. Secondly, there were the continental States that owned archipelagos, such as India and Greece. Although the two groups cooperated with each other, the first group realised, very early in the Conference, that the claim of

---

[158] Indonesia Act No. 4 of 18 February 1960. An English text of the Act was published in UN Doc A/CONF.19/5 Add. 1, p. 3 (1960). This document is also reprinted in Syatauw, *ibid.*, at pp. 175–176.

the second group was unlikely to win wide acceptance. Hence, the five abovementioned archipelagic States formed a group of their own to further their common interests. In order to gain leverage, they joined the 86-member group of coastal States, thus securing the support of approximately two-thirds of the members of the Conference. The archipelagic States had to negotiate their claim with the great maritime powers, especially the US and the USSR, and with some of the neighbours of the archipelagic States whose interests were adversely affected by the establishment of archipelagic baselines.

It will be recalled that in the case of passage through straits used for international navigation, a private negotiating group was convened by Fiji and the UK. In the case of archipelagos, no negotiating group was established. Instead, the Rapporteur of the Second committee, Satya Nandan, who was also the representative of Fiji, took it upon himself to negotiate a compromise text between the archipelagic States, on the one hand, and the major maritime powers and certain affected neighbouring States, on the other hand. This took place during the third session of the Conference held in 1975 in Geneva. By the end of that session, Nandan had succeeded in drafting a compromise text which was incorporated into the Informal Single Negotiating Text.[159] With only a few subsequent embellishments, the Nandan text has survived the test of time.

The Position Under the United Nations Convention

The 1982 Convention has accepted the claim of archipelagic States to draw straight baselines or "archipelagic baselines",

---

[159] *Supra,* note 145.

joining the outermost points of the outermost islands. The system of archipelagic baselines is not, however, applicable to archipelagos belonging to continental States. Thus, the islands of Hawaii,[160] the Nicobar and Andaman Islands, the Greek islands, amongst others, are not entitled to the system of archipelagic baselines.

Archipelagic Baselines

An archipelagic State may draw straight archipelagic baselines joining the outermost points of the outermost islands and drying reefs of the archipelago if four criteria can be satisfied. The first criterion is that the main islands of the archipelago must be included within such baselines.[161] The second criterion is that the area of water enclosed by such baselines must not be greater than nine times the area of land.[162] In other words, the ratio between the area of water and the area of land enclosed by such baselines must not exceed 9:1. If the ratio does exceed 9:1, then the archipelagic baselines must be redrawn in order to conform to the ratio. If this cannot be done, then the archipelagic State in question is not entitled to the system of straight archipelagic baselines under the Convention. For the purpose of calculating the area of land enclosed by archipelagic baselines, land includes atolls[163] and "waters lying within the fringing reefs of islands and atolls, including that part of a steep-sided oceanic plateau which

---

[160] "Archipelagoes and Archipelagic States under UNCLOS III: no special treatment for Hawaii," (1981) 4 Hastings Int'l & Comp. L. Rev. 509.

[161] 1982 Convention, *ante* note 1, Article 47, para. 1.

[162] *Ibid.*

[163] *Ibid.*

is enclosed or nearly enclosed by a chain of limestone islands and drying reefs lying of the perimeter of the plateau."[164]

The third criterion is that the length of archipelagic baselines shall not exceed 100 nautical miles.[165] There is an exception to this criterion. The exception is that 3 per cent of the baselines may be between 100 and 125 nautical miles.[166] If the baselines drawn by an archipelagic State do not satisfy this criterion either because more than 3 per cent of the total number of baselines exceed 100 miles or because some of the baselines exceed 125 miles, then, the baselines will have to be redrawn in order to conform to this criterion. If this cannot be achieved, then the archipelagic State in question is not entitled to the system of straight archipelagic baselines under the Convention. The fourth criterion is that the archipelagic baselines must not depart, to any appreciable extent, from the general configuration of the archipelago.[167]

An archipelagic State must show its baselines either on charts of a scale or scales adequate for ascertaining them or by listing their geographical coordinates.[168] The archipelagic State must give due publicity to such charts or lists of geographical coordinates and must deposit a copy with the Secretary-General of the United Nations.[169]

The breadth of the territorial sea, the contiguous zone the exclusive economic zone and the continental shelf shall be measured from the archipelagic baselines drawn in accordance

---

[164] *Ibid.*, Article 47, para. 7.

[165] *Ibid.*, Article 47, para. 2.

[166] *Ibid.*

[167] *Ibid.*, Article 47, para. 3.

[168] *Ibid.*, Article 47, para. 8.

[169] *Ibid.*, Article 47, para. 9.

with Article 47 of the Convention.[170] The waters enclosed by the archipelagic baselines are called archipelagic waters.[171]

Status of Archipelagic Waters

What is the status of archipelagic waters? It will be recalled that archipelagic waters are situated on the landward side of archipelagic baselines and archipelagic baselines are the baselines from which the territorial sea of an archipelagic State is measured. Normally the waters on the landward side of the baseline of the territorial sea are the internal waters of a State.[172] However, Article 8, paragraph 1 specifically provides that this proposition has an exception and the exception is in Part IV of the 1982 Convention dealing with archipelagic States. The implication that archipelagic waters generally do not constitute "internal waters" is confirmed by Article 50 which states, "Within its archipelagic waters, the archipelagic State may draw closing lines for the delimitation of internal waters, in accordance with Articles 9, 10 and 11." Article 9 deals with the drawing of a straight baseline across the mouth of a river; Article 10 deals with the drawing of straight baselines across the mouths of bays; and Article 11 deals with the problem posed by ports. The implication of Article 50 is clear: only the waters enclosed by the baselines drawn across the mouths of rivers and bays and the waters landward of the outermost permanent harbour works are the "internal waters" of an archipelagic State. It follows logically from the foregoing that archipelagic waters do not have the status of "internal waters".

---

[170] *Ibid.*, Article 48.

[171] *Ibid.*, Article 49, para. 1.

[172] *Ibid.*, Article 8, para. 1.

If archipelagic waters are not internal waters, what is their status? The Convention does not pin a label to describe the status of archipelagic waters. The Convention does, however, describe the rights and duties of archipelagic States and the rights and duties of the international community in archipelagic waters. The archipelagic State has sovereignty over its archipelagic waters, the air space above, the bed and subsoil and the resources contained therein.[173] The sovereignty which an archipelagic State enjoys over its archipelagic waters is, however, subject to two qualifications. The first qualification is that "Ships of all States enjoy the right of innocent passage through archipelagic waters."[174] In this respect, the status of archipelagic waters is similar to the status of the territorial sea because in both cases the sovereignty of the coastal State is subject to the right of innocent passage. Article 52, paragraph 2, permits an archipelagic State to suspend, temporarily, in specified areas of its archipelagic waters, the innocent passage of foreign ships if such suspension is essential for the protection of its security, and provided two conditions are met. First, the suspension must not discriminate, in form or in fact, among foreign ships.[175] Second, such suspension shall take effect only after having been duly published.[176]

Archipelagic Sea Lanes Passage

The second qualification to the sovereignty of archipelagic States over their archipelagic waters can be best explained by the following analogy. A strait State has sovereignty over its territorial

---

[173] *Ibid.*, Article 49, para. 1 and 2.
[174] *Ibid.*, Article 52, para. 1.
[175] *Ibid.*, Article 52, para. 2.
[176] *Ibid.*

sea. However, in the case of a strait used for international navigation, the sovereignty of the strait State over its territorial sea is qualified by the right of transit passage. Similarly, where routes normally used for international navigation traverse archipelagic waters, the sovereignty of the archipelagic State is qualified by the right of archipelagic sea lanes passage.[177] This was a concession that archipelagic States had to make in return for the support of the great maritime powers for the concept of archipelagic States.

What is archipelagic sea lanes passage? Archipelagic sea lanes passage is defined as "the exercise in accordance with this Convention of the rights of navigation and overflight in the normal mode solely for the purpose of continuous, expeditious and unobstructed transit between one part of the high seas or an exclusive economic zone and another part of the high sea or an exclusive economic zone."[178] The right of archipelagic sea lanes passage includes the right of overflight by civilian and State aircraft.[179] It also includes submerged passage by submarines.[180]

Where can the right of archipelagic sea lanes passage be exercised? If an archipelagic State designates sea lanes and air routes there above, suitable for the continuous and expeditious passage of foreign ships and aircraft through or over its archipelagic waters and the adjacent territorial sea, the right must be exercised in such sea lanes and air routes.[181] If the archipelagic

---

[177] *Ibid.*, Article 53.

[178] *Ibid.*, Article 53, para. 3.

[179] *Ibid.*, Article 53, para. 1, 2, 3, 4, 5, 12; Article 54.

[180] This conclusion is derived from textual construction. The argument is similar to that in the case of transit passage through straits used for international navigation.

[181] 1982 Convention, *ante* note 1, Article 53, para.1.

State does not designate such sea lanes and air routes, the right may be exercised through the routes normally used for international navigation.[182]

If an archipelagic State wishes to designate sea lanes and air routes, are there any criteria it must comply with? The 1982 Convention prescribes several criteria. First, the sea lanes and air routes must traverse the archipelagic waters and the adjacent territorial sea.[183] Second, the sea lanes and air routes shall include all normal passage routes used as routes for international navigation and overflight through or over archipelagic waters.[184] In the case of ships, the routes shall include all normal navigational channels. The third criterion is an extremely difficult one to explain. Article 53 paragraph 5, states that sea lanes and air routes shall be defined by a series of continuous axis lines from the entry points of passage routes to the exit points and that ships and aircraft in archipelagic sea lanes passage shall not deviate more than 25 nautical miles to either side of such axis lines during passage. There is also a proviso that ships and aircraft shall not navigate closer to the coasts than 10 per cent of the distance between the nearest points on the islands bordering the sea lane. Figure 3 may help to explain this complex rule. The figure shows a sea lane bounded by two islands, A and B. CD is the axis line. The dotted lines on either side of CD are 25 nautical miles away from the axis lines. Ships and aircraft in archipelagic sea lanes passage may travel within the two dotted lines, which is 50 nautical miles wide. Suppose that the distance between the nearest points on islands A and B is 100 miles.

---

[182] *Ibid.*, Article 53, para. 12.

[183] *Ibid.*, Article 53, para. 4.

[184] *Ibid.*

Ships and aircraft shall not navigate closer than 10 nautical miles of the coasts of islands A and B.

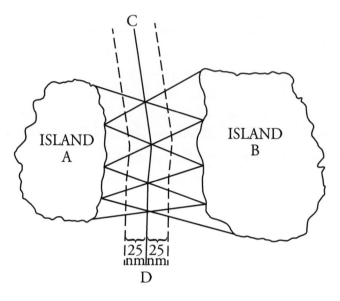

Figure 3

An archipelagic State that designates sea lanes may also prescribe traffic separation schemes for the safe passage of ships through narrow channels in such sea lanes.[185] Such sea lanes and traffic separation schemes shall conform to generally accepted international regulations.[186] Before such sea lanes and traffic separation schemes can be designated and prescribed respectively, they must first be adopted by the International Maritime Organization.[187] The archipelagic State shall clearly indicate the

---

[185] *Ibid.*, Article 53, para. 6.
[186] *Ibid.*, Article 53, para. 8.
[187] *Ibid.*, Article 53, para. 9.

axis of the sea lanes and the traffic separation schemes designated or prescribed by it on charts to which publicity shall be given.[188]

The rights and duties of strait States and the rights and duties of foreign ships and aircraft in transit passage, as contained in Articles 39, 40, 42 and 44 apply, *mutatis mutandis*, to archipelagic sea lanes passage.[189]

Accommodating Interests of Archipelagic States and Their Neighbours

The establishment of archipelagic waters, in some cases, adversely affects the rights and interests of the States immediately adjacent to the archipelagic States. Negotiations were therefore held between the archipelagic States in question and the affected neighbouring States. The negotiations were successfully concluded with the adoption of three provisions. First, Article 47, paragraph 5, says that the system of archipelagic baselines shall not be applied by an archipelagic State in such a manner as to cut off from the high seas or the exclusive economic zone, the territorial sea of another State. Second, Article 47, paragraph 6, says that if a part of the archipelagic waters of an archipelagic State lies between two parts of an immediately adjacent neighbouring State, existing rights and all other legitimate interests which the latter State has traditionally exercised in such waters and all rights stipulated by agreement between those States shall continue and be respected. An example of a situation to which Article 47, paragraph 6, applies in the case of Indonesia and Malaysia. A part

---

[188] *Ibid.*, Article 53, para. 10.
[189] *Ibid.*, Article 54.

of the archipelagic waters of Indonesia lies between East and West Malaysia.

Third, Article 51 says that an archipelagic State shall respect existing agreements with other States and shall recognise traditional fishing rights and other legitimate activities of the immediately adjacent neighbouring States in certain areas falling within archipelagic waters. The proposition that archipelagic States shall respect existing agreements with other States is axiomatic and needs no explanation. The second limb of the sentence can be illustrated by the following example. If Malaysia and Singapore, two immediately adjacent neighbouring States of Indonesia, can show that their fishermen have traditionally fished in certain areas of Indonesian archipelagic waters, Indonesia must recognise such traditional fishing rights. The rights of the immediately adjacent neighbouring States include "other legitimate activities", a some-what imprecise category, meant to accommodate Singapore's existing rights in Indonesia's archipelagic waters.

The terms and conditions for the exercise of such rights, including the nature, the extent and the areas to which they apply, shall be regulated by bilateral agreements between archipelagic States and their immediately adjacent neighbouring States. Such rights shall not be transferred to or shared with third States or their nationals.

The Convention also provides that archipelagic States shall respect existing submarine cables laid by other States and passing through its waters without making a landfall.[190] An archipelagic State shall permit the maintenance and replacement of such cables upon receiving due notice of their location and the intention to repair or replace them.

---

[190] *Ibid.*, Article 51, para. 2.

The New Passage Regimes and States Not Parties to the 1982 Convention

In the late 1960s, the primary interest of the US in convening a new conference on the law of the sea was to secure international agreement on navigational and overflight rights. In the face of unilateral claims by coastal States to extend their territorial seas from three to twelve miles, thereby abolishing the high seas corridor in 116 straits used for international navigation, and in the face of claims by archipelagic States such as the Philippines and Indonesia, the US felt the need for a new international legal consensus concerning the maximum breadth of the territorial sea, concerning a special regime of passage for ships, including submarines and aircraft through, under and over straits used for international navigation and through archipelagic waters.

The provisions of the 1982 Convention have strengthened the regime of innocent passage through the territorial sea compared to the corresponding provisions in the 1958 Territorial Sea Convention.[191] The 1982 Convention contains special regimes of passage through straits used for international navigation and archipelagic waters. The US government has decided not to become a party to the 1982 Convention. The question that arises is whether the US could stay outside the Convention and yet enjoy the special regimes of passage through straits and archipelagos.

Representatives of the US government have argued that it could stay outside the Convention and enjoy the regimes of transit passage and archipelagic sea lanes passage on the ground that they are not new law but are customary international law

---

[191] Moore, *ante* note 90.

or evidence of the emerging customary law.[192] At the meeting of the Conference, on 30 April 1982, the Chairman of the Group of 77 stated that no rights could accrue to States that were not parties to the Convention. He argued that the rights in the Convention were contractual in nature, that they were not customary law and that States had no right to pick and choose among the provisions of the Convention, taking those they like and rejecting the rest.[193] In his closing statement to the Conference, on 10 December 1982, the President of the Conference said:

> This Convention is not a codification Convention. The argument that, except for Part XI, the Convention codifies customary law or reflects existing international practice is factually incorrect and legally insupportable. The regime of transit passage through Straits used for international naviga-tion and the regime of archipelagic sea lanes passage are two examples of the many new concepts in the Convention.[194]

The question of when a rule in a Convention becomes part of the general international law was dealt with in the judgement of the International Court of Justice in the *North Sea Continental Shelf Case*.[195] The Court said that it could do so in three circum-stances. First, when the rule in the Convention merely codifies

---

[192] Statement of Brian Hoyle, Director of the Office of Oceans Law and Policy in the US State Department, at a Workshop of the Law of the Sea Institute in January 1984 in Hawaii, J Van Dyke (editor), *Consensus and Confrontation: The United States and the Law of the Sea Convention* (1985), pp. 292–293.

[193] Third UN Conference on the Law of the Sea, Off. Rec., Vol. XVII, (Resumed 11th Sess., 1982), 183rd Meeting, p. 3.

[194] *Ibid.*, 193rd Meeting, pp. 135–136.

[195] I.C.J. Rep. 1969, p. 1.

the pre-existing law. Second, when the rule in the Convention reflects the emerging customary law. Third, when the subsequent practice of States subsumes a rule of law in a Convention into the body of general international law. Using this analytical tool, we can proceed to examine the provisions of the new Convention on passage rights.

In the case of the regime of innocent passage through the territorial sea, although the Convention makes some improvements to the regime, as contained in the 1958 Territorial Sea Convention, it is probably correct to say that this aspect of the Convention satisfies the first and second criteria in the *North Sea Continental Shelf Case*. Therefore, a State that stays outside the Convention may, nevertheless, invoke the provisions of the Convention on innocent passage through the territorial sea.

In the cases of transit passage through straits used for international navigation and archipelagic sea lanes passage through archipelagic waters, the position is more doubtful. Under the 1958 Territorial Sea Convention, the regime of passage for ships (not aircraft) through straits formed by territorial sea is non-suspendable innocent passage. The regime excluded the submerged passage of submarines. The provisions of the new Convention on transit passage were the result of intensive negotiations among the parties and reflect a *quid pro quo*. In view of this, it is difficult to argue convincingly that it satisfies either the first or the second criteria. However, with the passage of time, and if the Convention is ratified by a large number of States, the third criterion could be satisfied and non-parties to the Convention, such as the US, would then enjoy the benefits of a free ride. This reasoning applies equally to archipelagic sea lanes passage.

The answer to the question, whether a non-party to the Convention, could enjoy the benefit of the Convention's provisions on transit passage and archipelagic sea lanes passage, is, to put it mildly, unclear. In practice, strait States and archipelagic States may apply the rules of the Convention uniformly, not differentiating between States which are parties to the Convention and those which are not. If this were the case, the non-parties would not be faced with any problem. However, one cannot exclude the possibility of a dispute arising between a non-party such as the US and a strait State or an archipelagic State over the assertion by the US of the right of transit passage or archipelagic sea lanes passage. The dispute could take place with countries that are generally friendly to the US. Spain and Indonesia, for example, have declared that they did not regard the regimes of transit passage and archipelagic sea lanes passage, respectively, as conforming to customary international law. It would be impolitic for the US to use force against such friendly countries. When force has to be used, it is surely better to use it with the law on your side than to do so with the law on the side of your adversary or in the context of legal uncertainty. The US may also find itself confronted by demands by some strait States and archipelagic States for the conclusion of bilateral agreements to regulate the passage of US ships, including submarines, and aircraft through, under and over critical sea lanes. Such bilateral agreements could be costly and would provide less security and certainty for the US than a widely accepted multilateral treaty.

The Exclusive
Economic Zone

In the previous article, we learnt that under the 1982 Convention,[1] every coastal State is entitled to claim a territorial sea and a contiguous zone and that their maximum permissible breadths are 12 and 24 nautical miles respectively. Under Part V of the Convention, every coastal State is entitled to claim an exclusive economic zone (EEZ). It is an area of the sea beyond and adjacent to the territorial sea.[2] The maximum permissible breadth of the EEZ is 200 nautical miles from the baselines from which the breadth of the territorial sea is measured or 188 miles from the outer limit of a 12-mile territorial sea.[3] If the coastal State has claimed a 12-mile contiguous zone, it will overlap with the EEZ.

---

[1] The Convention was adopted on 30 April 1982. The text is contained in U.N. Doc. A/CONF. 62/122, 7 October 1982, and is reprinted in 21 I.L.M. 1245 (1982).

[2] *Ibid.*, Article 55.

[3] *Ibid.*, Article 57.

The Genesis of the Exclusive Economic Zone

The EEZ is the result of two recent developments in the relations between coastal States and distant-water fishing States. The first development took place in the relationship between developed coastal States and distant-water fishing States; the second, between developing coastal States and distant-water fishing States.

Developed Coastal States and Distant-Water Fishing States

Following the failure of the Second United Nations Conference on the Law of the Sea in 1960 to agree on the limit of the exclusive fishing rights of coastal States, a number of developed coastal States resorted to national legislation to establish a nine-mile exclusive fishing zone beyond their three-mile territorial sea.[4] The first country to take this step was Iceland. The British and the French protested against Iceland's action. The dispute between Iceland and the United Kingdom led to the famous Cod War during which units of the British navy were sent to protect British trawlers against attempts by Iceland to enforce its legislation beyond the three-mile limit. The UK had to withdraw its naval escort when the crisis in the bilateral relationship between the UK and Iceland threatened the unity of NATO. The crisis was eventually resolved by an agreement between the two governments.[5] The UK agreed to respect Iceland's new

---

[4] For a brief description of the Second Conference, see the first article in the Malaya Law Review series on the evolution of the law of the sea, (1987) 29 Mal. L.R. 1 at pp. 13–14.

[5] Exchange of Notes Constituting an Agreement Settling the Fisheries Dispute between the Government of Iceland and the Government of the United Kingdom of Great Britain and Northern Ireland, 11 March 1961, 397 U.N.T.S. 275.

fishing limit in return for Iceland's agreement to phase out the British trawlers over a period of three years. It was also agreed that any dispute concerning the extension of fishing limits could be submitted to the International Court of Justice.

In 1962, the Fame Islands, which belong to Denmark, followed Iceland's example and established a 12-mile exclusive economic zone. In 1964, Ireland[6] and Canada[7] also established such zones. There was, however, an important difference between the Canadian and Irish legislation. The Canadian laws recognised the traditional fishing rights of eight distant-water fishing States and sought to accommodate them through bilateral negotiations. The Irish legislation did not do so. Nor did it contain a phasing out provision. New Zealand[8] in 1965, Australia[9] and Spain[10] in 1967, enacted national legislation extending their exclusive fishing zones to 12 miles. The legislation of all three countries contained provisions for phasing out the traditional rights of distant-water fishing States over a specified period of time.

United States

Until 1966, the United States had refused to recognise any national fishery legislation purporting to have effect beyond

---

[6] Maritime Jurisdiction (Amendment) Act, 1964 (No. 3 of 1964), reprinted in United Nations Legislative Series, *National Legislation and Treaties Relating to the Territorial Sea, the Contiguous Zone, the Continental Shelf, the High Seas and to Fishing and Conservation of Living Resources of the Sea* (1970), UN Doc. ST/LEG/SER.B15, at p. 641.

[7] Territorial Sea and Fishing Zones Act, 1964, Statutes of Canada, Ch. 22, reprinted in UN Legislative Series. *Ibid.*, at p. 52.

[8] Territorial Sea and Fishing Act 1965 (No. 11 of 1965), reprinted in UN Legislative Series, *supra*, note 6, at p. 653.

[9] Fisheries Act 1952–1967 (No. 116 of 1967), reprinted in UN Legislative Series, *supra*, note 6, at p. 571.

[10] Act No. 20 of 1967, reprinted in UN Legislative Series, *supra*, note 6, at p. 668.

three miles. It will be recalled that at the Second United Nations Conference in 1960, the US had led the opposition to a proposal which would have empowered coastal States to establish exclusive fishing zones up to 12 miles. In one of its recurrent U-turns, the US enacted national legislation in 1966 to establish a nine-mile fishing zone adjacent to its three-mile territorial sea.[11] Within the fishing zone, the US claimed the right to exercise the same exclusive rights in respect of fisheries as it has in its territorial sea, subject only to the continuation of traditional fishing by foreign States recognised by her. The reason for the schizophrenic behaviour of the US is that her national interests are divided. On the one hand, she has coastal communities in Alaska and the New England States which are dependent on fisheries of their coasts and which resented the competition of foreign fishing fleets. On the other hand, as we shall see later in this article, the US also possesses fishing fleets which fish at great distances from her own shores, especially for tuna.

The Fisheries Jurisdiction Case

In 1972, Iceland announced its intention to extend its fishery jurisdiction from 12 to 50 miles. The UK and the Federal Republic of Germany requested the International Court of Justice to declare that there was no foundation in international law for Iceland's claim to extend its fishery jurisdiction to 50 miles. In its judgement, the Court[12] stated that the concept of an exclusive fishing zone of up to 12 miles had become part of

---

[11] Contiguous Fishing Zone Act, 1966, Public Law 89-658, reprinted in UN Legislative Series, *supra.* note 6, at pp. 701–702.

[12] *The Fisheries Jurisdiction Case*, I.C.J. Rep. 1974, p. 266.

customary international law since the Second United Nations Conference of 1960. Beyond 12 miles, the Court held that coastal States could claim preferential fishing rights. However, "A coastal State entitled to preferential rights is not free, unilaterally and according to its own uncontrolled discretion, to determine the extent of those rights. The characterisation of the coastal State's rights as preferential implies a certain priority but cannot imply the extinction of current rights of other States, particularly of a State which, like the applicant, has for many years been engaged in fishing in the waters in question, such fishing activity being important to the economy of the country concerned. The coastal State has to take into account and pay regard to other States, particularly when they have established an economic dependence on the same fishing grounds."[13]

The Court declared that Iceland's unilateral action constituted an infringement of the principle in the Convention on the High Seas, which requires that all States, including coastal States, in exercising their freedom of fishing, pay reasonable regard to the interests of other States. The Court said that the appropriate method for resolving the dispute between Iceland and the UK was by negotiations between them, on the basis that Iceland had preferential rights in the fishing and the UK had a historic interest. The negotiations should aim to bring about an equitable apportionment of the fishery resources.

Ten of the judges of the Court subscribed to the majority opinion. Five of these ten judges, however, appended a separate opinion.[14] In their separate opinion, they said that they did not

---

[13] *Ibid.*, at p. 27.
[14] *Ibid.*, at p. 45.

regard the judgement as declaring that the extension of Iceland's jurisdiction was without foundation in international law. They said that the judgement was based on the special facts and circumstances of that case and not on the British argument that a customary rule of international law existed that prohibited the extension by States of their exclusive fisheries jurisdiction beyond 12 miles. They were of the view that no firm rule could be deduced from State practice as being sufficiently general and uniform to be accepted as a rule of customary law fixing the maximum extent of the coastal State's jurisdiction with regard to fisheries.

Developing Coastal States and Distant-Water Fishing States

The progressive extension of exclusive fisheries jurisdiction by developed coastal States, in response to competition by distant-water fishing States, was matched by similar action on the part of developing coastal States. Developing coastal States were, with very few exceptions, too poor and too underdeveloped, technologically, to have fishing fleets capable of competing with the modern fishing fleets of Japan, the USSR and US. The developing coastal States felt that the doctrine of freedom of fishing in the high seas, coupled with a three-mile territorial sea, was designed to serve the interests of the rich and the powerful because it enabled countries such as Japan, the USSR and US to fish close to their shores whilst they lacked the capacity to fish off the coasts of those or other developed coastal States. The movement to remould the international law of fisheries was led by the Pacific-coast Latin American countries which felt threatened by the tuna fleets of the US.

The first blow was struck by Chile on 23 June 1947.[15] The President of Chile issued a Declaration claiming national sovereignty over the continental shelf and over the seas adjacent to its coasts up to a limit of 200 miles from the coasts and islands. The Declaration contained a proviso that the declaration of sovereignty recognised the legitimate rights of other States on a reciprocal basis and it would not affect the rights of free navigation on the high seas. Two months later, on 1 August 1947, Peru issued a similar decree.[16]

Santiago Declaration (1952)

Representatives of Chile, Ecuador and Peru met in Santiago, Chile, from 11 to 19 August 1952 to discuss the maritime resources of the South Pacific. At the end of their conference, they issued a declaration which came to be known as the Santiago Declaration of 1952.[17] In it, the governments of Chile, Ecuador and Peru "proclaim as a principle of their international maritime policy that each of them possesses sole sovereignty and jurisdiction over the sea adjacent to the coast of its own country and extending not less than 200 nautical miles from the said coast." The declaration states that it "shall not be construed as disregarding the necessary restrictions on the exercise of sovereignty

---

[15] United Nations Legislative Series, *Laws and Regulations on the Regime of the Territorial Sea* (1957), UN Doc. ST/LEG/SER.B/6, at p. 4.

[16] Supreme Decree of 1 August 1947, reprinted in *Laws and Regulations on the Regime of the High Seas*, UN Doc. ST/LEG/SER.R1 (1951), pp. 16–18 and in UN Legislative Series, UN Doc. ST/LEG/SER.B/6, *ibid.*, pp. 38–39.

[17] S Oda, *The International Law of the Ocean Development, Basic Documents* (1972), pp. 345; SH Lay, R Churchill and M Nordquist, *New Directions in the Law of the Sea*, Vol. 1 (1973). p. 231.

and jurisdiction imposed by international law to permit the innocent and inoffensive passage of vessels of all nations through the zone aforesaid."[18]

The Santiago Declaration fixed 200 nautical miles as the limit of the sovereignty and jurisdiction of Chile, Ecuador and Peru over the seas adjacent to their coasts. Does the figure of 200 nautical miles coincide with the limit of any natural phenomenon? It does not coincide with the widths of the continental shelves of the three countries. They have relatively narrow continental shelves which vary in width from 8 to 80 nautical miles. According to DP O'Connell, Peru has tried to justify the figure of 200 nautical miles on the ground that it is the approximate width of the Peru Current.[19] The Peruvian estimation of the width of the current has been contradicted by the subsequent investigations of oceanographers. Cuchlaine AM King, for example, stated that, "The current extends to about 900 kilometres from shore."[20] What is the connection anyway, between the width of the Peru Current and Peru's claim to exclusive fishing rights?

The Peru Current, also known as the Humboldt Current, is an ocean current which flows north from the tip of Chile along the coasts of Chile and Peru. This ocean current carries cool, nutrient-rich sub-Antarctic water. The major nutrients in seawater are: phosphorus, nitrogen, silicon, copper and iron. The presence of these nutrients and the availability of sunlight will enable phytoplankton to grow. What are phytoplankton? They are microscopic plants, each consisting of a single cell. However difficult it may be to believe, it is, nevertheless, true

---

[18] Oda, *ibid.*, at 346; Lay, *ibid.*, at 232.

[19] DP O'Connell, *The International Law of the Sea* (1982), Vol. 1, p. 555.

[20] CAM King, *Introduction to Physical and Biological Oceanography* (1975), p. 95.

that "these finely scattered and microscopic plants ... really form a vegetation which has sufficient bulk to support all the teeming animal life of the sea: the dense populations of planktonic crustaceans, the vast shoals of fish and all the invertebrate animals on the seabed."[21]

Zooplankton are little animals which feed on phytoplankton. What are these little animals? They include miniature jelly fish, arrow worms, many kinds of protozoa, segmented worms and molluscs.[22] Fish larvae and juvenile fish, as well as some species of fish such as the herring, feed on the zooplankton. In turn, other fish feed on the herring and juvenile fish. This is the food web of the oceans.

I have already referred to the fact that the Humboldt Current brings cool, nutrient-rich water from the Antarctic. In addition, the prevailing winds in the area carry the surface water away from the coast thereby resulting in water being drawn to the surface from depths of generally less than 100 metres. This upwelling along the Chilean and Peruvian coasts brings nutrient-rich water to the surface and is the additional cause of an enormous growth of phytoplankton and zooplankton on which a huge school of anchoveta and other pelagic fish as well as their predators depend. The importance of the Humboldt Current to fisheries can be seen by the fact that by 1964, Peru had become the world's number one fishing nation. In the peak year, 1970, Peru accounted for 12 million metric tonnes of catch or over one-fifth of the global catch.[23]

---

[21] A Hardy, *The Open Sea: Its Natural History, Part1: The World of Plankton* (1971), p. 37.

[22] *Ibid.*, at p. 68.

[23] S Holt, "Marine Fisheries", in EM Borgese & N Ginsburg (Editors), *Ocean Yearbook*, Vol. 1 (1978), at p. 40.

Although Peru had said that, "the limit of 200 miles does not pretend to be a universal rule, but is valid only for those countries whose realities and responsibilities makes its acceptance possible and necessary,"[24] similar claims were made by other Latin American States whose situations were quite different from those of Peru. Regional solidarity, a heightened mood of economic nationalism in the Third World and the feeling that the old legal order was unjust and obsolete encouraged this trend.

The Montevideo Declaration on the Law of the Sea (1970)

From 4 to 8 May 1970, a meeting on the law of the sea was convened in Montevideo by the government of Uruguay. The meeting was attended by Argentina, Brazil, Chile, Ecuador, El Salvador, Nicaragua, Panama, Peru and Uruguay. The meeting adopted a Declaration of Principles on the Law of the Sea which states, *inter alia*, "the right of coastal States to avail themselves of the natural resources of the sea adjacent to their coasts and of the soil and subsoil thereof" and "the right to establish the limits of their maritime sovereignty and jurisdiction in accordance with their geographical and geological characteristics and with the factors governing the existence of marine resources and the need for their rational utilisation."[25]

---

[24] *Ministerio de Relaciones Exteriors del Peru, Soberania Maritima: Fundamentos dela Posicion Peruana* (1970), p. 16, as noted in O'Connell. *supra*. note 19, at p. 557.
[25] Oda, *supra*, note 17, at pp. 347–348; Lay, Churchill and Nordquist, *supra*, note 17, at pp. 235–236.

Declaration of the Latin American States on the Law of the Sea (1970)

Three months after the meeting in Montevideo, another meeting was held in Lima, Peru, and attended by 20 Latin American States: Argentina, Barbados, Bolivia, Brazil, Chile, Colombia, Dominican Republic, Ecuador, El Salvador, Guatemala, Honduras, Jamaica, Mexico, Nicaragua, Panama, Paraguay, Peru, Trinidad and Tobago, Uruguay, and Venezuela. The Declaration, *inter alia*, recognises the "inherent right of the coastal State to explore, conserve and exploit the natural resources of the sea adjacent to its coasts and the soil and subsoil thereof, likewise of the Continental Shelf and its subsoil" and upholds the "right of the coastal State to establish the limits of its maritime sovereignty or jurisdiction in accordance with reasonable criteria, having regard to its geographical, geological and biological characteristics, and the need to make rational use of its resources."[26]

Declaration of Santo Domingo (1972)

The Special Conference of the Caribbean Countries on Problems of the Sea met at Santo Domingo, the Dominican Republic, from 6 to 9 June 1972. The meeting was attended by the following 13 States: Barbados, Colombia, Costa Rica, Dominican Republic, Guatemala, Haiti, Honduras, Jamaica, Mexico, Nicaragua, Panama, Trinidad and Tobago, and Venezuela. El Salvador and Guyana attended as observers. The aim of the meeting was to harmonise the views of the participating States on fundamental questions of the law of the sea. The 15 participating States were, however, unable to agree and a vote had to be taken on

---

[26] Oda, *ibid.*, at pp. 349–350; Lay, Churchill and Nordquist, *ibid.*, at pp. 237–239.

the Declaration of Santo Domingo. The ten States that voted for the Declaration were: Colombia, Costa Rica, Dominican Republic, Guatemala, Haiti, Honduras, Mexico, Nicaragua, Trinidad and Tobago, and Venezuela. The remaining five States, Barbados, El Salvador, Guyana, Jamaica and Panama abstained.

The Declaration states, *inter alia*, that the "coastal State has sovereign rights over the renewable and non-renewable natural resources, which are found in the waters, in the seabed and in the subsoil of an area adjacent to the territorial sea called the patrimonial sea" and the "whole of the area of both the territorial sea and the patrimonial sea, taking into account geographic circumstances, should not exceed a maximum of 200 nautical miles."[27] The Declaration of Santo Domingo was significant for two reasons. First, it gave a name "patrimonial sea" to the zone in which the coastal State would have sovereign rights to the renewable and non-renewable resources of the water column, the seabed and its subsoil. Secondly, it fixed 200 nautical miles as the maximum permissible breadth of the territorial sea and patrimonial sea. It will be recalled that neither the Montevideo Declaration nor the Lima Declaration had mentioned any limit although it seemed to have been assumed that 200 nautical miles would not be regarded as an unreasonable limit.

The Asian-African Legal Consultative Committee

Representatives of four Latin American States, Argentina, Brazil, Ecuador and Peru attended the meeting of the Asian-African Legal Consultative Committee (AALCC) held in Colombo, Sri Lanka, in January 1971. They tried to persuade the Asian

---

[27] S Oda, *The International Law of Ocean Development, Basic Documents, Vol. II* (1975), at pp. 32–34; Lay, Churchill and Nordquist, *supra*, note 17, at p. 247.

and African States of the validity of the 200-mile claims of the Latin American States. The initial reaction of the Afro-Asians was sceptical. Most of them regarded the Latin American claims as being excessive and unlikely to win international acceptance.

However, at the next meeting of AALCC, held in Lagos, Nigeria, in January 1972, Kenya put forward a working paper entitled, "The Exclusive Economic Zone Concept".[28] The paper observed that attempts by developing countries to extend their territorial seas up to a distance of 200 miles, in order to compensate for their technologically disadvantaged position, had given rise to concern among the major maritime powers that such extensions would have a prejudicial effect on the freedoms of navigation and overflight within such zones. Kenya was, therefore, putting forward the concept of the exclusive economic zone as a compromise to the competing claims. The concept would embody a relatively narrow territorial sea of 12 miles together with exclusive coastal State jurisdiction for economic purposes in a zone extending to 200 miles from the territorial sea boundaries.

African States Regional Seminar on the Law of the Sea (1972)

In June 1972, an African regional seminar on the law of the sea was held in Yaounde, Cameroon. The meeting, in effect, endorsed the proposal submitted five months earlier by Kenya to the AALCC. The report of the meeting contained the following propositions:

The Territorial Sea should not extend beyond a limit of 12 nautical miles.

---

[28] Asian-African Legal Consultative Committee, Report of the Thirteenth Session Held at Lagos from 18 to 25 January 1972, pp. 369–374.

The African States have equally the right to establish beyond the territorial sea an Economic Zone over which they will have an exclusive jurisdiction for the purpose of control, regulation and national exploitation of the living resources of the sea and their reservation for the primary benefit of their peoples and their respective economies, and for the purposes of the prevention and control of pollution.

The establishment of the zone shall be without prejudice to the following freedoms: freedom of navigation, freedom of overflight, freedom to lay submarine cables and pipelines.[29]

Draft Articles on the Exclusive Economic Zone

On 7 August 1972, the delegation of Kenya submitted draft articles on the concept of the exclusive economic zone (EEZ) to the United Nations Seabed Committee.[30] The draft articles would entitle every coastal State to claim an EEZ beyond a territorial sea of 12 miles. The maximum permissible breadth of the EEZ would be 200 miles, measured from the baselines for determining the territorial sea. The coastal State shall have exclusive jurisdiction to the living and non-living resources of the water column, the seabed and subsoil thereof. The establishment of such a zone shall be without prejudice to the exercise of the freedom of navigation, the freedom of overflight and the freedom to lay submarine cables and pipelines as recognised by international law.

---

[29] Report of the Committee on the Peaceful Uses of the Seabed and the Ocean Floor Beyond the Limits of National Jurisdiction, UN Gen.Ass.Off.Rec., 17th Sess. (1972), Supp. No. 21, pp. 73–74 (UN Doc. A/8721); reprinted in Lay, Churchill and Nordquist, *supra*, note 17, at pp. 250–251.

[30] Submitted as UN Doc. A/AC.138/SC.II/L.10, Report of the Seabed Committee, *ibid.*, pp. 180–182; also reprinted in Oda, *supra* note 18, at p. 252.

These, then were the chief signposts on the road towards the evolution of the EEZ. To ward off the pressure of distant-water fishing fleets, a number of developed coastal States had claimed exclusive fishing rights in a nine-mile zone seaward of their territorial sea of three miles. One of the developed coastal States, Iceland, had purported to extend her exclusive fishing zone from 12 (measured from the territorial sea baselines) to 50 miles. Chile, Ecuador and Peru, faced with increasing pressure from American tuna fleets, extended their maritime zones to 200 miles. The figure of 200 miles was picked because Peru thought it was the width of the Humboldt Current. Although the geographical and biological situations of other Latin American States were significantly different from those of Chile and Peru, their example was widely copied in Latin America. The Declaration of Santo Domingo acknowledged a distinction between the territorial sea and a wider zone within which coastal States would have sovereign rights only to the resources and called the latter the patrimonial sea. Kenya crystallised the idea by calling the zone the EEZ, and drawing a clear distinction between the territorial sea and the EEZ. According to the Kenyan proposal, a coastal State would enjoy exclusive rights to the resources of the EEZ but the international community's freedoms of navigation, overflight, and the laying of submarine cables and pipelines would be unaffected.

Rights of Coastal States in the Exclusive Economic Zone

What are the rights of coastal States in the EEZ? First, the coastal State has sovereign rights to the resources of the EEZ.[31]

---

[31] Article 56, para. (1)(a), 1982 Convention, *supra* note 1.

This includes both living and non-living resources, in the water column, the seabed and its subsoil. The main forms of living resources in the water column are marine mammals and marine animals. The two most common species of marine mammals are whales and dolphins. Marine animals in the water column are mainly fish. Marine biologists classify fish into two categories: the pelagic fish or surface-living fish and the demersal fish or bottom-living fish. The marine animals that live on the bottom of the seabed are called benthos. The most important species of benthos to man are lobsters, crayfish, shrimp, oysters, scallops and clams. The most important forms of non-living resources in the seabed and subsoil are the hydrocarbons or oil and gas. The coastal State is said to have "sovereign rights" to all these resources in its EEZ. In respect of fish, does this mean that a coastal State has exclusive right to them? Some writers have argued that under the Convention, a coastal State has only preferential not exclusive right to the fish in its EEZ because the coastal State is under a legal duty to allocate to other States the difference between the total allowable catch and its own harvesting capacity.

Secondly, the coastal State has the exclusive right to undertake activities for the economic exploration and exploitation of the zone, such as the production of energy from the water, currents and winds.[32] The main sources of energy from the oceans are tides, waves, temperature differences, ocean biomass, offshore wind and salinity gradients. Of these, only the first three look promising. Tides are produced by the gravitational pull of the moon and the sun. The moon's gravity pulls the ocean

---

[32] *Ibid.*

towards her. The range between low tide and high tide is called the tidal range. A tidal range of ten metres or more is needed to make tidal power feasible. The technology of tidal power is similar to hydro-power. A dam will be built across a bay. At high tide, water will pass through the dam into the bay. As the tide ebbs, the water will pass through the dam, driving its turbines. France has a tidal power plant at La Rance. Canada has built a pilot project in the Bay of Fundy, which has the world's largest tidal range.

Waves in the ocean are produced by the wind and winds are, in turn, produced by the sun. The UK is known to have undertaken a large project on wave energy but has decided that it will not be economical for the next 20 years. The Government of Mauritius, with funding from the United Nations Development Programme, is building a pilot project. It will dam a coral reef and build an outlet where a turbine is installed.

The third potential source of energy from the ocean is the temperature difference between the warm surface layer of water and the cold water at depths of 1,000 metres or more. The temperature difference between the two layers of water is particularly pronounced in the equatorial regions and the tropics where the surface temperature may be between 28–30°C and the temperature of the bottom layer may be between 3–8°C. The concept is extremely simple: the temperature difference equals potential energy. A fluid, such as ammonia, is brought into contact with warm surface water. When this happens, the ammonia vapourises and the vapour drives the turbines in a generator. The ammonia vapour is then brought into contact with cold water from the ocean bottom. This causes the vapour to condense and the ammonia fluid is then pumped out to start the cycle all over again. The technology is called ocean thermal energy conversion (OTEC). Japan has built a pilot plant in Nauru.

According to information supplied by the United Nations,[33] the Netherlands and Indonesia will be building an OTEC plant on Bali, Indonesia, and Jamaica and Sweden will be building one near Kingston, Jamaica.

Jurisdiction of Coastal States in the Exclusive Economic Zone

What is the jurisdiction of the coastal State in the EEZ? The coastal State has jurisdiction in its EEZ over three matters.[34] First, over the establishment and use of artificial islands, installations and structures and secondly, over marine scientific research. Thirdly, over the protection and preservation of the marine environment. The provisions of the Convention affecting the jurisdiction of the coastal State over artificial islands, installations and structures are contained in Part V, entitled "Exclusive Economic Zone". The provisions dealing with the jurisdiction of the coastal State over marine scientific research are, however, contained in Part XIII, and the provisions dealing with the jurisdiction of the coastal State over the protection and preservation of the marine environment are contained in Part XII.

The Living Resources of the Exclusive Economic Zone

Although Article 56 characterises the right of the coastal State to the living resources of the EEZ as "sovereign", it is, in fact,

---

[33] I am grateful to Mr Lawrence Newman of the Ocean Economics and Technology Branch of the UN Secretariat for this information.

[34] Article 56, para. (1)(b), 1982 Convention, *supra* note 2.

qualitatively different from the right of the coastal State to the non-living resources of the zone. The Convention imposes two important duties on the coastal State in respect of the living resources in the EEZ. First, the coastal State has a duty to "ensure through proper conservation and management measures that the maintenance of the living resources in the exclusive economic zone is not endangered by overexploitation."[35] Second, the coastal State has a duty to promote the objective of optimum utilisation of the living resources in the EEZ.[36] The coastal State, therefore, has a duty to practice proper conservation and management of the living resources in its EEZ. The coastal State must ensure, through proper conservation and management, that the living resources in its EEZ are not endangered by overexploitation. One of the reasons advanced for the EEZ was that it would lead to the better conservation and management of the living resources. The argument was that under the traditional law, fish outside the territorial sea was the common property of all nations. Every nation and every fisherman was out to get as much of the fish in the high sea as possible. Although everyone paid lip service to the need for conservation, no one was, in fact, prepared to limit his catch because no one was prepared to sacrifice unless everyone had to make a sacrifice. The result was a classic zero-sum game and many fish stocks were dangerously overfished. It was said that the regional fisheries organisations could not solve the problem because their member States were not prepared to give them the power necessary to do the job. The establishment of the EEZ would end the common property problem and coastal States would have the power and the incentive to practice proper conservation and management.

---

[35] Article 61, para. 2, *ibid.*
[36] Article 62, para 1, *ibid.*

Optimum Utilisation

Why is the coastal State under a legal obligation to promote the optimum utilisation of the living resources in the EEZ? It is placed under such a duty because we live in a world of hunger, and fish is a very important source of animal protein.[37] It is also the premise from which the Convention proceeds to impose on the coastal State a duty to allocate to other States any surplus between the total allowable catch and its own harvesting capacity. It should be pointed out that optimum utilisation is not the same as maximum utilisation. A simple analogy will bring out the difference between maximum and optimum. Let us suppose that the maximum speed of a car is 100 kilometres per hour. Its optimum speed, based on the criteria of speed, safety and fuel-efficiency is, let us say, 55 kilometres per hour. Therefore, if our objective is the maximum utilisation of the living resources of the EEZ, the total allowable catch or maximum sustainable yield will be greater than the total allowable catch when the objective is optimum utilisation. When the objective is optimum utilisation, the coastal State, in fixing the total allowable catch or optimum sustainable yield, is entitled to take relevant biological, environmental, economic and social factors into account. The reason for the recent trend in fisheries science in moving from the concept of maximum sustainable yield to the concept of optimum sustainable yield is prudence. If you are harvesting the maximum sustainable yield of a species or biomass and an environmental mishap were to occur which reduces the population of the species or biomass, the capacity of the species or biomass to maintain itself at a stable level could be seriously endangered.

---

[37] SJ Holt & C Vanderbuilt, "Marine Fisheries," in EM Borgese & N Ginsburg (Editors), *Ocean Yearbook*, Vol. 2 (1980), at p. 28.

This is because maximum sustainable yield pushes the catch too close to the brink and does not contain any safety margin. Optimum sustainable yield is supposed to rectify that shortcoming.

Determining the Total Allowable Catch

How shall the coastal State establish the total allowable catch or optimum sustainable yield of the living resources in its EEZ? The Convention suggests various ways to assist the coastal State. First, the coastal State should take into account the best scientific evidence available.[38] Secondly, it could consult the Food and Agricultural Organization or the appropriate regional fisheries organisation.[39] Thirdly, in setting the total allowable catch, the coastal State shall be guided by the objective of maintaining or restoring "populations of harvested species at levels which can produce the maximum sustainable yield, as qualified by relevant environmental and economic factors, including the economic needs of coastal fishing communities and the special requirements of developing States, and taking into account fishing patterns, the interdependence of stocks and any generally recommended international standards".[40] The objective is to maintain the populations of the harvested species at a stable level. Where the population of a particular species has fallen below the desirable level, owing to overfishing or because of an environmental hazard or both, the total allowable catch may be lowered in order to restore the population to the desired level. The following are two examples of environmental factors that should be taken into account in fixing the total allowable catch.

---

[38] Article 61, para. 2, 1982 Convention, *supra* note 2.
[39] *Ibid.*
[40] Article 61, para. 3, *ibid.*

Suppose that we are fixing the total allowable catch of the anchoveta fishery in the EEZ of Peru. We know from historical record that every six to ten years a warm current, known as "El Niño", comes down the coast of Peru. The warm current stops the upwelling, which brings nutrients from the lower layer of water to the surface. When El Niño occurs the population of anchoveta is drastically reduced. We would take the temperature of the water in order to detect any warming trend. Let us suppose that the total allowable catch of anchoveta has been fixed at 10 million metric tonnes for the current year. Let us further suppose that the temperature of the water indicates that El Niño has occurred. This should be taken into account in fixing the total allowable catch of anchoveta for next year, which will be fixed at, let us say, 8 million metric tonnes.

Another situation would be the occurrence of a major oil spill in the EEZ. Let us suppose that the oil spill has seriously damaged a fishery, which will take five years to recover. This factor should be taken into account in fixing the total allowable catch for the next five years.

Fourthly, the coastal State shall take into consideration the effects of the total allowable catch of one species or another species that is associated with or dependent upon the former.[41] The coastal State should ensure that the total allowable catch of one species would not have the effect of reducing the population of the associated or dependent species below a desirable level. There is an intricate food web linking various species in the oceans. For example, the anchoveta and the sardine in the Peruvian EEZ, are associated species in the sense that they compete for food. In another case, one species may be dependent upon

---

[41] Article 61, para. 4, *ibid.*

another species. For example, cod feeds on herring; it can, therefore, be said that cod is dependent upon herring. The inter-relationships between different species in a biomass must, therefore, be understood and taken into account in fixing the total allowable catch of each of the species.

Finally, the coastal State should take into account statistics on catch, on fishing effort and other data relevant to the conservation of fish stocks.[42] Fisheries science has abandoned the use of "catch per unit effort" by a fishing vessel as a criterion for calculating the abundance of the species. In recent years, the total allowable catches have been based upon what fisheries scientists call, "virtual population analysis". The idea is to use the data on the total catch of a species and its age distribution to calculate its abundance. Fisheries biologists can tell the age of a fish. Therefore, if data on total catch and age distribution are available for a number of years, it is possible to estimate, retrospectively, the size of each year's class of that stock. Developing countries may, however, find it difficult to obtain the necessary data. Statistics on the total catch of each species may not be available. If statistics are available, they may not be reliable. There may not be available an adequate number of trained personnel to compile statistics on the age distribution of the catch. Meanwhile, fisheries science in the west has marched on and the latest thinking on fisheries management seems to emphasise the fact that the different species in a biomass form an interactive system and fisheries management must, therefore, take into account "the interactive and flexible community nature of the resource base".[43]

---

[42] Article 61, para. 5, *ibid.*

[43] LM Dickie, "Perspectives on Fisheries Biology and Implications for Management," (1979) 36 J. Fish. Res. Bd. Can. 838 at p. 843.

Harvesting Capacity and Surplus

After determining the total allowable catches of the different species in the EEZ, the coastal State should then determine its own harvesting capacity.[44] If the coastal State has the capacity to harvest the entirety of the total allowable catches of some or even all the species, it is entitled to do so. In that event, there would be no surplus in respect of some or of all the species. However, if the coastal State's harvesting capacity is less than the total allowable catch, the coastal State is under a legal duty to give other States access to the surplus.[45]

Criteria For Allocating the Surplus

If a surplus exists and only one State is seeking access to the surplus, no problem arises. A problem arises when the surplus is not big enough to satisfy the requests of all those seeking a share of it. How should the coastal State allocate the surplus? Who gets to the head of the queue? The Convention lays down a number of criteria on the allocation of the surplus.

First, the coastal State shall have particular regard to the provisions of Articles 69 and 70, especially in relation to the developing States referred to in those Articles.[46] Articles 69 and 70 deal, respectively, with the rights of landlocked States and geographically disadvantaged States.

Secondly, the coastal States shall take into account all relevant factors, including, *inter alia*, (a) the significance of the living resources of the area to the economy of the coastal State concerned and its other national interests; (b) the provisions of

---

[44] Article 62, para. 2, 1982 Convention, *supra* note 1.
[45] *Ibid.*
[46] *Ibid.*

Articles 69 and 70; (c) the requirements of developing States in the subregion or region in harvesting part of the surplus; and (d) the need to minimise economic dislocation in States whose nationals have habitually fished in the zone or which have made substantial efforts in research and identification of stocks.[47] In view of the use of the words "including" and "*inter alia*", we should read Article 62, paragraph 3 as meaning that the four factors mentioned are not exhaustive. The first factor, that is the significance of the living resources of the area to the economy of the coastal State concerned and its other national interests, would appear to be superfluous since the coastal State is entitled to harvest as much of the total allowable catch as it has the capacity to do. Are the second, third and fourth factors intended to indicate their rank in the hierarchy or their places in the queue? I think it would be reasonable to interpret Article 62, paragraph 3, as creating a hierarchy and giving the first place in the queue to landlocked and geographically disadvantaged States; the second place to developing States in the same subregion or region as the coastal State; and the third place to States which have habitually fished in the zone or which have made substantial efforts in research and identification of stocks. This interpretation is supported by the emphasis given to landlocked and geographically disadvantaged States in Article 62, paragraph 2, and by the fact that landlocked and geographically disadvantaged States have a "right" to a part of the surplus[48] whereas the States belonging to the other two categories do not have a "right" but a "privilege".[49]

---

[47] Article 62, para. 3, 1982 Convention, *supra* note 1.

[48] Articles 69 and 70, *ibid.*

[49] The terms "right" and "privilege" are used in accordance with Professor Hohfeld's taxonomy. See generally, WN Hohfeld, *Fundamental Legal Conceptions as Applied in Judicial Reasoning* (1946).

Landlocked and Geographically Disadvantaged States[50]

We have established that in applying for a part of the surplus, the first priority shall be given to landlocked[51] and geographically disadvantaged States. What are geographically disadvantaged States? The Convention defines them as: (a) coastal States that can claim no EEZs of their own and (b) coastal States, including States bordering enclosed or semi-enclosed seas, whose geographical situation makes them dependent upon the exploitation of the living resources of the EEZs of other States in the subregion or region for adequate supplies of fish for the nutritional purposes of their populations or parts thereof.[52] The first limb of the definition is very precise but, to the best of my knowledge, only one State, Singapore, has claimed to satisfy it. The second limb of the definition is less precise and would include the case of coastal States whose EEZs are extremely small as well as the case of coastal States whose EEZs are very poor in living resources. Jamaica, for example, has claimed that its EEZ is like a biological desert.

---

[50] See S Jayakumar, "The Issue of Rights of Landlocked and Geographically Disadvantaged States in the Living Resources of the Economic Zone," (1977) 18 Va. J. Int'l L. 69.

[51] The following 30 landlocked States participated in the Third United Nations Conference on the Law of the Sea: Afghanistan, Austria, Bhutan, Bolivia, Botswana, Burundi, Byelorussian SSR, Central African Republic, Chad, Czechoslovakia, Holy See, Hungary, Laos, Lesotho, Liechtenstein, Luxembourg, Malawi, Mali, Mongolia, Nepal, Niger, Paraguay, Rwanda, San Marino, Swaziland, Switzerland, Uganda, Upper Volta, Zambia and Zimbabwe.

[52] Article 70, para. 2, 1982 Convention, *supra* note 1. The following 25 States claim to qualify as geographically disadvantaged States: Algeria, Bahrain, Belgium, Bulgaria, Cameroon, Ethiopia, Finland, Gambia, German Democratic Republic, Federal Republic of Germany, Greece, Iraq, Jamaica, Jordan, Kuwait, Netherlands, Poland, Qatar, Singapore, Sudan, Sweden, Syria, Turkey, United Arab Emirates and Zaire.

Rights of Landlocked and Geographically Disadvantaged States

Landlocked States and geographically disadvantaged States have a right to an appropriate part of the surplus of the coastal States of the same subregion or region.[53] Developed landlocked and geographically disadvantaged States can assert their right only against developed coastal States of the same subregion or region.[54] It would appear that developing landlocked and geographically disadvantaged States can exercise their right against both developing and developed coastal States of the same subregion or region.

When a landlocked or geographically disadvantaged State applies to a coastal State for a part of its surplus, the terms and modalities for allocating a part of the surplus shall be governed by a bilateral, subregional or regional agreement.[55] In negotiating such agreements, account shall be taken of the following factors, amongst others. The first factor is the need to avoid effects detrimental to fishing communities or fishing industries of the coastal State.[56] This factor does not appear to be relevant when the right of the landlocked and geographically disadvantaged States is limited to a share of the surplus. When a surplus exists, it must follow that the interests of the fishing communities and fishing industries of the coastal State have already been taken care of. This factor is only relevant in a no-surplus situation.

The second factor is the extent to which the landlocked State or geographically disadvantaged State is, at present, participating in the exploitation of the living resources of the EEZs

---

[53] Article 69, para. 1, and Article 70, para. 1.
[54] Article 69, para. 4, and Article 70, para. 5.
[55] Article 69, para. 2, and Article 70, para. 3.
[56] Article 69, para. 2(a), and Article 70, para. 3(a).

of other coastal States or is entitled to do so, under existing bilateral, subregional or regional agreements.[57] In other words, account shall be taken of the extent to which a landlocked or geographically disadvantaged State is, at present, fishing in the EEZs of other coastal States or is entitled to do so under an existing agreement.

The third factor is the extent to which other landlocked and geographically disadvantaged States are fishing in the EEZ of the coastal State and the need to avoid a particular burden for any single coastal State or part thereof.[58] If, in a particular subregion or region, there are several landlocked and geographically disadvantaged States and several coastal States with a surplus, it would be unfair for all the landlocked and geographically disadvantaged States to apply to one coastal State only. The burden of accommodating the landlocked and geographically disadvantaged States should be shared among the several coastal States of the subregion or region. This factor would be inapplicable if, of all the coastal States of the subregion or region, only one has a surplus. It may also be inapplicable to a situation in which the surplus of the other coastal States is in respect of species which the landlocked or geographically disadvantaged States have no economic interest in harvesting.

The fourth factor is "the nutritional needs of the respective States".[59] Does the phrase, "respective States" refer to the landlocked and geographically disadvantaged States, on the one hand, and the coastal State, on the other? Does it refer to the landlocked and geographically disadvantaged States, *inter se*,

---

[57] Article 69, para. 2(b), and Article 70, para. 3(b).
[58] Article 69, para. 2(c), and Article 70, para. 3(c).
[59] Article 69, para. 2(d), and Article 70, para. 3(d).

when more than one has applied for a share of the surplus? In a situation where a surplus exists and only one landlocked or geographically disadvantaged State has applied for a share of it, this factor is irrelevant. However, if two or more landlocked and geographically disadvantaged States have applied and the sum of their request exceeds the surplus available, the coastal State may take this factor into account in deciding the priority and the amounts to be allocated to the applicants. In a no-surplus situation, it would be relevant to take into account the nutritional needs of the populations of the coastal State, on the one hand, and the landlocked and geographically disadvantaged State or States, on the other hand.

The four factors mentioned above apply to both developed and developing landlocked and geographically disadvantaged States. There is a fifth factor which is applicable only to developed landlocked and geographically disadvantaged States. The fifth factor requires us to give "regard to the extent to which the coastal State, in giving access to other States to the living resources of its EEZ, has taken into account the need to minimise detrimental effects on fishing communities and economic dislocation in States whose nationals have habitually fished in the zone."[60] I find this factor rather puzzling. We have previously established that the Convention creates a hierarchy of applicants for a share of the surplus and that landlocked and geographically disadvantaged States are placed at the head of the queue, ahead of States which have habitually fished in the zone. How can we reconcile this with the fifth factor? One way to reconcile the two is to posit that the priority of developing landlocked and geographically disadvantaged States is an absolute one whereas

---

[60] Article 69, para. 4, and Article 70, para. 5.

the priority of developed landlocked and geographically disadvantaged States is relative. In other words, if a developed landlocked and geographically disadvantaged State and a habitual fishing State apply for a share of the surplus of a coastal State and the surplus is not big enough to accommodate the requests of both to the full, the coastal State shall share the surplus between them, giving the former relatively more weight than the latter.

When No Surplus Exists

What happens when no surplus exists? In such a situation, the Convention makes a clear distinction between developed and developing landlocked and geographically disadvantaged States.[61] When no surplus exists there is nothing to be done for developed landlocked and geographically disadvantaged States. In the case of developing landlocked and geographically disadvantaged States, the Convention requires the coastal States of the subregion or region to cooperate in order to establish equitable arrangements so that the developing landlocked and geographically disadvantaged States can continue to fish. Such arrangements could be of a bilateral, subregional or regional nature. The terms on which continued access will be granted to developing landlocked and geographically disadvantaged States, in a no-surplus situation, must be satisfactory to all the States concerned. In implementing this provision, the four factors relevant to the allocation of the surplus, must also be taken into account.

Equal or Preferential Rights

Nothing in the Convention prevents the countries of any sub-region or region from agreeing upon arrangements whereby

---

[61] Article 69, para. 3, and Article 70, para. 4.

the coastal States will grant to the landlocked or geographically disadvantaged States of their subregion or region, equal or preferential rights for the exploitation of the living resources in the EEZs.[62] This provision was included in the Convention in order to take account of developments in Africa. The conclusions of the 1972 African States Regional Seminar on the Law of the Sea, held in Yaounde, Cameroon, contain the following:

> the exploitation of the living resources within the economic zone should be open to all African States both landlocked and near landlocked provided that the enterprises of these States desiring to exploit these resources are effectively controlled by African capital and personnel.[63]

The Declaration on Issues of the Law of the Sea, adopted by the Council of Ministers of the Organisation of African Unity in 1973, contained the following paragraph:

> That the African countries recognize, in order that the resources of the region may benefit all peoples therein, that the landlocked and other disadvantaged countries are entitled to share in the exploitation of living resources of neighbouring economic zones on an equal basis as nationals of coastal States on bases of African solidarity and under such regional or bilateral agreements as may be worked out.[64]

At the second session of the Third United Nations Conference on the Law of the Sea, draft articles on the EEZ were submitted

---

[62] Article 69, para. 5, and Article 70, para. 6.

[63] *Supra*, note 29.

[64] Para. 9, OAU Declaration on the Issues of the Law of the Sea, reprinted in the Report of the Committee on the Peaceful Uses of the Seabed and the Ocean Floor Beyond the Limits of National Jurisdiction, UN Gen. Ass. Off. Rec., 28th Sess. (1974), Supp. No. 21, Volt II. pp. 4–6 (UN Doc. A/9021).

by 18 African States.[65] The draft articles, *inter alia*, recognised that, "Developing landlocked and other geographically disadvantaged States have the right to exploit the living resources of the exclusive economic zones of neighbouring States and shall bear the corresponding obligations."[66] The nationals of the landlocked and geographically disadvantaged States were to "enjoy the same rights and bear the same obligations as nationals of coastal States".[67]

Restrictions

The rights conferred by Articles 69 and 70 on landlocked and geographically disadvantaged States cannot be exercised against a coastal State whose economy is overwhelmingly dependent on the exploitation of the living resources of its EEZ.[68] Iceland is an example of such a coastal State.

The rights conferred on landlocked and geographically disadvantaged States by the said articles cannot be transferred, directly or indirectly, to third States by lease, licence, joint ventures or otherwise, except with the consent of the coastal State.[69] This prohibition does not, however, preclude the landlocked and geographically disadvantaged States from obtaining technical or financial assistance from third States or international organisations so long as such assistance does not have the effect of transferring the rights of the landlocked and geographically disadvantaged States to third States.[70]

---

[65] UN Doc. A/CONF. 62/C.2/L.82, Third United Nations Conference on the Law of the Sea, Off. Rec., Vol. III, 2nd Sess. (1974), pp. 240–241.

[66] *Ibid.*, Article 6, para. 1.

[67] *Ibid.*, Article 6, para. 2.

[68] Article 71, 1982 Convention, *supra*, note 1.

[69] Article 72, para. 1, *ibid.*

[70] Article 72, para. 2, *ibid.*

Terms and Conditions for Access to Surplus

We have established that if a coastal State is unable to harvest the entire allowable catch, it has a legal duty to allocate the surplus to other States. Can the coastal State charge fees or other forms of remuneration for granting access to its surplus? Can the coastal State demand other terms and conditions? The following are the terms and conditions specified by the Convention. The list is, however, not exhaustive.

First, the coastal State may demand the payment of fees.[71] The amount of the fee and the manner in which it is calculated vary from jurisdiction to jurisdiction. The following are some of the licence fees in force in various parts of the world. Brazil (mainly for lobsters) charges US$1,215 per vessel annually.[72] Mexico (mainly for shrimp) charges US$18 per capacity tonne.[73] Ecuador (mainly for tuna) charges a registration fee of US$700 together with US$60 per registered tonne for 50 days or one full load, whichever comes first.[74] Peru charges a registration fee of US$500 annually together with US$20 per net registered tonne for 100 days.[75] Canada charges an access fee and a fishing fee.[76] The access fee is calculated on the basis of C$1.45 per GRT (gross register tonnage) of the vessel. The fishing fee is calculated on the bases of (a) the GRT of the vessel, (b) the number of days the vessel is fishing and (c) the species fished.

---

[71] Article 62, para. 4(a), *ibid.*

[72] FW Bell, "World-Wide Economic Aspects of Extended Fishery Jurisdiction Management," in LA Anderson, *Economic Impacts of Extended Fisheries Jurisdiction* (1977) at pp. 10–11.

[73] *Ibid.*

[74] *Ibid.*

[75] *Ibid.*

[76] Sections 3 and 4, Coastal Fisheries Protection Act, R.S.C. c. C-21, Coastal Fisheries Protection Regulations, CRC (1978) c. 413, p. 2911.

Thus, a foreign fishing vessel of 3,000 GRT that spends 30 days in the Canadian EEZ fishing for squid, will have to pay an access fee of C$1.45 × 3000 = C$4,350 + a fishing fee of C$0.377 × 30 × 3000 = C$33,930, making a total of C$38,280. In the case of a developing coastal State, the Convention permits it to demand, in place of cash payment, compensation in the field of financing, equipment and technology relating to the fishing industry. Thus, a developing coastal State can ask the State applying for the surplus to finance the construction of fishing vessels or to build fish processing plants in lieu of the payment of licencing fees.

Second, the coastal State could require the State or States to which the surplus is allocated to undertake specified fisheries research programmes.[77] This requirement can be very useful to developing coastal States which do not have the scientific capacity to carry out such necessary research programmes as assessing what living resources exist in its EEZ, where they are to be found, their life cycles, the interactions between the different species, the abundance of each species, etc.

Third, the coastal State can require the landing of all or part of the catch by the foreign vessels in the ports of the coastal State.[78] The purpose of this requirement is to capture the value added in the downstream activities such as processing and marketing. The coastal State should not, however, insist on this requirement unless it has adequate processing plants to process the fish landed at its ports and unless it has the capacity to market the end product.

---

[77] Article 62, para. 4(f), 1982 Convention, *supra* note 1.
[78] Article 62, para. 4(h), *ibid.*

Fourth, the coastal State can request the applicant State to enter into a joint venture or other cooperative arrangement to harvest the surplus.[79]

Fifth, the coastal State can ask the applicant State to train the former's personnel and to transfer fisheries technology, including enhancing the coastal State's capacity to undertake fisheries research.[80] One very important condition not mentioned in the Convention is access to the market of the State applying for a part of the surplus.

Are the Same Terms and Conditions Applicable to Landlocked and Geographically Disadvantaged States and Developing States?

Articles 69 and 70 accord first place in the queue for access to the surplus to landlocked and geographically disadvantaged States. Article 62, paragraph 3, accords the second place to developing States in the same subregion and region. States which have habitually fished in the zone or which have made substantial efforts in research and identification of stocks in the zone, which are probably all developed States, are accorded the third place. The question is whether the same terms and conditions for being allocated a part or the whole of the surplus, are applicable to all three categories of States or only the third category.

I think the correct answer is that the same terms and conditions are applicable to all three categories of States. Under Articles 69 and 70, the rights of the landlocked and geographically disadvantaged States to an appropriate part of the surplus, are to

---

[79] Article 61, para. 4(i), *ibid.*
[80] Article 61, para. 4(j), *ibid.*

be exercised, "in conformity with the provisions of ... Article 61 and 62". Article 62, paragraph 4, empowers coastal States, *inter alia*, to establish the terms and conditions for gaining access to the surplus. The provision makes no distinction between the three categories of States in the queue for access to the surplus. The conclusion is that a coastal State may require landlocked and geographically disadvantaged States as well as developing States of the same subregion or region to comply with the same terms and conditions for access to the surplus as States in the third category. This conclusion casts a new complexion on the whole question of priority in the queue for the surplus because if the coastal State demands the same terms and conditions from all three categories of States, the landlocked and geographically disadvantaged States and the developing States may find themselves unable to make use of their priority and the surplus will, therefore, be allocated to the highest bidder. Such an outcome seems contrary to the policy of giving priority to the landlocked and geographically disadvantaged States and to developing States. There is, however, no escape from this conclusion because the Convention does not state that the preferential access to the surplus is to be granted *gratis* or on terms more favourable than those applicable to States in the third category. The only cure lies in the coastal State itself deciding, as a matter of its regional and foreign policy, not only to grant preferential access to the States in the first and second categories but to do so on more favourable terms and conditions than those demanded of other States. Thus, Venezuela, for example, may decide to give preferential access to the small countries of the Caribbean and to demand less onerous terms from them than from developed countries in order to enhance Venezuela's ties with the countries of the Caribbean. Indonesia, to take another example, may well do the same in respect of her regional partners in the Association of South East Asian Nations.

Conservation and Management Measures

The Convention imposes on the coastal State a duty to ensure, through proper conservation and management measures, that the maintenance of the living resources in the EEZ is not endangered by overexploitation. In order to avoid the danger of overexploitation, the coastal State is required to determine the total allowable catch of the living resources in the EEZ. The coastal State is entitled to harvest as much of the total allowable catch as its fisheries industry is capable of doing.

In order to ensure that the total allowable catch is not exceeded, the coastal State should enact laws and regulations and establish an infrastructure to enforce such laws and regulations. The laws and regulations apply, in the first place, to the domestic fisheries industry. In a situation where there is a surplus to be allocated to other States, then the conservation and management laws and regulations, which may or may not be the same as those applicable to the domestic fisheries industry will also apply to the foreign States granted access to the surplus. Article 62, paragraph 4, requires the foreign States fishing in the EEZ, to comply with the conservation and management laws and regulations of the coastal States. That provision enumerates a long but not exhaustive list of the measures which the coastal State may adopt.

Types of Fishery Regulations

Kesteven and Williams have divided fishery regulations into four classifications: regulations with respect to catch; regulations with respect to fishing operations; regulations with respect to fishing gear; and regulations with respect to fishing units.[81]

Regulations with respect to catch belong to four subdivisions. First, the regulation may fix a quota of the total amount of the catch of a particular stock. The objective of such a regulation is the maintenance of the catch. Its expected effect is that the stock will remain stable. The second kind of regulation imposes a limit on the amount of fish per fishing unit, for example, limit per bag, limit per trip and limit per boat during the fishing season. The objective of this kind of regulation is to spread the employment or recreational opportunity. The main expected effect is the sharing of the allowable catch among the optimum number of participants. Kesteven and Williams have pointed out that this kind of regulation may lead to underexploitation or to an increase in operational inefficiency. The third kind of regulation controls the size or age of the fish that can be caught. The objective is to obtain the maximum yield from a fishable stock. The expected result is the survival and successful growth of a significant pro-portion of the undersize or underage individuals and hence the maintenance of the best average size in the catch. An undesirable effect of this kind of regulation is the rejection at sea of signifi-cant amounts of captured undersized fish unless this regulation is complemented by other regulations with respect to fishing operations and fishing gear. The fourth kind of regulation deals with the sex composition of the catch, for example, a prohibition against the taking of crayfish in berry. The objective of this regu-lation is also the maintenance of catch through the preservation of the reproductive capacity of the stock.

---

[81] GL Kesteven and GR Williams, "Fishing Regulations—Conflicts in Exploita-tion of Fishery Resources," in Kesteven, et al., *Essays in Fisheries* Science (1971), at p. 77.

Kesteven and Williams have also divided regulations with respect to fishing operations into four subdivisions. The first type of regulation deals with periods of fishing, for example, prohibiting fishing of certain species during a specified period of time. The objective of such a regulation could be either the maintenance of the catch or the prevention of the capture of unsaleable fish. The effect is to exempt from fishing, fish that would otherwise be vulnerable during the close season. In order to overcome this restriction, fishermen would, of course, concentrate their fishing capacity during the open season. Therefore, this kind of regulation may have to be supplemented by controls on the amount of catch or of fishing effort. The second kind of regulation either closes an area to fishing or partitions a fishing ground into two or more portions. The objective of closing an area is either to maintain the catch or to prevent the capture of unsaleable fish. The effect is to protect fish in the closed area from fishing. This will also result in the concentration of fishing capacity in the open area and may, therefore, have to be supplemented by controls on the amount of catch or fishing effort. The objective of partitioning a fishing ground is usually to spread employment opportunity. The effect is the development of separate fleets for the different portions of the fishing ground. The third type of regulation limits the frequency or amount of use of gear by each fishing unit. Its objective is the maintenance of catch. Its effect is to restrict fishing capacity as well as to limit the total catch. However, if the intention is to limit the total fishing effort, it can be defeated by increasing the number of fishing units. The fourth kind of regulation seeks to limit the total effort expended. Its objective is to maintain the catch. Its effect is the same as the third type of regulation. Kesteven and Williams warn that this type of regulation may produce intense competition among fishing units and that its enforcement requires very close supervision of fishing operations.

The third class of regulations, dealing with fishing gear, may be divided into three categories. The first category of regulation specifies the mesh size or escape gaps. Its objective is to promote the maximum yield from the fishable stock. Its effect is that small fish are allowed to escape and to grow to optimum size. The second type of regulation contains limits on gear dimensions such as the length or other dimension of the net or the width of the dredge. Its objective is the maintenance of the catch. Its effect is to restrict fishing power and to limit the total catch. Economically, this type of regulation has the effect of limiting the efficiency of the fishing unit. It can also be circumvented by improvements to the non-regulated characteristics of fishing gear. The third kind of regulation deals with the properties of materials of which fishing gear is constructed, for example, prohibiting the use of monofilament nylon nets. Its objective is to spread employment opportunity. Its effect is to restrict fishing power and to limit the total catch. Economically, it has the effect of preventing the development of improvements and of increased efficiency.

The fourth class of regulations, dealing with fishing units, can be divided into two categories. The first category of regulation limits the number of vessels allowed to fish a stock by a system of licencing. Its objective is to maintain the total catch and the catch per vessel. It is expected to have the effect of limiting the fishing effort thereby remitting in orderly operations to take the allowable catch. This kind of regulation can have two types of negative effect. On the one hand, it may have the effect of reducing the incentive to improve efficiency. On the other hand, the allowable effort and catch may be exceeded if the licensed vessels increase their fishing power. The second kind of regulation imposes limits on the fishing power of individual fishermen, for example, limits on the number of lobster pots or the number of dredges. The objective of this kind of regulation is to maintain the catch and to spread the employment opportunity. Its expected effect is to limit the fishing effort and the total catch. This kind of regulation can be defeated unless the number of fishermen is limited or the amount of fishing effort is directly limited.

Each coastal State should decide for itself what its fishery policy is. Within the framework of its fishery policy, it should then establish its conservation and management measures. In doing so, it should attempt to integrate the contributions of the fisheries biologist, the fisheries economist, the lawyer, sociologist, environmentalist, the representative of the fishermen and the politician. Difficult choices may have to be made in situations where conflicts occur, for example between the commercial fishermen and the sport fishermen, between the inshore fishermen and the offshore fishermen, between the artisanal fishermen and fishermen employing more sophisticated boat and gear, between economic efficiency and social equity and between competing social objectives. The fishery administrators should keep in mind the need to promote communication with the fishermen for no system of conservation and management will succeed unless the administrators can convince the fishermen that the system is in their interest.

The Canadian Model

The conservation and management measures applicable to domestic fishermen may not be wholly applicable to foreign fishermen who are only permitted to fish in the EEZ when the coastal State has a surplus. We shall examine the regime of one particular country, Canada, as it relates to the fishing fleets of foreign States granted access to its surplus.[82] It is given not as the only model but as one model that appears to work reasonably well.

As a result of scientific research by fisheries biologists, it has been determined that there are separate stocks of fish which tend to congregate in different areas of the Canadian EEZ. Each year, Canadian scientists determine the health of each stock and recommend its total allowable catch. Next, the portion of the total allowable catch of each stock, which Canadian fishermen are likely to harvest, is calculated. If there is a surplus in the total allowable catch of any of the stocks, this is available for allocation to other States. The allocation is done through bilateral negotiations between Canada and the foreign States applying for access to the surplus. The negotiations, if successful, will result in the allocation of a fixed quota (in metric tonnes) of catch and a quota of the number of fishing days in order to catch the allocated quota.

A country that has obtained the twin quotas will then apply for licences for their fishing vessels to utilise these quotas. The applicant State must have a representative in Canada with whom Canadian government officials can liaise in respect of the licencing procedure and of the activity of the vessel. The licence application is in the form of a specification and data sheet which details a vessel's identification, specifications, fishing gear, communications equipment, processing equipment, fish storage hold and a fishing

---

[82] I am grateful to RJ Prier, Chief Conservation and Protection Division, Scotia-Fundy Region, of the Canadian Department of Fisheries and Oceans for the information.

plan. The licence granted outlines the specific requirements of each vessel, regarding the mesh size of its net, the area of vessel's operation and the reporting requirements.

Once a vessel is licensed and fishing in the EEZ, it is required to submit certain reports concerning its catch and activities. The vessel must submit a report 24 hours before entering the EEZ. The report will specify the time and position of the vessel's entry into the zone and its anticipated activity while in the zone. The vessel must submit a report 24 hours before the estimated time of entry into any Canadian port. A vessel must report its departure from any Canadian port at the actual time of its departure. A vessel must also report 72 hours before departure from the EEZ. The purpose of this last requirement is to enable the Canadian authorities to schedule an inspection of the vessel's catch before she leaves the zone. In addition, a vessel must submit a weekly report giving details of fishing activities during the week, including, the area in which it fished, the species it was permitted to fish, the tonnage of the species caught, the species of the by-catch and their tonnage and any biological samples taken. If the vessel had not been fishing, it must explain why it had not done so. The vessel must also report any tran-shipments of fish to other vessels or of fish discarded.

At the time when a licence is issued to a vessel, it is also provided with three logbooks: a fishing log, a production log and a transhipment log. The fishing log indicates the catch of each tow and the type of fishing gear used. The production log gives a record of the amount and type of product rendered by the production plant on board the vessel. The transhipment log contains a record of fish transferred from the fishing vessel to a transport vessel. All the information collected is stored in a computer program called "Flash" which is used as a surveillance and management tool.

An important aspect of the Canadian system is the observer programme. The Department of Fisheries and Oceans has 42 observers. The observers are given instruction in navigation, marine biology, fisheries law and enforcement, as well as practical training. Each observer is assigned to a fishing vessel for a period ranging from 10 to 30 days. The observer has two primary duties. His first duty is to monitor the ship's compliance with Canadian fisheries regulations and policies regarding areas fished, fishing gear used, species caught, logbook record-keeping practice and reporting conditions. His second duty is to collect and record biological data from representative fish samples, such as age and sex determinations, length and weight measurements, detailed species morphologies, stomach content analysis as well as catch and effort data.

The information provided by the observers enables the Department of Fisheries and Oceans to manage the fishery more realistically and to pass on such information to the fishing industry. The observer endeavours to ensure that the captain of the vessel is aware of and understands the various fishing regulations. Regular reports by the observer help to keep the Canadian authorities informed of the vessel's activities. The observer programme has apparently worked well and forms an important component of Canada's surveillance and enforcement machinery.

Surveillance and Enforcement

It is not enough for a coastal State to adopt conservation and management measures. The coastal State must also develop a capacity to ensure compliance with its conservation and management laws and regulations. Unless the coastal State develops such a capacity, there will be no sanctions against violations of its laws and regulations. If fishermen, both domestic and foreign, know that violation will not attract sanction then some, if not all of the fishermen, will feel free to violate the coastal State's conservation and management laws and regulations. Therefore, it is very important for coastal States, within the limits of their financial, manpower and technical resources, to develop a capacity for surveillance and enforcement.

Surveillance and enforcement can be carried out in three ways: by using ships, by using aircraft and by placing observers on board fishing vessels. Ships patrolling the EEZ will identify the fishing vessels and determine their location, verify that they are licensed to be in the zone and in that particular location, observe their fishing activities and, where necessary, board and inspect the fishing vessels. When a fishing vessel is boarded, inspection should include the examination of its logbook entries, the nets in use, the catch on deck and the fish processing and storage facilities below deck.

The use of aircraft, in conjunction with ships, is extremely common and effective. There are many different types of aircraft being used for this purpose. Since the aircraft will be flying among and identifying fishing vessels, it must have a good low-level flying capability and be highly manoeuvrable. The aircraft must be equipped with radar; with accurate navigation equipment in order to determine if a violation is taking place; with good communications equipment to report violations, to communicate with patrol vessels and fishing vessels; with day and night photo capability; and night illumination or searchlight.

The use of observers by the Canadian government has already been referred to. By placing an observer on board a fishing vessel, the latter is deterred from violating the coastal State's laws and regulations. Under the Canadian observer programme, the observer will collect certain data, report violations and, where necessary, call for a boarding inspection. An interesting feature of the Canadian programme is that the cost of the observer is borne by the fishing vessel.

For many developing countries, developing a capacity for surveillance and enforcement will not be an easy task. This is because they lack finance, equipment, and trained manpower. This is, therefore, an area in which developed countries can assist developing countries in acquiring ships and aircraft, in manpower training and in financing. It must, however, be pointed out, in all candour, that helping developing countries to the necessary equipment and to train their manpower will be in vain if the developing countries do not, on their part, stamp out corruption and ensure that those who are charged with the tasks of surveillance and enforcement are men and women with integrity who cannot be bribed. One way in which the cost of surveillance and enforcement can be reduced is for the fisheries management to enlist the help of the armed forces in carrying out sea and air patrols. In Canada, the Department of National Defence assists the Department of Fisheries and Oceans in carrying out both sea and air patrols. The arrangement is cost-effective and appears to work well.

Straddling Stocks

If a fish stock spends its entire life cycle within the EEZ of one coastal State, the right to manage and conserve that fish stock lies exclusively with that coastal State. Reality is, however, sometimes more complex than our intellectual constructs. Thus, we find some fish stocks which straddle two EEZs in that the fish spawn in one EEZ and spend the rest of their lives in another EEZ. There are also cases in which a fish stock straddles three EEZs, for example, it spawns in one EEZ, grows up in a second EEZ and lives as adults in a third EEZ. In both situations, the

Convention enjoins the coastal States to seek, either directly or through appropriate subregional or regional organisations, to agree upon the measures necessary to coordinate and ensure the conservation and development of such straddling stocks.[83]

A fish stock may also straddle an EEZ and a part of the high sea adjacent to it. In such a situation, efforts of the coastal State to conserve the fish stock in its EEZ, will be undermined if it is overexploited in the adjacent high sea. Canada faces such a situation on its east coast. It tried unsuccessfully to persuade the Conference to expand the right of the coastal State, beyond its EEZ, to conserve the fish stock. The Conference rejected the demand because most delegations perceived it as another example of creeping jurisdiction by the coastal States. The Convention directs the coastal State and the states fishing for such stock in the adjacent high sea to seek, either directly or through appropriate subregional or regional organisations, to agree upon measures to conserve such stocks in the high sea.[84] The approach of the Convention contains two loopholes. First, some of the states fishing the stock in the high sea may not belong to the subregional or regional fisheries organisation. Second, the coastal States and the other states may not be able to agree on the measures necessary to conserve such stocks in the high sea.

Highly Migratory Species

Annex I of the Convention lists 17 species of highly migratory fish. The first eight are all tunas. The characteristic they share in common is that their normal migration covers great distances,

---

[83] Article 63, para. 1, 1982 Convention, *supra* note 1.
[84] Article 63, para. 2, *ibid.*

often covering thousands of miles. This fact raises a number of questions and problems. First, does a coastal State have sovereign right over a highly migratory species in its EEZ? Second, does another State have the right to harvest a highly migratory species in the EEZ of a coastal State without its agreement? Third, how and by whom are the highly migratory species to be managed and conserved?

Article 64 of the Convention states that the coastal State and other States whose nationals fish in the region for the highly migratory species shall cooperate, directly or through appropriate international organisations, with a view to ensuring conservation and promoting the objective of optimum utilisation of such species throughout the region, both within and beyond the EEZ. In regions where no appropriate international organisation exists, the coastal State and other states whose nationals harvest these species in the region, shall cooperate to establish such an organisation and participate in its work. I don't think Article 64 is intended to derogate from the rights of coastal States in Article 56. If this assumption is correct, then it follows that the sovereign right of coastal States to the living resources in its EEZ extends to the highly migratory species. Therefore, a third State may not harvest the highly migratory species in the EEZ of a coastal State without its agreement. This interpretation of Article 64, paragraph 1, would appear to be supported by paragraph 2 of the same article which states that, "The provisions of paragraph 1 apply in addition to the other provisions of this Part."

Anadromous Species

Anadromous species of fish are fish which spawn in rivers and live most of their lives at sea but which return to the places of their birth to spawn. Salmon is a paradigm example of an anadromous species. If an anadromous stock spawns in the river of State A and lives the rest of its life in the EEZ of that State, no particular problem is created.

Problems arise in the following situations. First, if an anadromous stock spawns in the river of State A and lives the rest of its life in the EEZs of States A and B. Second, if an anadromous stock spawns in the river of State X and lives the rest of its life in the EEZ of State X and in an adjacent part of the high sea. In the first situation, do the two States have equal right to the anadromous stock? If not, which State has the greater right? How and by whom is such a stock to be managed and conserved? In the second situation, do third States have the right to harvest the anadromous stock in the high sea? How and by whom is such a stock to be managed and conserved?

The Convention states that the State in whose river anadromous stock originate shall have the primary interest in and responsibility for such stock.[85] This seems to confer on the State of origin the primary right to such stock and to impose on the State of origin the primary responsibility for its management and conservation. In a situation where the anadromous stock originates in State A and lives in the EEZ of States A and B, the Convention imposes an obligation on State B to cooperate with State A with regard to the conservation and management of the stock.[86] Does this mean that State B has no right to harvest the stock in its EEZ? No, it does not mean that. Both States A and B have the right to harvest the stock in their respective EEZs. Of the two States, however, the State of origin, A, is recognised to have primary interest. This must, therefore, be taken into

---

[85] Article 66, para. 1, *ibid.*
[86] Article 66, para. 4, *ibid.*

account in the negotiations between the two States to apportion the total allowable catch between them. The Convention also imposes on the State of origin, A, the primary responsibility for the conservation and management of such stock. The responsibility of State B is to cooperate with State A in this regard.

In a situation where the anadromous stock originates in State A and lives its life in the EEZ of State A and in the high sea, can third States harvest the stock in the high sea? The general rule seems to be no, because Article 66, paragraph 3(a) states that, "Fisheries for anadromous stocks shall be conducted only in waters landward of the outer limits of exclusive economic zones." There is, however, an exception to this rule. The exception is where the application of the rule would cause economic dislocation for a third State.[87] The State of origin and a third State which would suffer economic dislocation if it were prevented from harvesting the anadromous stock in the high sea, shall consult with a view to achieving agreement on the terms and conditions of such fishing. The agreement shall give regard to the conservation requirements and the needs of the State of origin in respect of the stock. The State of origin shall minimise the economic dislocation for the third State by taking into account its normal catch and its mode of operations, as well as all the areas in which such fishing has occurred.[88] A third State which has incurred expenditures in participating, with the agreement of the State of origin, in measures for the renewal of the anadromous stock shall be given special consideration.[89] The enforcement of the regulations of the State of origin, beyond its

---

[87] Article 66, para. 3(a), *ibid.*
[88] Article 66, para. 3(b), *ibid.*
[89] Article 66, para. 3(c), *ibid.*

EEZ, shall be by agreement between the State of origin and the other States concerned.[90]

Catadromous Species

A paradigm example of a catadromous species is the eel. A catadromous fish has a life cycle which is the reverse of an anadromous fish. A catadromous fish spends most of its life in the fresh waters of rivers but spawns at sea. An anadromous fish spends most of its life at sea but spawns in rivers. The migratory pattern of eels from different parts of Europe is highly interesting. There is evidence to suggest that they swim thousands of miles to spawn in the Sargasso Sea. The young eels then make the opposite journey and return to the waters of their ancestors.

The Convention gives the coastal State, in whose waters a catadromous stock spends the greater part of its life cycle, the responsibility for the management of that stock.[91] A catadromous stock will traverse the high sea, both on its way to its spawning ground and on its way back. Can States harvest the catadromous stock in the high sea? The answer is apparently no because the Convention states that, "Harvesting of catadromous species shall be conducted only in waters landward of the outer limits of exclusive economic zones."[92] There is no exception to this rule.

A catadromous stock may migrate through the EEZ of another State, whether as mature fish on their way to the spawning ground or as juvenile fish on their return journey. In such a situation, can the coastal State through whose EEZ the

---

[90] Article 66, para. 3(d), *ibid.*

[91] Article 67, para. 1, *ibid.*

[92] Article 67, para. 2, *ibid.*

catadromous stock is migrating, harvest the stock? The answer is yes, but the harvesting must be regulated by agreement between such State and the State in whose waters the stock spends the greater part of its life cycle.[93] The management of the stock shall also be regulated by agreement between the States concerned.

Marine Mammals

Marine mammals consist of three main groups. The first group, cetaceans, comprise whales, dolphins and porpoises. The second group, pinnipeds, comprise seals and sea lions. The third group, sirenians, comprise manatees and dugongs. Throughout history, the marine mammals have been hunted by man for their meat, fur, blubber, ivory and bone. Among the marine mammals, whales are the most endangered species. During the past decade, a worldwide movement, spearheaded by environmentalists, has been campaigning to stop the commercial hunting of whales. In 1972, the United Nations Conference on the Human Environment recommended a ten year moratorium on commercial whaling.[94] This recommendation was endorsed generally by the United Nations General Assembly during the same year.[95] On 23 July 1982, the International Whaling Commission approved, by a vote of 25 in favour, 7 against, with 5 abstentions, an amendment to paragraph 10 of its Regulatory Schedule which has the effect of banning all commercial whaling from 1985 until 1990. The seven States which voted against the decision

---

[93] Article 67, para. 3, *ibid.*

[94] Recommendation 33, Report of the UN Conference on the Human Environment, (1972) I I I.L.M. 1416 at 1434. (UN Doc. A/CONF.48/14/Rev.1)

[95] UN General Assembly Resolution 2994, UN Gen. Ass. Off. Rec., 27th Sess. (1972), Supp. No. 30, at p. 42 (UN Doc. A/8730).

were: Brazil, Iceland, Japan, Republic of Korea, Norway, Peru and the USSR.[96]

The Convention contains one article, Article 65, on marine mammals. Although the article is located in Part V, dealing with the EEZ, Article 120 gives effect to Article 65 in the conservation and management of marine mammals in the high seas. What principles or rules does Article 65 prescribe? First, the duty of coastal States to promote the optimum utilisation of the living resources of their EEZs does not apply to marine mammals. Thus, a coastal State or a competent international organisation can decide to prohibit altogether the exploitation of marine mammals. They may also limit or regulate the exploitation of marine mammals more strictly than provided for in Part V of the Convention. Second, States shall cooperate with a view to the conservation of marine mammals.

Third, in the case of cetaceans, States shall work through the appropriate international organisations for their conservation, management and study.

Jurisdiction of Coastal States in the Exclusive Economic Zone

In the EEZ, the coastal State has jurisdiction with regard to: (1) the establishment and use of artificial islands, installations and structures; (2) marine scientific research; and (3) the protection and preservation of the marine environment.[97]

Although the terms, "artificial islands", "installations", and "structures" are not defined in the Convention, they refer to

---

[96] See P Birnie, "The International Organization of Whales," (1984) 13 Denver J. Int'l L. & Policy 309 at p. 321.

[97] Article 56, para. 1(b), *ibid.*

things which are, by now, quite familiar. Man's search for oil and gas began to move offshore after the end of the Second World War. Artificial islands, installations and structures have been constructed to search for and exploit offshore deposits of oil and gas. In the Beaufort Sea, the Canadians have constructed artificial islands to exploit offshore petroleum because of the danger of icebergs. Installations and structures used for offshore oil exploration include the submersible oil rig and the jack-up oil rig.

In the EEZ, the coastal State has the exclusive right to construct and to authorise and regulate the construction, operation and use of artificial islands, installations and structures.[98] The customs, fiscal, health, safety and immigration laws and regulations of the coastal State shall apply to them. There is, however, a lacuna in the law with respect to drillships and semi-submersible oil rigs. Are they vessels or are they structures? They are registered as vessels and fly the flag of the registering State. As vessels, they are subject to the laws and regulations of the flag State. However, once the drillship or semi-submersible oil rig arrives at their drill site, they function just like an installation or structure. Do they then cease to be vessels and become structures? Are they subject to the laws and regulations of the coastal State, as well as of the flag State? The law is unsettled and this has given rise to difficulties over such questions as whose safety regulations apply and, in the event of an accident, whose courts have jurisdiction.

If an artificial island, installation or structure is to be constructed, the coastal State must give due notice of such construction.[99] The coastal State must also ensure that permanent means

---

[98] Article 60, para. 1, *ibid.*
[99] Article 60, para 3, *ibid.*

for giving warning of their presence will be maintained.[100] If an installation or structure is abandoned or disused, it shall be removed to ensure safety of navigation but "taking into account any generally accepted international standards established in this regard by the competent international organization."[101] Obviously, the Inter-Governmental Consultative Organization (IMCO) does not require removal in all cases because paragraph 3 of Article 60 goes on to state that, "Appropriate publicity shall be given to the depth, position and dimensions of any installations or structures not entirely removed." The removal of such installation or structure shall have due regard to fishing, the protection of the marine environment and the rights and duties of other States.

A coastal State may, where necessary, establish safety zones around artificial islands, installations and structures.[102] The breadth of safety zones shall be determined by the coastal State.[103] In general, such zones shall not exceed a distance of 500 metres, measured from each point of their outer edge, unless authorised by generally accepted international standards or recommended by the competent international organisation. A coastal State shall give notice of the extent of safety zones. All ships must respect these safety zones and shall comply with the generally accepted international standards regarding navigation in the vicinity of artificial islands, installations, structures and safety zones.[104]

Artificial islands, installations and structures and the safety zones around them may not be established where interference

---

[100] *Ibid.*
[101] *Ibid.*
[102] Article 60, para 4, *ibid.*
[103] Article 60, para 5, *ibid.*
[104] Article 60, para 6, *ibid.*

may be caused to the use of recognised sea lanes essential to international navigation.[105]

Finally, artificial islands, installations and structures do not possess the status of islands.[106] Consequently, they have no territorial sea of their own and their presence does not affect the delimitation of the territorial sea, the EEZ or the continental shelf.

The Status of the Exclusive Economic Zone

One of the most difficult questions relating to the EEZ is its legal status. Is the EEZ a zone of national jurisdiction? Is it part of the high seas? Is it a *sui generis* zone? The negotiations over this question at the Conference took several years. It was finally resolved at the sixth session of the Conference in June–July 1977, thanks to the initiative of the leader of the Mexican delegation, Dr Jorge Castañeda.[107] On 25 June 1977, Castañeda invited to dinner the leaders of the following delegations: Australia, Brazil, Bulgaria, Canada, Egypt, India, Kenya, Mexico, Nigeria, Norway, Peru, Senegal, Singapore, Tanzania, the UK, US, USSR and Venezuela. Castañeda proposed to the group that it set about the task of resolving the issue of the legal status of the EEZ. The group agreed and started work that very evening. Between 25 June and 12 July, a total of 13 meetings were held. The group succeeded in agreeing on a number of amendments to the Revised Single Negotiating Text.[108] The amendments were

---

[105] Article 60, para 7, *ibid*.

[106] Article 60, para 8, *ibid*.

[107] See KC Brennan, *The Evolution of the Sui Generis Concept of the Exclusive Economic Zone* (1983) at p. 8.

[108] The Revised Single Negotiating Text consists of four parts: Parts I, II and III appear in the Third United Nations Conference on the Law of the Sea, Off. Rec., 4th Sess. (1976), Vol. V, pp. 125–185 (UN Doc. A/CONF.62/WP.8/Rev.1);

accepted by the Chairman of the Second Committee and incorporated into the text.[109]

First, it was agreed that the EEZ was neither territorial sea nor part of the high seas but was *sui generis*.[110] This agreement is reflected in Article 55, the very first article of Part V, which states: "The exclusive economic zone is an area beyond and adjacent to the territorial sea, subject to the specific legal regime established in this Part V, under which the rights and jurisdiction of the coastal State and the rights and freedoms of other States are governed by the relevant provisions of this Convention." The words, "subject to the specific legal regime established in this Part" are intended to convey the sense that the EEZ is *sui generis*.

Second, it was agreed that no State could subject the EEZ to its sovereignty.[111] How is this agreement reflected in the text? Article 89 states that, "No State may validly purport to subject any part of the high seas to its sovereignty." Article 58, paragraph 2 states that, "Articles 88 to 115 and other pertinent rules of international law apply to the exclusive economic zone in so far as they are not incompatible with this Part." The application of Article 89 to the EEZ is not incompatible with Part V of the Convention. Therefore, no State may validly purport to subject any part of the EEZ to its sovereignty.

Article 53 contains the rights and freedoms of the international community in the EEZ of coastal States. Bernard Oxman

---

Part IV appears in Third United Nations Conference on the Law of the Sea, Off. Rec., 5th Sess. (1976), Vol. VI, pp. 144–145 (UN Doc. A/CONF.62/WP.9). The RSNT provisions on the EEZ are contained in Vol. V at pp. 160–161.

[109] The revised provisions were incorporated into the ICNT (Informal Composite Negotiating Text) (UN Doc A/CONF.62/WP.10), Third United Nations Conference on the Law of the Sea, Off. Rec., Vol. 8, 6th Sess. (1977), pp. 13–16.

[110] Brennan, *supra*, note 108, p. 10.

[111] *Ibid.*

classifies those rights and freedoms into two groups.[112] The first group of rights and freedoms are unqualified: the freedoms referred to in Article 87 of navigation, overflight and the laying of submarine cables and pipelines. What is the significance of the cross-reference to Article 87? The significance is that Article 87 is the basic article listing the freedoms of the high seas. Therefore, the freedoms which the international community enjoys in the EEZ, of navigation, overflight and the laying of submarine cables and pipelines are qualitatively identical to those in the high seas. The cross-reference to Article 87 also makes clear that "treaties regulating these freedoms on the high seas apply in the same way to the exercise of these freedoms in the exclusive economic zone."[113]

The second group of rights and freedoms of the international community in the EEZ is qualified. It is subject to a compatibility test. What are these rights and freedoms? Article 58, paragraph 1, refers to "other internationally lawful uses of the sea related to the freedoms of navigation, overflight, and the laying of submarine cables and pipelines, such as those associated with the operation of ships, aircraft and submarine cables and pipelines, and compatible with the other provisions of this Convention." Article 58, paragraph 2 makes Articles 88 to 115 the basic articles elaborating the high seas regime, applying to the EEZ in so far as they are not incompatible with Part V of the Convention.

Another difficult issue has to do with the residual rights. If the Convention does not attribute a right or jurisdiction to the coastal State or to third States within the EEZ, who gets

---

[112] BH Oxman, "An Analysis of the Exclusive Economic Zone as Formulated in the Informal Composite Negotiating Text," in T Clingan (editor), *Law of the Sea: State Practice in Zones of Special Jurisdiction* (1982) at p. 68.
[113] *Ibid.*

the residual right or jurisdiction? The coastal States, of course, argued that residual rights should go to the coastal State. The maritime powers, understandably, argued that they should go to the international community. The solution contained in Article 59 is that, "the conflict should be resolved on the basis of equity and in the light of all the relevant circumstances, taking into account the respective importance of the interests involved to the parties as well as to the international community as a whole." Thus, the residual rights do not automatically belong either to the coastal State or to the international community. Each case has to be judged on its merit.

Letter on the
Law of the Sea

I have vivid memories of the year 1982. I remember the high emotion in the conference room, at the United Nations in New York, on 20 April 1982, when I put the United Nations Convention on the Law of the Sea (UNCLOS), to the vote. The vote was 130 in favour, 4 against with 17 abstentions. I also remember the final session of the Conference, held in Montego Bay, Jamaica, from 6 to 10 December 1982. When the Convention was opened for signature on 11 December, it was signed by 119 States. Let me share a few thoughts and reflections.

First, I mourn the passing of so many of our dear friends and colleagues. Those who played a leadership role in the negotiations include Andrés Aguilar, Shirley Hamilton Amerasinghe, Hans Anderson, Alfonso Arias-Schreiber, Christopher Beeby, Alan Beesley, Keith Brennan, Jorge Casteñeda, Tom Clingan, Paul Engo, Jens Evensen, Reynaldo Galindo Pohl, SP Jagota, Elizabeth Mann Borgese, Arvid Pardo, Elliott Richardson, Willem Riphagen and Shabtai Rosenne.

Second, I am gratified that the Convention has enjoyed universal support. The Convention has 162 Parties (161 States plus the European Union). The few States, such as, the United States of America, which have not yet acceded to the Convention, have accepted the Convention as the applicable law. I would discourage the efforts of some of our friends who wish to revise the Convention or to convene a new conference to negotiate a new treaty on the high seas. The Convention has served us well and it would be extremely unwise to undermine its integrity and effectiveness.

Third, my dream that the Convention will become the "constitution" of the world's oceans has come to pass. It is the constitution of the oceans because it treats the oceans in a holistic manner. It seeks to govern all aspects of the resources and uses of the oceans. In its 320 Articles, and 9 Annexes, as supplemented by the 1994 General Assembly Resolution 48/263 relating to Part XI of the Convention and the 1995 Agreement relating to the conservation and management of straddling fish stocks and highly migratory fish stocks, the Convention is both comprehensive and authoritative.

Fourth, in recent years, some environmentalists have expressed the view that the Convention gives too much weight to navigational rights and too little to protecting the marine environment. This view is mistaken. When I was chairing the negotiations at the Earth Summit, I included Chapter 17 in Agenda 21, in order to harmonise the UNCLOS and United Nations Conference on the Environment. Over the past three decades, the International Maritime Organization (IMO) has, in conformity with the UNCLOS, enacted new treaties, rules and procedures to protect the marine environment from ship-based pollution. What is not generally known is that 80 per cent of marine pollution is caused by land-based pollution. It is much harder to stop land-based marine pollution because States hide behind their sovereignty.

Fifth, the Food and Agriculture Organization has repeatedly called the world's attention to the crisis in fisheries. The crisis is being caused by overfishing, by illegal, unreported and unregulated fishing, by the ineffectiveness of the regional fishery management organisations and by the use of destructive and unsustainable methods of fishing, such as, bottom trawling and dredge fishing. Urgent action is needed to tackle these problems. The world can learn from the successful experiences of Iceland and New Zealand in the management of their fisheries. The IMO should consider requiring all commercial fishing boats to be licenced and to carry transponders. We should also consider eco-labelling for fish. Regional fishery management organisations should be established in all regions, and they should be allowed to make their decisions by majority votes rather than by consensus. Certain destructive methods of fishing should be banned.

Sixth, the nexus between climate change and the oceans is insufficiently understood. People generally do not know that the oceans serve as the blue lungs of the planet, absorbing CO_2 for the atmosphere and returning oxygen to the atmosphere. The oceans also play a positive role in regulating the world's climate system. One impact of global warming on the oceans is that the oceans are getting warmer and more acidic. This will have a deleterious effect on our coral reefs. In view of the symbiotic relationship between land and sea, the world should pay more attention to the health of our oceans.

Seventh, I wish to express a serious concern about the tendency by some coastal States to expand their jurisdictions and their rights in violation of the Convention. Some States have drawn straight baselines when they are not entitled. Other States have enacted laws and regulations governing activities in the exclusive economic zones even though they have no jurisdiction over such activities under the Convention. Some States have acted in contravention of the regime of transit passage. States have shown very little integrity and fidelity to law when it comes to deciding whether a feature is a rock or an island. I think States should be less reluctant to protest against such actions by other States and be more willing to refer such disputes to dispute settlement.

Professor Tommy Koh
President, Third United Nations Conference on the Law of the Sea

———❧———

This letter was published in 2013 in the United Nations publication, *United Nations Convention on the Law of the Sea at 30: Reflections.*

Index